GW01191831

This book traces the history of an oath for Catholics in the hundred years from the Treaty of Limerick to the Catholic Relief Act of 1793, chronicling the various attempts by the government and others (the Synges and Fr Nary in the 1720s and 1730s, Lord Clanbrassil in the 1750s and Bishop Hervey in the 1760s) to formulate an oath of allegiance for Catholics. The oaths invariably included an abjuration of the Stuarts and a renunciation of the Pope's alleged powers to depose kings, two matters on which there was contention within the Catholic body itself. If there had been agreement among Catholics on these matters, the emancipation process could have started as early as the 1720s. The Oath issue was thus to dominate Catholic politics from the 1690s to the 1790s, representing a single connecting thread within this period.

Divided Loyalties

The Question of the Oath for
Irish Catholics in the Eighteenth Century

PATRICK FAGAN

FOUR COURTS PRESS

This book was typeset by
Carrigboy Typesetting Services
in 10.5 on 12.5 point Ehrhardt for
FOUR COURTS PRESS
55 Prussia Street, Dublin 7, Ireland
e-mail: fcp@ indigo.ie
and in North America for
FOUR COURTS PRESS
c/o ISBS, 5804 N.E. Hassalo Street, Portland, OR 97213.

A catalogue record for this title
is available from the British Library.

ISBN 1-85182-252-6

Printed in Great Britain
by Antony Rowe Ltd, Chippenham, Wilts.

Contents

Preface

My sincere thanks are due, firstly, to Fr Hugh Fenning OP for reading the original typescript, for his advice and assistance thereon and for bringing additional sources of information to my attention. I am also indebted to him for the translation of one document from the Italian and for help with the translation of some documents from the Latin. I should like to thank Fr Benignus Millett OFM, editor, *Collectanea Hibernica*, for the use of material from the Vatican Archives edited or calendared in that journal by the late Fr Cathaldus Giblin OFM. My thanks are also due to the Congregation for the Evangelisation of Peoples, Rome for permission to make use of documents from the Vatican Archives, and to my son, Desmond, for helping with the checking of the proofs.

I am indebted to the staff of the following institutions for their help and co-operation in my research work: National Library of Ireland, Royal Irish Academy, Gilbert Library (a branch of the Dublin Public Libraries), the National Archives, the library of the Dominican Priory, Tallaght, the library of Trinity College, Dublin and the library of St Patrick's College, Maynooth.

Limerick and After

The question of what kind of oath should be applicable to catholics, both lay and clerical, was to dominate Irish catholic politics, such as they were, for the hundred year period from the Treaty of Limerick in 1691 to the Catholic Relief Act of 1793, and this question constitutes a single, persisting, connecting thread throughout that period. This book seeks to chronicle the various attempts by the government and others to formulate such an oath and to show how, for so many years, such efforts were thwarted by a significant section of Irish catholics with, on the one hand, a misplaced loyalty to the Stuart cause and, on the other hand, an ultramontane compliance with outmoded papal claims. It is a chronicle of sharp disagreements and missed opportunities on the catholic side and of efforts on the protestant side to come to terms with and to control the spectre of popery.

The ninth article of the Treaty of Limerick provided that the oath to be administered to such catholics as submitted to their Majesties', William and Mary's, government, should be the oath of allegiance and no other. The oath here mentioned was stated in Article 2 of the treaty to be that provided for in 1 William and Mary c. 2 and was as follows:

I, A.B., do solemnly promise and swear that I will be faithful and bear true allegiance to their Majesties King William and Queen Mary.

Section 14 of 3 William and Mary c. 2 provided that any person over the age of eighteen years could be summoned by two justices of the peace and required to take this oath. There were penalties prescribed in the case of persons refusing. The oath might appear at first sight to be simple, clear and very reasonable but in fact it left a large question mark as to whom and in what circumstances it applied. Did it apply only to those who were present in Limerick or Galway – for similar terms were negotiated in respect of the latter city – at the time of the surrender of those cities, or did it apply to the whole of Ireland and to persons not born at the time in question? Were there any concessions to be granted to catholics taking this oath? Could other forms of oath be required of catholics in particular circumstances?

It was not long – a matter of weeks in fact – before the situation was clar-
ified to some extent by an act of the British parliament[1] which provided that
no person could sit in the Irish parliament, nor hold any government office,
civil, military or ecclesiastical, nor practise law in Ireland, until he had subscribed to

1 the oath of allegiance set out above,
2 a new oath as follows:

> I, A.B., do swear that I do from my heart abhor, detest and abjure as
> impious and heretical that damnable doctrine and position, that princes
> excommunicated or deprived by the Pope, or any authotity of the see of
> Rome, may be deposed or murdered by their subjects, or any other what-
> soever. And I do declare that no foreign prince, person, prelate, state or
> potentate hath, or ought to have, any jurisdiction, power, superiority,
> pre-eminence or authority, ecclesiastical or spiritual, within this realm.

3 the declaration against Transubstantiation.

The same act (section 2) abrogated the old oath of supremacy, but the new
oath at 2 above came to be commonly known as the oath of supremacy.[2] The

---

1 Section 8 of 3 William & Mary c. 2 (English). Under section 3 of 1 William & Mary
c. 2 (English) (1689) the oath of supremacy had already been abrogated in England and
the new oath in lieu thereof set out here was provided for in that act. Some writers
incorrectly state that practitioners of medicine were also required to take the oaths and
to make the declaration mentioned, whereas only professors of physic were so required.
Ordinary physicians never came within the ambit of the penal laws and throughout the
eighteenth century there was always a significant number of catholic physicians practising in Ireland.   2 An oath of supremacy was first introduced under Henry VIII in
the Act of Supremacy 1537. This was repealed by the catholic Queen Mary by 3 & 4
Philip & Mary c. 8. The Act of Supremacy was revived by Queen Elizabeth 1 in 1560
in an act restoring to the Crown the ancient jurisdiction over the State Ecclesiastical
and Spiritual, and abolishing all foreign power repugnant to the same (2 Elizabeth c.1),
section 7 of which provided for a revised oath of supremacy as follows: 'I, A.B., do
utterly testify and declare in my conscience, that the Queen's Highness is the only
supreme governor of this realm, and of all other her Highness dominions and countries, as well in all spiritual or ecclesiastical things or causes, as temporal, and that no
foreign prince, person, prelate, state or potentate hath or ought to have any jurisdiction, power, superiority, pre-eminence or authority, ecclesiastical or spiritual, within
this realm, and therefore I do utterly renounce and forsake all foreign jurisdictions,
power, superiorities and authorities, and do promise, that from henceforth I shall bear
faith and true allegiance to the Queen's Highness, her heirs and successors, and to my
power shall assist and defend all jurisdictions, privileges, pre-eminences and authorities, granted or belonging to the Queen's Highness, her heirs and successors, or united and annexed to the imperial Crown of this realm, so help me God, and by the

new 'oath of supremacy', since it denied the spiritual authority of the pope, was unacceptable to catholics. Likewise, the declaration against Transubstantiation could not, of course, be made by anyone calling himself a Roman Catholic. However, in respect of such catholics as were entitled to the benefit of the Articles of Limerick, there was a saving clause to the effect that they should be obliged to take the oath of allegiance only.

Although much of the penal legislation enacted in subsequent years was a violation of the Articles of Limerick, and of the saving clause in the 1691 act just mentioned, nevertheless there were occasional nods in the direction of the ninth and other articles of the Treaty, notably in the Popish Solicitors Acts 1698, 1707 and 1734 and the acts for disarming Papists 1695 and 1739, all of which had saving clauses in respect of those who could show that they were covered by the Articles of Limerick. Of course, with the effluxion of time all those who could claim entitlement to the Articles would have passed away. It is of interest that perhaps the last of the catholic solicitors to practise publicly in accordance with the Articles of Limerick was Thady Dunne, who died in Dublin in 1748, aged eighty-four.[3]

With catholics effectively excluded from parliament and from civil, military and ecclesiastical positions, the question of an oath for catholics, as far as the government was concerned, arose only as a factor in how the catholic clergy, and to a lesser extent the catholic laity, were to be controlled, and how the voting rights of catholics in parliamentary elections were to be circumscribed – until 1728, that is, when the right was withdrawn. Specifically, if the clergy were to be recognised and controlled by a system of registration, should a necessary corollary be that they would be required to take an oath of allegiance or

contents of this book.' This was the oath which was abrogated by 3 William & Mary c. 2 (English). The declaration against Transubstantiation, as set out in the act to prevent the further growth of popery 1704, read as follows: 'I, A.B., do solemnly and sincerely, in the presence of God, profess, testify and declare, That I do believe, that in the sacrament of the Lord's-Supper, there is not any transubstantiation of the elements of bread and wine into the body and blood of Christ, at or after the consecration thereof, by any person whatsoever; that the invocation or adoration of the Virgin Mary, or any other saint, and the sacrifice of the mass, as they are now used in the Church of Rome, are superstitious and idolatrous. And I do solemnly, in the presence of God, profess, testify and declare that I do make this declaration, and every part thereof, in the plain and ordinary sense of the words read unto me, as they are commonly understood by Protestants, without any evasion, equivocation, or mental reservation whatsoever; and without any dispensation already granted me for this purpose by the Pope, or any other authority or person whatsoever, or without any hope of a dispensation from any person or authority whatsoever, or without believing that I am, or can be, acquitted before God or man, or absolved of this declaration, or any part thereof, although the Pope or any other person or persons, or power whatsoever should dispense with or annul the same, or declare that it was null and void from the beginning.' 3 *Dublin Weekly Journal*, 24 December 1748.

fidelity to the king. In this connection the presence on the continent of James II until his death in 1701, of the latter's son James until his death in 1766 and grandson Charles Edward until his death in 1788, and the constant scheming of these people to topple the reigning monarch, was a complicating factor. Did an oath of allegiance to the reigning monarch necessarily entail the abjuration of the Stuart claimant to the throne? The Irish and British administrations clearly believed that it did, and this was one of the matters that was to bedevil all attempts at formulating an oath acceptable to catholics for the best part of a century. The prevailing catholic stance was that an oath which entailed abjuring the Stuarts went further than the Oath of Allegiance provided for in the Ninth Article and was thus a violation of that article. I say 'prevailing catholic stance' because, it will be seen, there was always a segment of catholic opinion which found no difficulty in abjuring the Stuarts.

A second besetting problem in the formulation of an oath for catholics later in the century was the claim by the pope to have power to depose monarchs and to dispense their subjects from their oaths of allegiance. This evident challenge to civil authority by an external ruler was a further matter which the British and Irish authorities required to be taken care of in any oath to be taken by catholics. Curiously, it was not a requirement of the oath of abjuration first imposed in England in 1701 and incorporated in the Irish acts of 1704 and 1709 to prevent the further growth of popery.

The papal claim to have power to depose princes (i.e. kings, queens, emperors, rulers) and to release their subjects from oaths of allegiance to them had its roots in the struggle between the Holy Roman Emperor and the papacy in the eleventh century and in particular in the declarations of Gregory VII on this subject. A high point of papal power was reached when the Emperor Henry IV, excommunicated by Gregory and faced with a rebellion by his subjects, came to the pope's castle at Canossa in 1077 to offer his submission to Gregory, thereby admitting that a king or emperor, as a son of the church, was subject to its ruler, the pope. These deposing and dispensing powers were later to be enshrined in the third canon of the Fourth Lateran Council convoked in 1215 by Innocent III,[4] who brought the church to the height of its power in medieval Europe.

By the eighteenth century the first of these powers, that of deposing princes, could be said to be nothing more than a relic from the past. Outside of his own papal states the pope was in no position to depose anyone or to bring anyone to heel. Indeed the boot was firmly on the other foot in that the Emperor and the catholic kings of France, Spain and Portugal were in a position to pressurise and influence reigning popes and, in the case of the emperor, to exercise a veto in conclaves on the election of a new pope. Catholic monarchs,

4 Fenning, Hugh, *The Irish Dominican province, 1698–1797*, Dublin 1990, 271–2.

including the throneless James III of Britain and Ireland, also had the privilege of nominating bishops to vacant sees and of nominating some members of the sacred college of cardinals. It was all a far cry from the penitence of Canossa but nevertheless the deposing power was still tenaciously upheld by the pope and the ultramontane faithful. However, since it could not be enforced, there was no question of its being taken seriously by rulers and governments.

The papal dispensing power was, however, a different matter altogether. This could be said to be nothing less than a gratuitous intrusion into the minds and consciences of men and women. It facilitated, if it it did not indeed encourage, persons to take false oaths, a practice recognised by the church itself as one of the gravest sins. It was a claim that struck at the heart of all civil law and authority. Monarchs, whether they are such *de jure* or *de facto*, have a right to expect allegiance from their subjects, and when a subject swears an oath of allegiance not involving any articles of faith, the monarch has the right to expect that such an oath will not be negatived by outside papal interference. It was a situation which it was difficult, if not impossible, to take care of in the framing of oaths of allegiance and abjuration, since the problem was to provide against mental reservations which could be held by the person taking an oath. Even when a person in the course of an oath renounced the pope's power to dispense him from that oath, that did not mean that he could not in the future be absolved by the pope from the effects of such an oath. Furthermore, even where a person swore in the course of an oath that he had no mental reservations, the pope could still conceivably absolve him from the effects of that oath which he might claim to have taken under circumstances of duress. All in all, it would be difficult to describe the papal claim to dispense with oaths of allegiance as other than an unwarrantable interference with the things that are Caesar's.

An extension of the papal deposing and dispensing powers was the doctrine that princes excommunicated by the pope might be deposed or assassinated by their subjects. A renunciation of this concept was also to figure in proposals for oaths of allegiance and indeed is to be found in the 1774 oath, ultimately accepted by catholics. This doctrine, amounting to a Vatican *fatwah*, will appear chilling to modern ears, but it was on a par with the power of the Inquisition to hand over persons found guilty of heresy to the civil power for execution by burning at the stake.

The papal deposing and dispensing powers, and indeed other papal powers, had been under attack in the church itself for some time. The catholic church in France, urged on by their king, Louis XIV, had been to the fore in challenging the papal position. The Eldest Daughter of the Church had ever displayed a wayward disposition and was inclined to show a scant regard for the authority of the Holy Father in Rome, as witness the Albigensians in the twelfth and thirteen centuries, the Jansenists in the seventeenth and eighteenth centuries and Napoleon's humiliation of Pope Pius VII at the beginning of the nineteenth century. The Gallican Articles agreed by the assembly of the French clergy in 1682 were a further example of French disenchantment with papal pretensions. The assembled hierarchy of France pulled no punches when they solemnly agreed that

1 The pope has jurisdiction only in spiritual matters; kings are not subject to him in temporal matters, nor can the subjects of kings be released from their oaths of allegiance by the pope.
2 The decree of the Council of Constance that a General Council had to be obeyed by all Christians, including the pope, is to be observed by the Gallican Church.
3 The apostolic authority of the Roman church must be exercised in accordance with canons inspired by the Holy Ghost and in accordance with the rules, constitutions and customs of the Gallican Church.
4 Though the pope has the chief part in determining questions of faith, and though his decrees have force in the entire church and in each particular church, yet his decisions are not unalterable, at least until they are approved by the verdict of the entire church.[5]

This declaration was approved by the king who ordered in particular that it was to be observed by all teachers and professors of universities in France and its overseas territories and by all candidates for theological degrees. The great majority of the Irish secular clergy throughout the eighteenth century were educated in France, and these would all have been influenced in greater or lesser degree by Gallican principles. Indeed those of them who took degrees in French universities would have been required to subscribe specifically to the Gallican Articles. Provisions in oaths of allegiance renouncing the pope's deposing and dispensing powers would have been nothing new to such people.

Outside of France too there was opposition to these papal pretensions, in particular in the university of Louvain, a major centre of catholic theological education since its founding in the early fifteenth century. Some members of the Strict Faculty of the university were outspoken in their denunciation. Foremost among these was an Irish member of the Faculty, Fr Francis Martin of Galway, whose book on the allegiance due to princes sought to show that the ecclesiastical jurisdiction which Christ had settled in his church was neither directly or indirectly vested with a power of deposing princes or of absolving subjects from their allegiance. Martin would not allow that the decree of the Fourth Lateran Council enshrining this concept contained any matter of doctrine, but rather of discipline wherein the church might be mistaken in her methods.[6]

5 McCaffrey, James, *History of the catholic church from the renaissance to the French revolution*, vol. 1, 319.   6 I have been unable to discover a copy of Francis Martin's book.

At home in Ireland there was always throughout the century a degree of opposition among clergy and laity to the papal deposing and dispensing powers. It will be seen that a denial of these powers formed part of Fr Cornelius Nary's proposed form of an oath of allegiance in the 1720s. Later in the 1750s prominent laymen such as Charles O'Conor of Belanagare and Dr John Curry are on record as opposing these powers, and they were also opposed in a controversial pastoral proposed (but never issued) in 1757 by Primate Michael O'Reilly and other bishops. The oath of allegiance ultimately accepted by catholics in the 1770s also contains a denial of these powers.

Of the two main ingredients of the various forms of a catholic oath proposed by the authorities during the first three-quarters of the eighteenth century, the abjuration of the Stuarts was arguably the one which was to cause most division among catholics. A permanent thorn in the sides of successive British and Irish administrations, there were actual attempts by the Jacobites at invasion or insurrection in Scotland or England in the years 1708, 1715, 1719 and 1745, but apart from these there was hardly a year up to the 1750s when the Jacobites were not plotting with some great European power or other, with the invasion of Scotland or England as the desired end, and it was always on the cards that if Britain was brought to heel in any of the wars she engaged in over this period, the restoration of the Stuart dynasty in Britain would have been one of the conditions of the peace. In view of this persistent Jacobite challenge, the British and Irish authorities could scarcely be faulted for insisting on a provision for the abjuration of the Stuarts in any oath to be taken by catholics.

From the catholic point of view there was the highly important consideration that from 1719 onwards James Stuart was housed in Rome in a papal palace, protected by a papal guard, subvented by a papal pension, and, most important of all, recognised by the pope as the only rightful king of Great Britain and Ireland. The fact that this man held the right of nomination to vacant Irish sees copperfastened his hold on the Irish church since it behoved any Irish cleric with episcopal ambitions to demonstrate his loyalty to James.[7] It is not surprising, then, that it was only in the 1750s, when it was obvious that the Stuart star had waned, that catholic clerics were to be found in any numbers ready to forsake the Stuart cause. But even at that stage it was apparent that as long as the pope continued to recognise the Stuart claimant as king (and such recognition only ended with the death of James Stuart on 1 January 1766), he could not agree to a form of oath for Irish catholics in which that claimant was renounced and abjured.

It is not listed in the British Library or Bibliothèque Nationale catalogues. For the title I am relying on a letter dated 21 June 1722 from Archbishop Edward Synge to Martin in which Synge stated *inter alia*: 'Your book concerning the allegiance due to princes was lent to me by a gentleman in this town [Dublin] who was directed by your brother to let me have the reading of it.'.   7 See Fr Cathaldus Giblin's article 'The Stuart nomination of Irish bishops 1687–1765' in *Irish Ecclesiastical Record*, vol. 105 (1966), 35–47.

So much for the main ingredients of the various oaths of allegiance and abjuration proposed over the following century. A word or two will not be amiss at this stage as to what was not included in these oaths. Some catholic historians and apologists, particularly in the last century and early in the present one, appeared to go out of their way to exaggerate the extent of catholic disabilities with the aim of making the dark penal night a lot darker than it really was. Some achieved this by putting a partisan gloss on a particular situation, some by suppression of information and some by outright misrepresentation. Notable among such apologists were Cardinal Patrick Moran, Canon William Burke and Fr Reginald Walsh. It is necessary to draw particular attention to an example of misinformation by the latter-named since it impinges directly on the present work and is of such critical importance that it must be refuted. Fr Walsh, in an article in a series 'Glimpses of the Penal Times' in *Irish Ecclesiastical Record*, volume 30, 4th series, confuses the new oath of supremacy with the oath of abjuration and goes on to state that registered priests were also required to make the declaration against Transubstantiation.[8] The fact of the matter is a catholic priest was not required to do any such thing and a moment's reflection will show that it simply would not make sense for the authorities to require a catholic priest, as a condition of being registered as such, to take the Oath of Supremacy or make the declaration against Transubstantiation, since by taking such an oath and making such a declaration, he could no longer be regarded as a catholic priest.

A word about the various divisions in the Irish catholic body and how these were reflected in attitudes to the various forms of oath, is also pertinent at this point.

Firstly, among the catholic clergy themselves there was the great divide between seculars and regulars. Bad relations between the regular and secular clergy had been brewing for some considerable time and a bitter animosity between the two groups had become entrenched by the seventeenth century. Although the regular clergy had been banished from the country by the Banishment Act of 1697, several managed to stay on and these were reinforced to such an extent by friars returning surreptitiously in the early decades of the eighteenth century that by the 1740s the regulars were believed to have a strength of about 700 members. This compared with a total of about 1400 secular priests in Ireland at that time.[9] Some 90 per cent of the regulars belonged to the four great orders of

8 Walsh, Reginald, 'Glimpses of the Penal Times' in *Irish Ecclesiastical Record*, 4th Series, vol. 30, 374.   9 Murphy, Ignatius, *The diocese of Killaloe in the eighteenth century*, Dublin 1991, 74. Murphy here revises radically the figure for secular clergy in John Kent's report on the Irish church in 1742. Kent believed the seculars and regulars were about equal in numbers at around 700 members each while Murphy, relying on information in the 1731 report on popery, concluded that the seculars were double that number. Murphy's total figure of 2,100 for the 1740s compares with a total of 1,824 in 1800, of which 400 were regulars (see Desmond J. Keenan, *The catholic church in nineteenth century Ireland*, Dublin

friars – Franciscans, Dominicans, Augustinians and Calced Carmelites – and governments were inclined to regard them as wasters supported by an organised form of begging which they called questing. The primary cause of the rift between them and the seculars was that they were both competing for monetary support from a catholic laity, the majority of whom were very poor and unable adequately to support both groups.

A further cause of dissension between seculars and regulars, and one of great importance in the context of an oath of allegiance, was the difference in theological outlook between the two groups. As much as 80 per cent of the seculars were educated in colleges in France, in particular at Paris, but also at Nantes, Lille, Bordeaux, Rouen, Charleville, Douai and Toulouse, and we have already noted the extent to which these clerics were imbued with Gallican principles.

On the other hand, very few regular clergy were trained in France; they had their colleges abroad chiefly in Flanders, Rome, Prague, Spain and Portugal. They did not, therefore, run any great risk of being influenced by the antipapal principles of the French church. On the contrary they were conditioned by their training to an ultramontane outlook of extreme loyalty to the pope, which included an unwavering acceptance of the papal deposing and dispensing powers. Their extreme loyalty to the pope as well as to James Stuart had its reward in the high numbers of regulars who were appointed bishops; it reached a high point in the 1740s when nine of the Irish bishops belonged to the regular clergy. The same extreme loyalty to pope and pretender was another reason for their unacceptability in the eyes of the Irish and British administrations.[10]

The regulars' disinclination to recognise the authority of the bishops and their insistence on their privileges, while failing generally to live according to the rules of their orders, were further factors tending to accentuate the rift between them and the seculars.

The second great division in the catholic body was between clergy and laity, that is, the middle and upper class laity. The religious provisions of the Penal Laws had by the 1730s become largely a dead letter – the only country-wide persecution of catholics after that date was that of 1744. Toleration by connivance, as it was called, was something which the clergy learned to live with so comfortably that the majority came to prefer such a situation to the acceptance of an oath of allegiance which inevitably would include controversial provisions which were likely to cause divisions among themselves. The position

1983, 73). Keenan's figures confirm the low ebb the regulars had reached by the end of the century, the reasons for which will be found in Hugh Fenning, *The undoing of the friars of Ireland*, Louvain 1972. That the number of seculars should be much the same in 1800 as in the 1740s is at first sight surprising, but it was due to the disruption, because of war and revolution on the continent, in the supply of priests from the colleges in France and elsewhere and the fact that Maynooth College had not yet come on stream. 10 Fagan, Patrick, *Dublin's turbulent priest: Cornelius Nary 1658–1738*, Dublin 1991, 101.

of the better-off catholic laity *vis-à-vis* the Penal Laws was quite different. There was no question of the laws in regard to catholic property becoming dead letters, since they only required the motor of human greed, a commodity always in plentiful supply, to put them in operation, and the activities of the dreaded discoverers as well as the operation of the gavel law were to plague catholic property owners right up to the Relief Act of 1778, and after that date in cases where proceedings had already been started. The catholic laity saw the formulation of an oath of allegiance as a necessary preliminary to a possible repeal of these laws. Furthermore, the exclusion of catholics from parliament and official bodies and from the legal profession was deeply resented, the more so as large numbers of them, especially in the cities, grew increasingly affluent but found that no recognition was accorded them to match this affluence. There was thus the spectacle of a catholic laity, in particular the Dublin merchants, ever ready to sign addresses of loyalty and to accept proposed oaths of allegiance to the king in the hope of some alleviation of their disabilities, while the catholic hierarchy advocated a policy of *laissez faire* and of keeping a very low profile, lest by attracting attention to themselves even by an address of loyalty they might draw down upon themselves the envy or malice of the often bigotted local magistrates and perhaps of the parliament and the administration generally. Archbishop Skerrett of Tuam put it this way in a letter to Charles O'Conor of Belanagare dated 1 May 1778:

> The secular gentlemen of that city [Dublin] assume an authority, which I think they have no right to do, that is to put everything their wise heads suggest in the name of the whole kingdom. I was always of the opinion that the less we meddled and the more insignificant we appeared in the eye of the Government, the better, but they by their addresses and representations make the Government think us to be of some consequence, consequently to be guarded against.[11]

O'Conor in his letters to Dr Curry refers more than once to this less disadvantageous position of the catholic clergy as compared with the laity, but his taunt that the clergy were 'the only licensed Roman Catholics in the Kingdom' was surely wide of the mark when it was made in 1761,[12] since very few if any of the priests who had registered in 1704 could have been still alive at that date.

The third great divide in the catholic body was between the poor and the middle and upper classes. The various Catholic Relief Acts, even the much vaunted act of 1829, meant little or nothing to the poorer classes of catholic. Even the poor struggling forty shilling freeholders' right to vote (granted to

---

11 Ward, R.E & Ward, C.C. (eds), *The letters of Charles O'Conor of Belanagare*, 2 vols., Ann Arbor, Michigan, 1980, addendum to letter no. 68 of 21 February 1760.   12 Ward, Robert E. et al. (eds), *Letters of Charles O'Conor of Belanagare*, Washington D.C. 1988, 97.

them under the 1793 Relief Act but taken from them in 1829) proved to be a poisoned chalice since in many cases it amounted to no more than a right to vote as their landlord ordered or face the possibility of eviction. The catholic tenant farmers had to await the land agitation of the 1880s and the resulting Land Acts to see justice done to them, while the poor labourers experienced no amelioration in their housing conditions until the end of the nineteenth century and any significant improvement in their wages and conditions of employment came about only in the present century. The poor catholics of the eighteenth century, ignored by the Catholic Committee, found expression in such aggressive agrarian associations as the Whiteboys in Munster and South Leinster and the Defenders in Ulster and North Leinster or in street demonstrations by the mob in Dublin city. The Catholic Committee, founded in 1756, was never anything other than a middle/upper class organisation which indeed was at pains to disassociate itself from the activities of the Whiteboys and was content to lie low for a few years in the 1760s until the unrest generated by the Whiteboys had levelled off.[13]

On the protestant side also different layers of conflicting interests can be detected. Throughout the eighteenth century about 25 per cent of the population of Ireland was protestant, and this can be divided about 15 per cent established church and about 10 per cent dissenter.[14] The entire apparatus of government was in the hands of the 15 per cent who belonged to the established church, although there were, even from the beginning of the century, a few members of the house of commons who were dissenters. Even after the 1719 Toleration Act dissenters remained excluded from county and local government and from the magistracy.[15] Their right to vote in parliamentary elections was of very restricted significance in practice because there was no meaningful contest for about 75 per cent of seats in the commons and anyway their votes were of little account numerically outside the Ulster counties. For the same reasons the chances of a dissenter becoming a member of the house of commons were small indeed.

Turning to the established church, we find it too composed of disparate elements. While the Cromwellian and earlier planters were the core component, this was added to very significantly as the century advanced by converts from catholicism bent on eluding the anti-popery provisions of the penal laws. The first generation of these converts were in the main notoriously partial to their former co-religionists, many were married to catholics and had some of their children, usually the daughters, reared in the catholic faith. Some converts became MPs and those who were appropriately ennobled took their seats in the house of lords. The special preserve of converts was the legal profession. The list of lawyers, in particular solicitors, issued in connection with the 1734

13 Wyse, Thomas, *Historical sketch of the late Catholic Association*, London 1829, vol. 1, 89–90. 14 Fagan, Patrick, *The second city: portrait of Dublin 1700–1760*, Dublin 1986, 11. 15 Dickson, David, *New foundations: Ireland 1660–1800*, Dublin 1987, 74–5.

Popish Solicitors Act could be a list of members of the profession today.[16]
There were relatively few lawyers of planter stock on this list, the reason presumably being that planter families, coming to this country primarily as land
owners in the second half of the seventeenth century, had to wait a generation
or two before they could gain a foothold in the legal and other professions.
Those of planter stock had an almost paranoic fear of a Stuart restoration,
deriving from the expectation that, in such an eventuality, catholics who had
been dispossessed in the seventeenth century would have their estates returned
to them and the planters ousted. For more than half the century the Pretender
or his son thus remained the great bogey-man of the protestant planters, while,
on the other hand, it was being said that the converts to protestantism secretly
hoped for a Stuart restoration. But in the parliament the planter element invariably had its way when, with the Pretender threatening yet another descent on
the British Isles, it appeared requisite to dampen down any possibility of Irish
catholic support by issuing a proclamation bringing the popery laws into operation or indeed by initiating new measures against catholics.

Parliament was divided not so much into Whigs and Tories as into a Court
Party which undertook to implement the administration's parliamentary pro-
gramme, and an opposition called the Country (later the Patriot) Party. After
Queen Anne's time the labels Whig and Tory did not truly reflect, in the Irish
context, the composition of the government party and of the opposition. Apart
from two brief periods in the 1760s and the 1770s the Whigs in the period
1714–1800 were permanently in power in Britain but in Ireland it was not
unusual in that period to find Whigs both on the government side and in opposition. From Chesterfield's time onwards the lord lieutenant and the administration were generally more liberally disposed towards the catholics than the
majority in the commons or lords or the local magistracy. It has to be remembered that, apart from a necessary leavening of lawyers, members of parliament
were predominantly country gentlemen, who found themselves daily confronted
in their constituencies with, as they saw them, this seething mass of papists
who must at all costs be kept in check, and who saw any slight concession to
Papists as a nail in the coffin of the protestant interest. While succeeding lords
lieutenant down to the 1770s were to find the parliament quite intransigent in
the matter of concessions to catholics, the other side of the coin was that the lord
lieutenant and privy council were sometimes able to act to frustrate the designs
of parliament to introduce further anti-catholic measures, as witness the suppression on four different occasions in the 1760s and 1770s by the lord lieutenant
or privy council of heads of bills passed by parliament to legalise quarterage
payments to city guilds by catholic merchants and tradesmen. These payments
had been declared illegal by a judgement of the court of king's bench in 1759.[17]

16 See Haliday pamphlet, vol. 121/1735 in Royal Irish Academy.   17 Wall, Maureen,
Catholic Ireland in the eighteenth century, Dublin 1989, 61–73.

The merchants and tradesmen of the cities and large towns were another sizeable stratum of protestants with little connection with the landed gentry. The vast majority particularly of protestant tradesmen – we are talking about weavers, tailors, barbers, bakers, blacksmiths, butchers, carpenters, coopers, bricklayers etc. – could be described as no more than lower middle class, if not indeed as working class. These as freemen of their respective guilds had a vote in parliamentary elections, but the cities were grossly under-represented in the matter of parliamentary seats; Dublin city, for example, had only two seats when on a population basis at the mid-century it would have been entitled to nearly twenty. Furthermore, a candidate seeking these freemen votes was highly unlikely to be one of themselves, but rather some lawyer or esquire. Considering that the protestant population of the cities of Dublin, Cork, Limerick and Waterford numbered about 105,000 in the 1730s and that there was a further considerable number in such boroughs as Drogheda, Kilkenny, Galway, Clonmel, Sligo, Youghal, Athlone and Wexford, the numerical importance of the cities and larger towns is apparent as comprising near a half of the members of the established church in Ireland.[18] And yet the cities and towns mentioned were represented by only 24 MPs in a house of 300, the inescapable conclusion being that in effect the country was governed, not so much by a protestant ascendancy, as by an oligarchy of country gentlemen within that ascendancy. Proposals in the 1780s to reform the parliamentary system failed to obtain the necessary majority in the Irish house of commons. It was, of course, too much to expect that the oligarchs would vote themselves into oblivion.

18 *Abstract of the number of protestant and popish families*, Dublin, 1736; Arthur Dobbs, *Essay on trade and improvement in Ireland*, Dublin 1731, part 2, p. 9. I have omitted the Ulster cities and towns from these calculations since their populations were predominantly of the dissenter persuasion.

2

To Abjure or Not to Abjure

It appears that for five or six years following the Treaty of Limerick Irish catholics enjoyed a degree of toleration. A census of catholic clergy carried out for the authorities in 1697 by poll tax clerks,[1] shows in the case of Dublin diocese, which is the only area for which detailed records of this census have survived, that catholic priests, both secular and regular, were living quite openly in the diocese. The census showed that there were 892 secular and 495 regular clergy in the country as a whole.[2] As already noted, the government had ever viewed the regulars with a jaundiced eye because of their extreme loyalty to the pope and because they could be said to be an unnecessary burden on the poor. It appears, then, that the government had plans for the banishment of the regulars in mind for some time but the fact that the War of the League of Augsburg was in progress until 1697 meant that such plans had to be shelved until the return of peace, since it would not have been feasible to banish large numbers of regulars to the European continent while there was a war going on there. It is not surprising then that the first bill (or rather heads of a bill) to be processed by the parliamentary session of 1697 was one for the banishment of the regular clergy from Ireland. The heads of bill were quickly passed and sent to London where they were approved by the privy council and received the royal assent on 25 September 1797. The original bill applied only to regular clergy and it was in that form it was agreed by William III. On its return to Ireland, however, it was expanded by the Irish parliament somewhat surreptitiously to include also the banishment of bishops and secular clergy exercising ecclesiastical jurisdiction. The expulsion of the regulars was carried out in a highly efficient manner and 424 of them were recorded as having been transported from Irish ports.[3]

1 Burke, W.P., *The Irish priests in the penal times*, Shannon 1969, 120.   2 Ibid., 128
3 Simms, J.G., 'The bishops banishment act 1697' in *Irish Historical Studies*, vol. 17 (1970), 185–99. This figure taken in conjunction with the figure of 495 in the 1697 census might imply that there were only seventy regulars left in the country following the banishments. However, there is evidence – see in particular *Collectanea Hibernica* no. 8 (1965) – that there were several hundred regulars in the country *c*.1700. The figure in

The speed with which the bill was processed may have taken the catholic body by surprise. In any event it appears that the bill was already law when the Irish catholic lobby saw fit to make representations to the Imperial ambassador in London, Count Auersperg. Since through the operation of Poynings' Law the Irish parliament was powerless itself to pass laws, the proper time to make representations against projected bills was before they had received approval in London. As Britain's catholic ally on the continent – and he was to remain such until the start of the Seven Years War in 1756 – the Austrian emperor was seen by the catholics of Ireland as a powerful intermediary with the British government for the quashing of anti-catholic measures proposed by the Irish parliament.

Count Auersperg's belated intervention elicited from Henry de Ruvigney, earl of Galway, one of the lords justices in charge of the administration in the absence of the lord lieutenant, the reply that the banishment of the regulars was 'what has always been wished for by the secular clergy', but the seculars made a statement denying this.

On 9 May 1698 the count informed the internuncio in Brussels, who had *inter alia* responsibility for Irish affairs, that the Irish lord chancellor, Lord Methuen, had informed him that the Banishment Act would not be fully enforced and that some regular clergy would be allowed to stay, especially those who were too old to be sent away.[4] However, a dispatch from the internuncio to Cardinal Secretary of State Spada in Rome puts a somewhat different slant on the situation in that the internuncio records that Auersperg had seen a letter written by Lord Galway in which he gave assurances that moderation would be used in dealing with catholics, that it was not intended to make any further changes in Irish ecclesiastical affairs apart from the expulsion of the regular clergy, and that this latter measure had been taken for grave reasons of state.

The intervention by Austria, while it came too late to have any effect on the actual expulsions, must have had some effect in staying the hand of the Irish authorities in the matter of taking action against those regulars who evaded the act by remaining on in Ireland or who dared to return to Ireland following transportation. In the event the regulars began to filter back to such an extent that by the 1720s they were believed to be as numerous as at any time since Charles II's reign.[5]

The fact that the seculars had not been included in the Banishment Act implied that they were to be allowed a degree of toleration, but since bishops

the census could have been deficient due to regulars going to ground or by concealing their true identity by working in parishes like seculars. **4** Giblin, Cathaldus, 'Catalogue of material of Irish interest in the collection Nunziatura di Fiandra, Vatican Archives' in *Collectanea Hibernica*, no. 4 (1961), 72. **5** Gilbert Library MS 28. In the 1720s there were around 650 regular clergy in Ireland – see H. Fenning, *The undoing of the friars of Ireland*, Louvain 1972, 201.

were included in the act, the government's hope apparently was that in time the number of seculars would through deaths be drastically reduced, since there would be no bishops to ordain new priests, and an act of 1703 (2 Anne sess.1 c. 3) prohibited catholic clergy of any kind from entering the country.

The oath of abjuration first made its appearance in England in the first year of Queen Anne's reign. On the death of James II in 1701 Louis XIV had recognised his son as James III and the English parliament felt it necessary to pass an act entitled 'an act to declare the alterations in the oath appointed to be taken' (1 Anne c. 22 Eng.), which imposed a special oath on state officials, expressly denying the right of the Stuart claimant to the throne. This oath is word for word exactly the same as that in the Irish acts of 1704 and 1709 which will be dealt with later.[6]

The first appearance of this English oath of abjuration, as directed specifically against catholics in Ireland, was in the act to prevent the further growth of popery 1704, section 24 of which provided that, 'for preventing Papists having it in their power to breed dissension among Protestants by voting in elections for members of parliament', from and after 24 March 1704 no catholic

---

6 The oath of abjuration was worded as follows: 'I, A.B., do truly and sincerely acknowledge, profess, testify and declare in my conscience, before God and the World, that our sovereign Lady Queen Anne is lawful and rightful queen of this realm and of all other her Majesty's dominions and countries thereunto belonging. And I do solemnly and sincerely declare that I do believe in my conscience, that the person pretending to be Prince of Wales, during the life of the late King James, and since his decease pretending to be, and taking upon himself the style and title of King of England by the name of James the Third, hath not any right or title whatsoever to the crown of this realm or any other the dominions thereto belonging. And I do renounce, abjure and refuse any allegiance or obedience to him; and I do swear that I will bear faith and true allegiance to her Majesty Queen Anne and her will defend to the utmost of my power against all traitorous conspiracies and attempts whatsoever which shall be made against her person, crown or dignity; and I will do my best endeavour to disclose and make known to her Majesty and her successors all treasons and traitorous conspiracies which I shall know to be against her or any of them; and I do faithfully promise to the utmost of my power to support, maintain and defend the limitation and succession of the crown against him the said James, and all other persons whatsoever, as the same is and stands limited by an act intitled "An act declaring the Rights and Liberties of the Subject, and settling the Succession of the Crown, to her present Majesty and the Heirs of her Body being Protestants"; and as the same by one other act, intitled, "An act for the further Limitation of the Crown, and better securing the Rights and Liberties of the Subject, is and stands limited after the decease of her Majesty, and for default of Issue of her Majesty, to the Princess Sophia, Electress and Dutchess Dowager of Hanover, and the heirs of her body being Protestants". And all these things I do plainly and sincerely acknowledge and swear according to the express words by me spoken and according to the plain and common sense and understanding of the same words, without any equivocation, mental evasion or secret reservation whatsoever. And I do make this recognition, acknowledgment, abjuration, renunciation and promise, heartily, willingly and truly, upon the true faith of a Christian. So help me God.'

freeholder, burgess or freeman or inhabitant of this kingdom should be capable of voting in elections for members of parliament unless he had taken the oaths of allegiance and abjuration. The form of the oath of abjuration to be taken was that set out in the English act 1 Anne c. 22 above. There was no requirement in the act for anyone else of the catholic persuasion in Ireland to take the oath except those catholics who wished to retain the right to vote. Although clearly the intention of the act was to make it difficult for catholics to qualify for a vote in parliamentary elections, Dr Simms's researches show that a substantial number of catholics took the required oaths in order to so qualify.[7] Indeed it is said that the large number of catholics who voted in the 1727 general election, and the influence they had in the success of some Tory candidates, was what determined Primate Boulter to put in train the 1728 act to deprive catholics of the right to vote altogether.

The oath of abjuration next appeared in the act of 1707 to explain and amend the 1698 act to prevent papists being solicitors. Under section 1 of this act a person practising as a solicitor in any suit of law or equity was required to take the oath and make the declaration against Transubstantiation in the 1698 act and in addition to take the oath of abjuration. However, section 8 provided a saver in respect of persons comprehended by the Articles of Limerick who had practised as common solicitors, managers or agents in the courts in the reign of Charles II and who had taken the oath of abjuration before 1 July 1707.

Turning to barristers, there has been some confusion as to what was required of them in the matter of oaths and declarations. Section 4 of the English act 3 William & Mary c. 2 required Irish barristers at law and attorneys to take the oath of allegiance, the new oath replacing the oath of supremacy and to make the declaration against Transubstantiation 'from the first day of Hilary term next' (that is, January 1692) but there was a saver in section 8 of that act in respect of persons who on 3 October 1691 were in Irish garrisons and had submitted to the king.

Dr Simms mentions that 'the oath of abjuration was demanded from barristers in 1703', but it seems to me that they were included in the category 'every person or persons whatsoever ... who shall bear any office or offices, civil or military' in section 16 of 2 Anne c. 6 (that is, the act to prevent the further growth of popery 1704) which required such persons from Easter term 1704 to take the oath of supremacy, make the declaration against Transubstantiation and receive the Sacrament of the Lord's Supper according to the usage of the Church of Ireland. It should also be noted in this connection that the records of the King's Inns include notice of an order made in 1704–5, but probably in May 1704, which stipulated that no person was to be admittted to the bar and practise as a barrister 'until he shall produce an authoritative certificate of his

7 Simms, J.G., *War and politics in Ireland 1649–1730*, London 1986, 228–9.

receiving the Sacrament according to the usage of the Church of Ireland ... the said admittance pursuant to the late act'.

However, not surprisingly, there appears to have been some doubt as to whether barristers were in fact covered by the description, persons bearing civil or military offices, in the 1704 act. At any rate, section 1 of 1 George II c. 20 (1727) sought to clarify the situation by requiring barristers, six clerks, attornies, solicitors and officers of the court to take the several oaths and subscribe the declaration against transubstantiation in the 1704 act to prevent the further growth of popery. There was a saver in respect of the Articles of Limerick and Galway for solicitors only.

It is also relevant that section 2 of the Popish Solicitors Act 1734 provided that barristers-at-law and attorneys should take a new oath, set out in the 1734 act, that they would not suffer any disqualified (i.e. catholic) barrister or solicitor to act or practise in their name, in addition to taking all the oaths and subscribing the declaration 'required of persons to be admitted into offices of state by the statute made in the second year of the reign of Queen Anne', that is, 2 Anne c. 6 mentioned above.

As to the situation catholic lawyers found themselves in, Fr Cornelius Nary in *The case of the Roman Catholics of Ireland*, written in 1724, is quite clear when he states:

> All Roman Catholic Lawyers, Attorneys and Solicitors are disabled to practise their respective callings, except they take the Oath of Abjuration, the Oath of Supremacy and the Test, that is, become Protestants. So that of about an hundred Roman Catholic Lawyers and Attorneys, that attended the Courts of Dublin, and in the country, not one of them is allowed to get a Morsel of Bread by those studies upon which they spent their youth and their time.[8]

Nary does not mention the saver in the 1707 Solicitors Act in respect of solicitors comprehended by the Articles of Limerick, perhaps because after a period of over thirty years the saver mattered very little. There was no such saver in respect of barristers and this appears to have been quite deliberate, for the act of 1727 and 1734, which covered barristers, attorneys and solicitors, allowed such a saver only in respect of solicitors.

Sir Toby Butler is often mentioned as a catholic barrister who took the oath of abjuration, and indeed he could have been little faulted if that was his only fall from grace. However, he would also have had to make the declaration against Transubstantiation and to receive the Sacrament according to the usage of the Church of Ireland if he wished to continue practising as a counsellor-

8 Reilly, Hugh, *Genuine history of Ireland*, Dublin 1762, 116.

at-law. This would have put him outside the fold of the Catholic Church, and Swift was probably accurate enough when he described him as one of his flock.[9] But he may have returned to the catholic church before he died in March 1721, for a notice of his death in *Whalley's Newsletter* has him competing with the former Jacobite chief justice, Denis Daly, who died at the same time, for 'the chief seat in Purgatory'.

The government wished to continue to maintain control over the numbers and movements of the secular clergy and this was the aim of the Act for registering popish clergy 1704 (2 Anne c. 7). Under the act each priest was required at the next general quarter sessions or assizes after 24 June 1704 to return his name, place of abode, age, parish of which he pretended to be popish priest, time and place of ordination and ordaining bishop. He was further required to enter into sufficient sureties, each in the sum of £50, and to be of peaceable behaviour and not to remove out of such county where his place of abode lay into any other part of the kingdom. The act was interpreted as allowing one catholic priest per civil parish although some catholic parishes comprised two or more civil parishes.

Despite the restrictions on the numbers and on the movement of clergy, the act afforded the secular clergy a degree of official recognition that they were not to experience again until the passing of the relief act of 1782. It is not surprising, then, that there was apparently no reluctance on the part of the clergy to register. In fact some 1089 did so and this was 197 more than the number of seculars in the country according to the census taken a few years before.[10] The discrepancy was probably due to some regulars, illegally in the country, registering for parishes and to some error in the census figure.

It is surprising that this act, in view of the obvious benefits conferred thereby on the catholic secular clergy, had no strings attached in the form of an oath of allegiance to Queen Anne or an oath of abjuration of the Stuarts by priests registering, more particularly as there was already, as noted above, an oath of abjuration readymade in section 24 of the act to prevent the further growth of popery 1704. In fact there was a requirement for such an oath in the heads of bill as submitted to the British privy council but it was omitted at the behest of that council.[11]

However, the Irish parliament was not disposed to let the matter rest and in any event loopholes, in need of attention, had begun to emerge in the act to prevent the further growth of popery. A commons committtee was, therefore, set up to prepare the heads of a bill for explaining and amending that act. Henry Tenison, member for County Louth, presented the resulting heads of a bill to the house on 7 August 1707, when they were received and committed

9 Williams, Harold (ed.), *The correspondence of Jonathan Swift*, vol. 2, 341. 10 Corish, P.J., *The catholic community in the seventeenth and eighteenth centuries*, Dublin 1981, 76. 11 Simms, J.G., op. cit., 229.

to a committee of the whole house for consideration. The heads were again before the house on 9 and 11 August. On 12 August Prime Serjeant Caulfield reported from the committee that the heads had been gone through paragraph by paragraph. The heads were then agreed by the house with some further amendments and were ordered to be conveyed to the lord lieutenant for transmission to London for approval.[12]

The *Commons Journal* gives no inkling as to what was contained in these heads of bill, and what information we have in the matter comes from a report sent by someone in London to the internuncio in Brussels who transmitted the report on 22 December 1707 to Cardinal Secretary of State Paolucci in Rome. This report states that it was proposed during the last (i.e. 1707) session of the Irish parliament that it was necessary to formulate some law to check the growth of Catholicism in Ireland; that commissioners had been named to draw up a plan which would compel "religious [*sic*] and parish priests" to take the oath of abjuration; that this move was in accordance with a law drawn up by the English parliament to guarantee the succession to the throne of Princess Sophia of Hanover and her heirs; that this guarantee was embodied in an oath of fidelity to the princess and her heirs which renounced any right to the throne which might be claimed by the Prince of Wales (James Stuart) on the death of the reigning queen. Penalties were prescribed for refusal to take the oath and awards for informers were provided for.

The report goes on to state that when the heads of the bill were sent to the English privy council, Irish catholics sent a delegation to London to implore the queen to withhold her consent and also to make it clear that it was impossible for the religious to take such an oath; that recourse was also had by the delegation to the envoys in London of the catholic powers to enlist their help; that the queen's advisers insisted that the oath was in no way opposed to the catholic religion but that it merely demanded loyalty to a monarch who had been declared heir to the throne in accordance with the law of the land, and accordingly the religious as subjects of the queen could not refuse to take the oath.[13] However, since the queen and her council were not in favour of oppressing anybody, her advisers would examine the heads to see if they could

---

12 *Commons Journal Ireland*, vol. 2, part 1 under dates mentioned. 13 Giblin, C., op. cit., no. 15 (1972), 12–13. The use of the word 'religious' in the report is confusing since this is a word which is generally applied only to the regular clergy. The oath would have applied only to registered priests, all the regular clergy and unregistered priests having been banished from the country. For 'religious', then, we should read 'registered priest'. It should be kept in mind that this report was originally written probably in English, the internuncio had it translated into Italian for transmission to Rome, and then, in our own day, it was translated back into English by Fr Giblin. A letter dated 22 November 1707 sent from London to the internuncio (op. cit., p. 14) was of course incorrect in stating that, when parliament was on the point of being prorogued on 30 October, an *act* was passed obliging priests to take the oath of abjuration.

moderate their terms in any way. Certain changes were, therefore, made in the heads, which were then approved by the queen and sent back to Ireland.

The heads had now gained the status of a bill which, the *Commons Journal* tells us, was presented to the house and read a first time on 10 October. It was read a second time and committed to a committee of the whole house on 13 October. On 18 October it was reported that the committee had gone through the bill paragraph by paragraph and had agreed on every paragraph except one. Apparently because they were not prepared to accept the changes made in London, the house then resolved that the bill be rejected.

As a sort of parting shot, as the last item on the last day of the session (30 October), the house passed two resolutions, nem. con., as follows:

1 That all Popish priests within the Kingdom were obliged to take the Oath of Abjuration by the laws in force in this Kingdom; and that all such priests refusing or neglecting to take the same, ought to be prosecuted for such refusal or neglect.
2 That it was the indispensible duty of all Judges and Magistrates to put the said laws in execution against Popish priests.

As regards the legal status of these resolutions, the report, mentioned above, commented that they were not given the force of law in the usual way, magistrates being directed to keep them in mind and to enforce them as they saw fit. But the report also says that, should priests refuse to take the oath of abjuration, then the 'old laws' were to be put into execution against them. Accordingly, the report concludes, the implementation of the resolutions depended on the clemency of Irish courts and judges.

This report shows Queen Anne in a new and revealing light. While her name has always been associated with the worst enactments of the penal laws, this report shows that she herself favoured toleration for catholics but was apparently unable to control the legislative excesses of her parliaments and ministers in Dublin and London. The two resolutions passed in the Irish house of commons were apparently *ultra vires* since at that time the oath of abjuration applied in Ireland only in the particular situations provided for in the act to prevent the further growth of popery. But it will be seen that priests were to be faced with the Hobson's choice of either taking the oath or of having the 'old laws' put into execution against them.

In the meantime, events outside Ireland were having an influence on the Irish administration to the further detriment of catholics, lay and clerical. The prospect of a grandson of Louis XIV becoming king of Spain and the consequent implications for the concept of the balance of power in Europe, added to Louis' seizure of the barrier fortresses in the Spanish Netherlands, had propelled the Grand Alliance of Britain, Holland and the Empire into a war with

France and Spain in 1701, known as the War of the Spanish Succession, which
was to continue until 1713. As a somewhat minor offshoot of the French campaign, in the spring of 1708 James Stuart, with the aid of French troops,
planned an invasion of Scotland. When, however, the French ships arrived in
the Firth of Forth the expected Scottish support did not materialise and indeed
there was no pilot to guide the ships into the harbour. In a subsequent attack
by British ships James was lucky to escape and he was back in Paris by the end
of April 1708.

On the first rumour of James Stuart's projected invasion the authorities in
Dublin took action to eliminate any possible support for him in Ireland. On
16 March 1708 the lords justices and privy council issued a proclamation for
seizing and apprehending the 'pretended Prince of Wales' and all his traitorous confederates and adherents; for taking the arms, ammunition, horses etc
belonging to any Papist or disaffected person; and for seizing and committing
to jail all Popish priests till further orders.[14]

On 23 March 1708 the lords justices and council issued a further proclamation for the apprehending of all popish priests not already secured and
forbidding any person to conceal, comfort or support any priest in his home
or other place, upon pain of incurring her Majesty's highest displeasure and
of being prosecuted with the utmost severity.[15]

About the same time in Dublin city the lords justices sent for Messrs Elmor,
Bagot, Butler, Daly (a judge in James II's time) and Cooke, and Drs Fitzpatrick
and Wogan. They are reported to have been tendered the oath of abjuration,
which they refused. They were then confined to their chambers and a guard
put over them.[16] Meanwhile the lord mayor of Dublin put out a proclamation
with the names of 31 of the popish priests of the city, who had withdrawn
themselves from their usual places of abode, requiring them to appear.

One of the priests apprehended at this time, Fr Oliver Doyle, parish priest
of Castleknock, Co. Dublin, wrote in the following terms from Kilmainham
jail to his landlord, Sir Richard Bellings, who lived in London:

Upon a report that the Prince of Wales is to land in Scotland, all the registered clergy of this kingdom and all persons having commissions from King
James, his father, are taken into custody and are committed into the several gaols of this kingdom without bail or mainprise. Among whom Father
Walter Cruise and I are committed here, which is the common gaol for this
county, where we are to continue during Government pleasure, which in all
probability will be whilst the differences in Scotland continue.[17]

14 Brady, John, *Catholics and catholicism in the eighteenth century press*, Maynooth 1965, 9.
15 Ibid., 10. 16 Ibid., 9. 17 Fagan, Patrick, *Dublin's turbulent priest: Cornelius Nary
1658–1738*, Dublin 1991, 64.

In other parts of the country moves were also made against catholic clergy and laity in accordance with the proclamation. The mayor of Kilkenny complained of the beleaguered situation in which protestants found themselves in that city and county; they were, he said, 'but a handful in respect of the Popish inhabitants who will not take the Oath of Abjuration, it being refused by the chief of them though tendered by me'. Outside the city they were 'in a way surrounded by that inveterate and implacable enemy'. He therefore entreated that arms and ammunition be sent as also the Commissioners of Array (for raising the militia).[18] A report from Queen's County (Laois) dated March 1708 stated that 'the priests are all in custody and we are now sending to all to take the Oath of Abjuration and such as refuse shall be committed'.[19] From Kerry in April 1708 it was reported that Lord Kenmare, Col. Maurice Hussey, MacCarthy More and others had refused the oath of abjuration and were prisoners in Tralee.[20] In Galway city all the popish inhabitants had been turned out of the town and Col. Dominick Browne and Sir Walter Blake had been 'secured' after refusing the oath. Likewise a large number of gentlemen from Galway county had been confined in the city because they would not take the oath.[21]

It might appear surprising that none of those reported to have been arrested agreed to take the oath of abjuration, since some catholics would have already taken it for the purpose of securing a vote in parliamentary elections. However, the authorities were apparently acting *ultra vires* in demanding the oath in circumstances other than those provided for in the 1704 act. In refusing the oath, then, those arrested were simply standing by the letter of the law.

Thomas Earl Wharton was appointed lord lieutenant in 1709 with Joseph Addison, the noted writer, as chief secretary. A notorious Whig, Wharton saw it as his mission to unite both strands of protestantism, established church and dissenter, against 'the common enemy', the papists. His own background – he was reared a calvinist – rendered him eminently suitable for such a mission. He had the name of being the greatest rake in England and, according to Swift's well-known character of him, he was a presbyterian in politics and an atheist in religion who chose to whore with a papist.[22] Although the dissenters remained second class citizens – the application of the Sacramental Test rendered them ineligible for public office, military commissions and membership of municipal corporations[23] – their antipathy to Catholicism was so extreme that they were quite willing to sink their differences with the established church, as long as the papists remained even more downtrodden than themselves. The term 'presbyterian' at this time appears to have been synonymous with 'Whig' and to have derived from the Scottish, Low Church and Parliamentarian origins of

18 Burke, W.P., op. cit. 320. The purpose of the Commissioners of Array was to arm the militia.   19 Ibid., 337.   20 Ibid., 390.   21 Ibid., 413.   22 Scott, Temple (ed.), *The prose works of Jonathan Swift*, London 1908, vol. 5, p.9.   23 Dickson, David, *New foundations: Ireland 1660–1800*, Dublin, 1987, 74–5.

that party. Swift uses the word in this sense when he describes Wharton as a presbyterian in politics, as indeed when he described his own housekeeper, Mrs Brent, as a presbyterian.[24] This usage of the word was also known on the Continent where we find the Brussels internuncio referring to presbyterians when he means Whigs.

In an address to Wharton the Irish house of commons acknowledged his tender regard of their welfare by putting them in mind of the great inequality there was between the number of protestants and catholics in the kingdom and of 'the dispositions of this sort of men among us'. They had found, they said, by deep-bought and fatal experience that the protestant religion and British interest in the kingdom were 'no longer safe than while it is not in the power of the Papists to distress or destroy them; and with abhorrence they called to mind the satisfaction which too visibly appeared in their faces and by the insolent behaviour of the generality of them when the late attempt was made by the Pretender upon the North part of Great Britain'. To preserve themselves against the danger from these enemies of their peace, they should consider of such laws as should be necessary for their own security and not be amused by those who endeavour to represent them (catholics) as neither inclined or able to do them harm. Lest the papists might be encouraged with hopes of succeeding in their wicked designs by the disagreement in matters of religious worship which unhappily divided the protestants of the Kingdom, they craved leave to assure his Excellency that 'as it shall be our chiefest care inviolably to preserve, support and maintain the church as by law established, so we cannot be so negligent of our common safety ... as to think it reasonable that those [Dissenters] who have hitherto given and shall continue to give all testimonies and assurances of their being faithful to the government and abjure the Pretender, should be laid under any uneasiness in the exercise of their religious worship; a liberty enjoyed by our most dangerous enemies.'[25]

Wharton was therefore to find himself at one with the majority in the Irish parliament in his aim further to oppress the catholics. As we have seen the heads of a new anti-popery bill had been amended by the English privy council in 1707 and so had not been proceeded with by the Irish parliament. The danger of a Jacobite invasion, which had become a near reality in March 1708, was now an additional impetus to revive this piece of legislation. Accordingly, on 10 May 1709 the heads of what is generally known as the second act to prevent the further growth of popery were introduced in the Irish house of commons by Sergeant Caulfield, and were ordered to be discussed in a committee of the whole house. In the ensuing six weeks this committee met on ten occasions and so must have subjected the heads to a very detailed examination. Part of their time was spent in interviewing representatives of protestant merchants

24 Williams, H. (ed.), op. cit., vol. 3, 434.   25 Brady, John, op. cit., 11.

and tradesmen from Dublin who complained about the inroads being made on their businesses by their catholic counterparts. The heads were eventually passed on 18 June and were sent to the lord lieutenant for transmission to London.[26]

What emerged was a rather lengthy bill, the most significant part of which was that all registered priests were required to take the oath of abjuration by 25 March 1710 on pain of being treated as regulars. Laymen also could be required to take the oath by any two or more justices of the peace. The penalty for a layman refusing to take the oath was, for a first offence, three months imprisonment or a fine of forty shillings and a perpetual ban on his being licensed to own or bear arms. There were stiffer penalties prescribed for second offences. Upon refusal of the oath a third time a layman was guilty of a *Praemunire*, that is, forfeiture and confiscation of all his real and personal estate and perpetual imprisonment.

The remaining highly important sections of the bill, with which we are not here concerned, related mainly to tightening up on the property and such like provisions of the 1704 act, but there were also provisions in regard to converts to the established church, both lay and clerical; on registered priests keeping a curate – they were both to be treated as regulars – and on the transportation of regulars and bishops.[27]

Meanwhile the Irish Catholic lobby had not been idle in regard to the bill. They swung into action on two fronts, firstly by mustering the support of the ambassadors of the catholic powers in London with a view to having the legislation negatived by the British privy council, and, secondly, by dispatching a priest from Dublin to Louvain to get the opinion of the Strict Faculty of that university on the question of Irish catholic priests and laymen taking the oath of abjuration, and to bring the oath and indeed the other provisions of the bill to the attention of the Brussels internuncio, Grimaldi.[28] A later commons address to the lord lieutenant mentions that the bill had been returned to Dublin by the British privy council in the same form as it had been 'retransmitted' 'notwithstanding the strong efforts made against it by the Irish Papists in Great Britain'.[29] From this we gather that the Irish lobby tried to have the bill negatived when it came before the British privy council but failed to achieve that end.

In July 1709 the Brussels internuncio, Grimaldi, engaged the Austrian Count Zinzendorf, then at the Hague, to make representations to London, but apparently these representations were made too late to have any effect on the decision

---

26 *Commons Journal Ireland*, vol. 2, part 1, 579–624. The heads were approved by the privy council in London on 31 July. On return to Dublin the bill was formally passed by the commons on 17 August and by the lords on 24 August 1709. 27 8 Anne c. 3, sections 22–4. 28 Giblin, Cathaldus, op. cit., 115. 29 *Dublin Intelligence*, 6 September 1709. The use of the word 'retransmitted' probably means that there was very little difference between the 1709 and the 1707 bills.

of the British privy council.[30] Later on 30 August 1709 Count Gallas, the imperial envoy in London, sent Grimaldi a report on the efforts he had made against
the bill. Gallas was emphatic that the delays in carrying out what he was asked
to do were not his fault, but were due to the tardiness of those in charge of
the negotiations on the English (Irish?) side. He saw that little good would come
of his efforts to block approval of the bill by verbal representations, as he would
receive only the usual, meaningless answers. Consequently he decided to present
his case in writing in the hope that he would procure a more logical and precise
reply, but he received answers from the two secretaries of state so inconsistent
and evasive that he decided to write to them again in a more vigorous strain,
but he heard nothing further of the matter. He believed that the whole opposition was the work of a faction which looked on the destruction of the catholics
as the extermination of an enemy. He had some hope that the British house of
lords, which had been opposed to such violent persecution from the very beginning, might yet intervene, but he was very doubtful if the lords would have
enough courage to make such a stand.[31] Presumably Gallas concentrated on the
other lengthy provisions of the bill rather than on the oath of abjuration, for it
is difficult to see how the imperial ambassador could be expected to work up
much enthusiasm against an oath abjuring James Stuart, considering that the
latter was actively engaged in plotting against the Anglo-Austrian alliance and
indeed had served with Austria's enemy, the French, at Oudenarde and
Malplaquet.

A letter from Grimaldi to Cardinal Paolucci at Rome dated 26 September
1709 shows that the Portuguese ambassador in London had also been active in
making representations to the English first minister.[32] At the beginning of
October Internuncio Grimaldi, on orders from Rome, wrote again to the catholic
ambassadors in London beseeching them to do everything in their power to
have the execution of the act deferred. He hoped that the ambassadors would
exert themselves to the best of their abilities for a cause which was so merito-
rious before God and so acceptable to the Holy See. He could see little prospect
of success, however, given the then state of the English government in which
the presbyterians (Whigs) predominated and sought their own ends without
mercy. He singled out the earl of Wharton as one of the leaders of the presbyterian party who was most powerful in the parliament and kept the more
moderate members of the court in subjection, so that they dared not offer any
opposition to him. However, God might intervene in some unexpected way to
make those evil counsels futile.[33]

Meanwhile the priest deputed to obtain the opinion of the Strict Faculty of
Louvain on the admissibility of the oath of abjuration for catholic priests and
laymen, had been less than successful in that mission. About July 1709 the

30 Giblin, C., op. cit., 117.   31 Ibid., 119–20.   32 Ibid., 123.   33 Ibid., 124.

priest informed Grimaldi that the regents of the faculty had not given any judgment, but that some theologians he had consulted declared that they considered the oath to be unlawful. These latter based their opinion on the iniquity of the oath itself and on two briefs written in 1606 and 1607 by Pope Paul V, condemning an oath for catholics decreed by James I. The priest was waiting to procure a document from Louvain which would give some satisfaction to the faithful in Ireland.[34]

On 1 August 1709 Grimaldi reported to Rome that the Irish priest was returning home in a few days without having obtained from the Strict Faculty the documents he had sought. The priest asked Grimaldi to give him a letter to the archbishop of Dublin advising the latter that he should not come to any decision on the oath without having first heard the opinion of the pope on the matter, and Grimaldi agreed to do this.[35]

Later on 24 August 1709 Grimaldi informed Paolucci that he had written to the archbishop of Dublin and by various channels had informed the bishops and clergy in Ireland that the formula of the oath had been examined at a meeting in the presence of the pope, and that the pope had decided that the oath was neither lawful nor binding; consequently that Irish catholics must abide by this judgment of the Holy See and pay no attention to whatever others might say on the point. As this direction from Grimaldi would have reached Ireland shortly after the arrival there of the priest who had been sent to Louvain, Grimaldi felt that any dangerous move on the part of the clergy or faithful had been opportunely forestalled.[36]

On 12 September 1709 Grimaldi informed Cardinal Paolucci that, in conveying the papal decision to the archbishop of Dublin, he had thought it as well to proceed with circumspection so as not to create further trouble for Irish catholics by disclosing the opinion of the Holy See on the oath. Accordingly, he sent the letter containing the decision to an Irish religious in Louvain with the request that he should return the letter to him (Grimaldi) as soon as he was satisfied he would be able to pass on the information in it to the archbishop in coded language and using assumed names as was usual in such cases in order to avoid discovery. The religious, however, considered the judgment was of such importance that he should send the internuncio's letter to the archbishop exactly as he had received it, while expressing the hope that no use would be made of the letter except in case of necessity. Grimaldi stated that he had informed the other bishops in Ireland through intermediaries of the pope's opinion of the oath and he hoped that all doubts about the matter would be removed since they could if necessary have recourse to the archbishop of Dublin for further confirmation.[37]

---

34 Ibid., 115. 35 Ibid., 115–17. 36 Ibid., 118–19. 37 Ibid., 120–1.

On 15 November 1709 the imperial ambassador, Gallas, reported to Grimaldi that even though the act would be put into execution in a short time and some of the principal Irish catholics, to avoid trouble, had gone to England, nevertheless there was a likelihood that it would be enforced with some moderation.[38] A letter received in the nunciature dated 17 November 1709 from Fr Edmund Knavin, a parish priest of Clonfert diocese, stated that in some parts of Ireland the law had already been enforced; that some (laity?) had taken the oath, while others had refused and had paid the fine for the first offence. Knavin feared, however, that most catholics would take the oath rather than run the risk of losing everything they had; he said the clergy had until 25 March 1710 to take the oath and that no terms were expected and no mercy.[39] In mid-December Grimaldi made further representations to the ambassadors of the catholic powers in London to do what they could towards having the greatest possible moderation used in enforcing the act.[40]

It can be deduced from the correspondence of the Brussels internuncio outlined above that the Strict Faculty of Louvain were not prepared to say that the oath of abjuration was such as could not be taken by Irish catholics. It appears that some of the catholic laity took the oath without much delay and that left to themselves, without any papal pronouncement in the matter, many more of the laity and clergy would have found the oath unobjectionable. As regards the pope's decision, it could hardly have been otherwise since he could scarcely have allowed Irish catholic clergy and laity to declare that they believed in their conscience that the man who in his capacity as James III was to nominate nearly every Irish catholic bishop for the next 56 years, had not any right or title whatsoever to the crown of Great Britain and Ireland.

The question, then, of whether the oath could be taken by catholics was far from being cut and dry, particularly as the oath did not transgress on any articles of the catholic faith. The pope's pronouncement could be explained away as a political decision stemming from his acknowledgment of James Stuart as the rightful king of Great Britain and Ireland. The most eloquent case against the oath is to be found in Fr Cornelius Nary's *The case of the Roman Catholics of Ireland* written in 1724 in reply to the anti-popery bill of 1723. While Nary would have no difficulty in swearing an oath of allegiance to the British monarch, there were three clauses in the oath of abjuration to which he could not in conscience swear. He outlined these as follows:

First, I am required by this oath to swear that I believe in my conscience that the late King James or the Pretender have no right or title whatsoever to the crown of England. Now, I am so far a stranger to the right and titles of kings and princes (and I am sure most of my profession, if not all, in this

38 Ibid., 128.   39 Ibid., 129–30.   40 Ibid., 130.

kingdom are so) that I would not take such an oath to any king, prince or potentate in Europe, with respect to all such pretenders to their crowns as they should require me to abjure. For to be able to swear it, I must have sure and certain motives to ground my belief upon, else I perjure myself. But this is what I could never yet find in anything that I read, or from any person with whom I conversed. Nay, many divines and persons of note and learning of the Church of England and of the Church of Scotland, and Ireland as by law established, have believed and do still believe that neither the late King James nor the Pretender have forfeited their right to the crown of England. And I am sure all the divines and lawyers in France, Spain and Italy are of the same opinion. How can I then, or any other Roman Catholic in this kingdom, ground my belief so as to swear that he has not? But whether he has or has not, I am no ways concerned at taking the oath of allegiance, which the law of nature and the common practice of all nations, allows me to take with a safe conscience to any prince who conquers me, and the country of which I am a member, tho' he be never so great a tyrant or usurper, even to the Zar of Muscovy or to the Grand Turk. But surely I could not swear that I believed King George had no right to the crown of England or Ireland, should either of these conquer me. Secondly, there is another clause in the Oath of Abjuration requiring men to swear they will maintain the succession to the crown in the Protestant line &c. Now, how any Roman Catholic, continuing such, can in conscience take such an oath, I own I do not understand. For by this clause I am sworn (should I take the said oath) to withdraw my obedience from (and the allegiance I swore before to) King George and his successors, in case he or his successors should become Roman Catholics: Nor is this an imaginary case: for what was, may be. [He proceeds to give examples of protestant kings who turned catholic.] Now if it should so happen to the royal family in Great Britain in time to come, and that they should embrace the religion which I profess: Could I in conscience violate my oath of allegiance to them, and to my power be aiding and assisting in dethroning them for doing that which it is in my opinion and belief they ought to do? No surely!

The third clause I remarked in the oath runs thus, 'And I make this recognition, declaration &c heartily, freely and willingly'. I shall only remark upon this clause that to my certain knowledge many a man as well Protestant as Catholic, have taken the oath of abjuration with aching hearts and no other way willingly than as a merchant or sailor in a storm, throws his goods over board into the sea, to save his life: Now whether such men do not perjure themselves, (since the laws of God require we should not only part with our goods, but even lay down our lives rather than sin against conscience) I leave the world to judge.[41]

41 Reilly, Hugh, op. cit., 119–21.

It should be noted that Cornelius Nary was a doctor of civil and canon law of Paris university, and like all good lawyers, he could probably have made an equally plausible case for the acceptance of the oath.[42] In opposition to the case made by Nary it could be argued that it was all a question of whether one believed in the supremacy of parliament or in the divine right of kings. If one believed in the supremacy of parliament, then one should have no problem in declaring that one believed in one's conscience that James III had no right or title to the crown of England, since the English parliament decided in 1688 to deprive James II of the throne and to give it to William and Mary, and since parliament furthermore decided in 1701 that the succession to the throne should be maintained in the protestant line. The supremacy of parliament, even of parliaments as corrupt and unrepresentative as the British and Irish parliaments of the eighteenth century, is a much more credible and sustainable concept than the divine right of kings, which was an Old Testament concept latched on to by the kings of France, Britain and elsewhere in the sixteenth to the eighteenth centuries for their own selfish purposes. Since nearly all claims to kingship depend ultimately on the acquisition of the crown in question by physical force by some ancestor, near or distant, it is a little short of blasphemy to claim a divine right for a crown originally acquired in such dubious or sordid circumstances.

It should also be noted that the oath, no doubt because it was taken over in its entirety from an English act, refers only to the crown of England. There is no reference at all to Ireland which was a separate kingdom with its own parliament. Anyone looking for a legal loophole could surely argue, silently to himself of course, that he was renouncing James Stuart only as king of England but not as king of Ireland. This would not amount to a mental reservation, disavowed later on in the oath, since it could be claimed to be a rational and strict interpretation of the oath.

It should also be kept in mind that catholics wishing to vote in parliamentary elections were required under the 1704 act to take the oath of abjuration, and the evidence is that many of them did so. Furthermore, as we have seen, catholic solicitors, covered by the Articles of Limerick, were required under the 1707 popish solicitors act to take the oath of abjuration in order to take advantage of the saver in that act. It is also of some little relevance that the facility granted to catholics to take degrees in Trinity College, Dublin under the 1793 relief act was subject to their taking the oaths of allegiance and abjuration.

Another telling point in favour of taking the abjuration oath in the 1709 act was the fact that the oath eventually accepted by all catholics under the 1774

42 Cornelius Nary was for nearly forty years parish priest of St Michan's parish, Dublin. The author of several works of religious controversy and the translator of the New Testament, he was arguably the most prominent catholic in Ireland in the first half of the eighteenth century.

act was not a great deal different. The 1774 oath required the taker to utterly renounce and abjure any obedience or allegiance unto the person ... who was said to have assumed the style and title of king of Great Britain and Ireland by the name of Charles III. If it was wrong to abjure James III in 1709, it should follow that it was equally wrong to abjure his son, Charles III, in 1774. Indeed, the 1774 oath contained further provisions denying the pope's powers to depose princes and to dispense their subjects from oaths of allegiance, not included in the oath in the 1709 act. And yet following some initial objections from some bishops, the 1774 oath was sworn by thousands of catholics mostly as a requirement under the relief acts of 1778 and 1782. True, by the 1770s the Stuarts were on their last legs and any possibility of a restoration had long since vanished. Nevertheless it has to be said that the principle remained the same. It may be argued that there was a difference between the two oaths in that the 1709 one required the swearer to declare that he believed in his conscience that James II and his son had no right or title whatsoever to the crown of England. But surely in order to utterly renounce and abjure Charles III, as required by the 1774 oath, one had necessarily to believe in one's conscience that he had no right to the crown.

Some cogent arguments in favour of taking the oath were made in a pamphlet published in Dublin in 1710 and said to have been written by Fr Garret Darcy of Navan, County Meath.[43] Darcy afterwards claimed in *Dublin Intelligence* that he never consented or gave orders directly or indirectly that any such paper should be printed, and 'inasmuch as his name had been made use of without his consent or knowledge, and that there were several ridiculous, incoherent and injurious expressions therein contained of which he never was or ever could be the author, he doth declare that upon discovery of the printer ... he would prosecute him with all the rigour the law would allow in such a case'.[44] Darcy was registered for the parishes of Navan, Donoughmore, Ardsallagh and Bective under the 1704 act, being aged forty at the date of registration. He was ordained at Kilkenny in 1687 by the bishop of Ossory, James Phelan.[45] It seems reasonably clear that he was one of the priests who took the oath, since in the beginning of this *Dublin Intelligence* notice, he says that the pamphlet in question 'pretended to contain Dr Garrot Darcy's reasons for taking the oath of abjuration'. Also, in a contemporary piece of verse on the oath (dealt with more fully below) it is inferred that he took the oath:

but soon after they followed Darcy's way
to damn their soul lest the flock should stray.[46]

43 *Dr Father Darcy's reasons, showing that the clergy and laity of the church of Rome might safely take the oath*, Dublin 1710. This is a short pamphlet of two folio pages. The Gilbert Library, Dublin has a copy.   44 Brady, John, op. cit., 14.   45 *List of the names of popish priests* 1705.   46 Burke, W.P., op. cit., 467.

But irrespective of who the author of the pamphlet was, it is pertinent to quote some passages from it in favour of taking the oath:

> If our case had been without example, even in Catholic times, our submitting to the laws of the present Government, might with some grounds be censured, but if we look back into history as we must do on such occasions, what shall we say of the Clergy and Laiety's oath to King Stephen in prejudice to the Empress Maud and her lawful issue, without being censured for the same by the Pope.[47] [He goes on to give other like examples – King John seizing the crown, Henry III a usurper's son, Henry IV's claim to the crown not properly grounded.]
>
> There is none that is acquainted with the present government of France, but will allow that if Lewis XIV desired of his bishops and other clergy of his Kingdom to take an oath abjuring all Pretenders to his Crown except his own family but they would immediately obey, though it be notoriously known over all Europe that there is a Prince yet living directly and lawfully descended from the House of Valois.[48] And if the Pope should threaten to come in person to excommunicate the said clergy for taking this Oath to strengthen their Monarch's title, they would tell his Holiness as they did before upon such occasions: *Excomunicaturus advenis: Excommunicatus abibis.*[49]
>
> To conclude it is but folly and madness in any private Man to dispute the right or title of Princes; for I never could read of any that was settled on the throne, but could have what Oaths he pleased of his subjects, and I look on this Oath required of us to be no more. Identically then that the Law Established has taken away all right and title to the Crown of England from this Pretender, and that he is not in possession thereof, for in the body of the Oath you may observe there is mention made to the several Acts of Parliament that have attainted and divested him of all right, by virtue of which another Act followed to tender and take the said oath.
>
> ... I can only pray to Almighty God to comfort and direct us in this for the best; and to preserve us from being instrumental to bring darkness upon

---

47 Stephen was king of England from 1135 to 1154. On the death of his uncle, Henry I, Stephen seized the throne from Henry's daughter, Matilda, in Darcy's pamphlet called Empress Maud. Stephen was engaged in civil war with Matilda for much of his reign but the year before he died he came to an agreement with her under which he accepted as his successor her son, Henry of Anjou, later Henry II.   **48** Louis XIV's grandfather, Henry of Navarre, succeeded to the French throne as Henry IV in 1589 on the assassination of Henry III, the last of the Valois kings. Henry IV's claim to the throne was based on his being tenth in descent from Louis IX (1226–70). Although about forty senior branches of the Valois family had become extinct, nevertheless Henry IV's claim to the throne, and by extension Louis XIV's, was indeed tenuous. **49** Translation: Ready to excommunicate you come: having been excommunicated (yourself) you will go away.

the Flock, misery and banishment into foreign countries upon ourselves, where we should be not much pitied but hit in the teeth with want of Learning, Sense and Policy to avoid our misfortune.

I might here add that our Non-juring Brethren ought not to reflect upon those that think it no sin to confirm [sic] themselves to the Government; and ought not to be reflected upon for the tenderness of their Conscience, though their nicety may be hereafter looked upon to be occasional of the Catholic religion in this Kingdom.

... So that I wish you all may do no worse than I have done; for my part, I think it no Sin to take the Oath.

The oath indeed appears to have generated its fair share of public controversy among the catholic population. I have come across three poems in Irish and one in English on the subject of the oath, and no doubt there were more.[50] Seán Ó Neachtain in his poem *Dhá fhear déag agus píobaire* makes a scathing attack on some Westmeath priests who took the oath at Mullingar:[51]

Twelve men and a piper of the mad clergy of Ireland went to the Muileann gCearr together, grinding lies voluntarily.
The oaths they swore, no devil's spawn would swear them; but against conscience and all that's right, voluntarily they swore them.
That the rightful heir was not the true son of his father, this crew without pity, swore. Excommunication on the churls!

Ó Neachtain implies that the erring priests could expect to be forsaken by their flocks and so be reduced to poverty:

If the Abjuration Oath is a failure, their hopes are henceforth dashed; what will the wretches do then since all Ireland will scowl on them?
It is certain the piper will drown himself with his bag of spits and the twelve will hang themselves straight away.
The entire body of the clergy, in their last gasp as they are, this faction by their lies aimed to drag down all together.
But the Lord God turned the card, and his hate fell on the betrayers; they got no reward but hardship and they have nothing now but poverty.

There is also a very interesting piece of verse in English on this Mullingar episode which sets out in dialogue form some arguments for and against the

50 One by Aogán Ó Rathaile, one by Seán Ó Neachtain (*Dhá fhear déag agus píobaire*) and a third by an anonymous writer (*Meilt bratha don Mhuileann Cearr*). The latter two can be read with English translations in Pádraig Ó Fágáin, *Éigse na hIarmhí*, Baile Átha Cliath 1985. 51 What follows are translations from the original Irish.

oath.[52] The arguments against are put by a Fr James Dillon who did not take the oath, while the arguments for are put by some of those who took the oath.[53] Those in favour open the discussion with the view that it is safe to take the oath if one does so subject to a mental reservation. Fr Dillon objects that the use of this stratagem is forbidden by scripture and the synods of Namur and Lorraine; he makes the point that if mental reservation is allowed, you cannot tell whether a person taking an oath is serious or not. One of the juring priests then changes tack:

> Hear me, good Sir, and you'll plainly find
> I don't reserve my oath unto my mind.
> I swear the Prince by law no right to these
> three kingdoms hath because his right doth cease.
>
> The right your Caesar had by law is void,
> his property and title both destroyed;
> then if I swear that Prince no right to have
> the law from guilt will my good conscience save.[54]

The priests complain of the severity of a law which requires them to take this oath or else face transportation; in modern parlance they find themselves pitched between a rock and a hard place. They argue that they must take the oath if they are to remain with their flocks and look after their pastoral needs. But Fr Dillon will have none of this: they are mistaken if they think God desires them to damn their souls (by taking the oath) for the sake of remaining with their flocks.

As to how the oath was implemented by the Irish authorities, it may be that the representations made by the imperial and other ambassadors in London in favour of Irish catholics had the effect of staying in some measure the hand of the Irish authorities. There is also the point that the Whigs were ousted from power in Britain in mid-1710, and the new Tory government, with Ormond as lord lieutenant, could be expected to be more accommodating to catholics, since the Tories, by and large, had a tradition of being more tolerant of catholics than had Whigs. Apart from these considerations there was one very practical reason for not proceeding immediately with implementation and that was the fact that transportation (the penalty for non-concurrence) of priests to European ports was not feasible in time of war, and the war with France and Spain was

---

52 Burke, W.P., op. cit., 464–7.   53 This appears to be the James Dillon who was registered parish priest of Ardnurcher and Kilbride, Co. Westmeath under the 1704 act. He was aged forty-five at the time of registration and had been ordained in 1683 by Thady Keogh, bishop of Clonfert. (*List of the names of popish priests* 1705). 54 Burke, W.P., op. cit., 465.

to continue until 1713. With the return of the Whigs to power in 1714 on the death of Queen Anne, the very considerable support both in Britain and Ireland for the restoration of James Stuart as king made the authorities very edgy and rendered all the more relevant an oath abjuring James and swearing allegiance to the new king, George of Hanover. The defection of Ormond and Bolingbroke to James Stuart at this time was further proof of how serious the situation was.

It appears, then, that very little was done towards enforcing the oath in the early years of its operation, although there were some straws in the wind. For example, in County Derry in 1710 there was correspondence between William Jackson, seneschal of Draperstown, and the Dublin authorities about bringing in a Fr Terence McRory with a view to his taking the oath, but we do not know whether there was any sequel to this.[55] In March 1711 the grand jury in County Clare presented a long list of priests who had not taken the oath,[56] while in neighbouring Limerick in July 1711 six priests were listed as having taken the oath and one as having refused.[57] In Westmeath at the assizes at Mullingar in March 1711 thirteen priests were presented by the grand jury for saying Mass not having qualified themselves by taking the oath.[58] It should be mentioned that the activities of Edward Tyrell, the priest-catcher, in various parts of the country in 1712–13 were not directed towards enforcing the oath of abjuration but rather towards apprehending bishops, vicars general, friars and unregistered priests.

A definite fillip was given to the enforcement of the oath when on 19 December 1713 the house of commons ordered all justices of the peace and clerks of the crown and peace throughout the kingdom immediately after the next quarter sessions, to certify 'what popish registered priests had taken the oath of abjuration, and what priests, having neglected to take the said oath, did still continue their functions of priests'. The house further ordered the same magistrates and officers after the next quarter sessions to certify to the house 'what popish priests not registered, or who having neglected to take the abjuration oath, have exercised their functions ... and what prosecution hath been had against them for so doing'.[59]

From late 1712 until 1715 there is evidence of a much more active campaign against non-juring priests, with frequent references to presentments, indictments, examinations and warrants granted by magistrates or grand juries. In County Derry in October 1712 magistrates meeting at Bellaghy issued summonses to several priests to appear before them and take the oath. For County Fermanagh there was a list dated June 1714 of twenty registered priests who had not taken the oath.[60] At a general quarter sessions held in Cavan in April 1714 sixteen priests were named as not having taken the oath and it was ordered

55 Ibid., 278. 56 Ibid., 399. 57 Ibid., 393. 58 Brady, John, op. cit., 15. 59 Index of *Commons Journal Ireland*, vol. 1, Accounts no. 2130. 60 Burke, W.P., 278–9.

that arrangements be made for their appearance at the next assizes or quarter sessions.[61]

In Kilkenny informations were taken in July 1714 against several priests for not taking the oath;[62] in the same county in July 1714 Fr Martin Archer was ordered to be transported for not taking the oath.[63] In Carlow in June 1714 warrants were granted for several priests who had not taken the oath.[64] At Naas, County Kildare, in June 1714 examinations were received against a number of priests for saying Mass without having taken the oath.[65] In Westmeath in 1714 a diligent search was being made in the barony of Moycashel for Fr James Dillon, a registered priest who had not taken the oath.[66] Presumably this was the same James Dillon who argued against the oath in the piece of verse already noted. In Offaly in March 1713 there were six bills of indictment against priests for not taking the oath, but Fr Thomas Geoghegan was allowed bail because he was ill.[67]

In Nenagh, County Tipperary, three registered priests were listed as not having taken the oath in July 1714.[68] In Cork in June 1714 two priests were convicted and transported for not taking the oath, while in a list of 55 priests five were noted as having taken the oath and seventeen as having refused.[69] In Kinsale in January 1716 the principal papists were tendered the oath 'which none here have refused'.[70] But in October 1712 Fr Donogh Sweeny, parish priest of Macroom, was sent to jail in Cork for refusing the oath.[71] In County Kerry under date June 1714 there is a long account of the catholic clergy of the county, two of whom are mentioned as having refused the oath.[72] In Clare in March 1715 the grand jury presented 51 priests, two of whom had taken the oath and fifteen of whom had not.[73]

As regards Galway, Vesey, church of Ireland archbishop of Tuam, complained in February 1712 that 'there is a great resort of the Roman Catholic gentlemen out of the other provinces to Galway to avoid the oath of abjuration', and that 'the judges will find much opposition from the Roman Catholic lawyers and gentry of this province'.[74] A report dated February 1712 stated that most of the constables of County Galway were Papists,[75] while in June 1714 a great number of priests were presented for celebrating Mass without having taken the oath.[76] In Sligo in June 1714 some nineteen catholic laymen, being summoned, refused to appear and take the oath.[77] In Roscommon in October 1712 the popish inhabitants of the parish of Athleague were summoned but all refused the oath. However, one Edmund Corr alleged he had taken the oath before, 'whereupon we asked him whether since [then] he had not confessed it as a sin to his priest. By his evasive answers we judge he did confess it and

61 Ibid., 285.   62 Ibid., 321.   63 Ibid., 322.   64 Ibid., 324.   65 Ibid., 328.   66 Ibid., 330.   67 Ibid., 344.   68 Ibid., 356.   69 Ibid., 374.   70 Ibid., 380.   71 Ibid., 378. 72 Ibid., 385.   73 Ibid., 403.   74 Ibid., 423.   75 Ibid., 423.   76 Ibid., 425.   77 Ibid., 435.

received absolution, and it is a general report that all the Papists who formerly took the oath have done in like manner. Which occasions in us the melancholy reflection of living among men whom neither oath can bind nor justice and lenity oblige to fidelity.'[78] In Roscommon the grand jury in March 1715 stated that they knew no priests who had taken the oath though they had been summoned.[79] In July 1714 several Leitrim priests were presented for not taking the oath.[80]

But making presentments and issuing indictments and warrants was one thing, to capture your priest and put him on trial was another. The truth was that those who objected to taking the oath found it all too easy to lie low and avoid arrest. The number, then, who were actually brought to trial and imprisoned or transported was very small. Canon W.P. Burke's trawl of the state papers (since destroyed in the fire in the public record office in 1922) comes up with only four, one in Kilkenny and three in Cork, as already noted above.

Mention should also be made of the following catholic lords who, the *Lords Journal* tells us, on being summoned before the house of lords, agreed to take the oath of allegiance but refused the other oaths and the declaration against Transubstantiation, viz. Viscounts Kingsland, Dillon and Netterville and Baron Cahir at different dates during 1715 and Viscount Mountgarrett in 1721.

No comprehensive data on the number of priests or laity who took the oath appears to have survived. The anti-oath lobby mounted such a strident campaign that few priests at any rate would have had the temerity to take the oath but it is probable that the proportion of the laity who did so was much higher. Fr Cornelius Nary states in his *The case of the Roman Catholics of Ireland* that out of 1,100 priests who registered under the 1704 act, no more that thirty-three took the oath.[81] Thomas Burke, bishop of Ossory, in his *Hibernia Dominicana* published in 1762, gives the same number.[82] Both these would of course have had an interest in keeping the number as low as possible. Dr David Dickson gives the figure as 'less than a hundred'.[83]

Given the unpopularity of the oath, it would not be surprising if those priests who took it went to some pains to conceal their transgression from their flocks and fellow priests. The *Supplement* in February 1710 reported:

---

78 Ibid., 441.   79 Ibid., 450. It is remarkable that W.P. Burke reports no cases at all of court proceedings in respect of the oath of abjuration for Dublin city and county. A perusal of Nicholas Donnelly's *Short histories of Dublin parishes* likewise reveals no such cases. Although Dublin was treated with greater lenity than most parts of the country in the matter of enforcement of the penal laws (see *Dublin Gazette* for January 1713), it can hardly be the case that there were no proceedings there for not taking the oath, and Burke's and Donnelly's failure to note any such cases must be due to the loss or non-availability of the relevant records.   80 Ibid., 443.   81 Nary, Cornelius in Reily, Hugh, op. cit., 127.   82 Burke, Thomas, *Hibernia Dominicana*, 1762, 152.   83 Dickson, David, op. cit., 61.

This term several Popish priests came to town and took the oaths and subscribed the declaration according to the late act. They refused to do it in
the country at the sessions because they would not have the parishioners
know they would do the same. They came incognito to town. The judge
made them stand in open court and speak aloud in their recantation.[84]

Of the priests who took the oath the twelve or thirteen who did so from
Westmeath undoubtedly achieved the greatest notoriety, with, as already noted,
poems in Irish and English written about their misdeeds. The names of only
nine of them have come down to us, viz. James Dalton, Ballymore/Drumraney;
Philip Tyrell, Mullingar; Charles Reilly, Taghmon; Michael Dillon, Tubber;
Hugh McDonogh, Castletown-Geoghegan; William Cullen, Castlepollard;
Thomas Dillon, Multyfarnham; John Pierce, Ballynacargy; Anthony Coughlan,
Rochfortbridge/Kilbeggan.[85] In Meath Fr Garret Darcy of Navan is believed,
as noted already, to have taken the oath. In Waterford Fr Theobald Burke of
Drumcannon took the oath,[86] while in Cork there were five who did so, name-
ly, Donogh Callaghan, Ballyhooly; John Sullivan, Rahan, Whitechurch; Daniel
Keeffe, Kilmeen and Cullen; James Nagle, Kilworth; Morris Condon,
Mitchelstown. As regards the latter, it was stated that 'one Butler his coadjutor [was] put on him for that reason' and that Butler was indicted at the recent
assizes at Limerick and Cork.[87]

In County Limerick there were six priests who took the oath, namely,
William Ryan, St Michael's; John Connelan, St Nicholas's; Murtagh Hehir, St
Michael's; Bartholomew Duffy, Ballycommin; Bartholomew Coughlan, St
John's; Francis Grady, Kilteely.[88] In Clare two are mentioned as taking the
oath – Symon Shinor, Kilfintenan and Killely and William Doogan, Killaloe.[89]
From Mayo it was reported that John Durkin of Killedan and Bohola was the
only priest in the county who had taken the oath, and that he had been turned
out of his parish by Dominick Bera, 'registered but of no parish'.[90] In Sligo
there was one unnamed priest who had taken the oath.[91]

The sanctions taken in particular instances by the catholic authorities against
priests who took the oath and the latter's unpopularity generally among their
flocks, not to mention the lacerations of the poets, no doubt acted as a strong

84 Brady, John, op. cit., 13.   85 Ó Fágáin, Pádraig, op. cit., 93. Although the various poems in Irish and in English indicate that the Westmeath priests took the oath in
Mullingar, Nicholas Donnelly in his *Short histories of Dublin parishes* (Part 2, 43–4)
states that they took the oath in Dublin, presumably in one of the Four courts. Donnelly
states that they stayed in Mrs Whyte's lodging house in Rosemary Lane, off Merchant's
Quay and proceeded from there to court. This Mrs Whyte was presumably the first
wife of Laurence Whyte, the poet and Maths teacher from Westmeath, who lived for
most of his life in Rosemary Lane.   86 Burke, W.P., op. cit., 364.   87 Ibid., 374–6.
88 Ibid., 393.   89 Ibid., 403.   90 Ibid., 430.   91 Ibid., 435.

deterrent to others who might see the oath as unobjectionable. It appears too that at least in some dioceses taking the oath by clergy and laity was regarded as a reserved sin, which could be absolved only on certain conditions, as witness the following instruction dated 16 March 1711 from Dominick Lynch, vicar general of Tuam, to a rural dean under him:

> You know the Abjuration as public and scandalous perjury was hetherto reserved specially, and shall be still in this our district. Save the few we design shall act for us or by our own power which we cannot subdelegate. Wherefore if any abjurer in this our district should pretend to be absolved, you must know by whom, that such [priest] may be punished and made sensible of his error and ignorance, and the [person] so unlawfully absolved must be by you again absolved, as one of the new authors upon the following conditions and terms:
>
>   First. That each of them shall sign and acknowledge the annexed declaration which you must be sure to keep private for we do not design to expose any body but as little as we can.
>
>   Second place; they must oblige themselves henceforth never to pretend to defend or commend the taking off the said oath to any body but rather as far as shall lay in them, censure it as the church does and it deserves.
>
>   Third. That each of them without delay shall cause the Holly Sacrifice of the Mass bee at least once offered for them, and perform what pilgrimage, fast, alms and prayinge you shall think fitt to impose according the condition and constitution of each person, and
>
>   Finally. That for the future they protest against these or any other such oaths censured by their pastors and church. Upon performing and engaging to perform all which you will admit as many as shall come to you to the Holly sacraments of penance and the rest but not otherwise.[92]

That the taking of the oath of abjuration at this time should be given the status of a reserved sin, is an indication of the extent to which expediency can govern the teachings of the church when political and temporal considerations are allowed to take precedence over spiritual ones. It is significant that, once the political heat had been removed from the equation, it was obviously no sin at all for a catholic to take the oath of abjuration in order to obtain a degree in Trinity College, Dublin following the 1793 relief act.

It will be gathered from the foregoing that references to the taking of the oath by the laity are scanty, but it should be remembered that we are here dependent largely on Canon W.P. Burke and he, having regard to the title of his book, no doubt concentrated his research work on priests rather than laity.

92 Ibid., 245.

The behaviour of the laity in Kinsale, County Cork and in Athleague, County Roscommon as well as the movement of catholic gentry to County Galway to avoid the oath are already mentioned above. The Kerry poet, Aogán Ó Rathaile, celebrates thus another layman, Donncha Ó hIcí, who evidently took it all too seriously and emigrated to England to avoid taking the oath.

Tréig do thalamh dúchais,
dein ar choiste Londain,
ag seachaint móide an amhgair
do chuir do thír faoi bhrón.

Cuir do dhócas cuimseach
i gCríost, do thiarna dílis,
ná tabhair ar bheatha an tsaoil seo
an tsíoraíocht tá id chomhair.[93]

It appears too that the oath of abjuration was used as a means of compelling catholic laymen to pay certain levies to which they were not subject by law. Fr Cornelius Nary in his *The case of the Roman Catholics of Ireland* mentions in this connection the levies called quarterages imposed on catholic merchants, tradesmen, craftsmen etc. by the relevant guilds.[94] There was no legal basis for these quarterages (and this, as mentioned in Chapter 1, was confirmed by a decision of the court of king's bench in 1759),[95] but nevertheless, Nary claimed, catholics were frightened into paying them by a threat of being summoned to take the oath of abjuration. A pertinent example of something of the same nature is to be found in the council book of Cork Corporation which on 2 April 1708 ordered that 'the several Popish merchants who have abatement of their petty duties be summoned before the Mayor and tendered the oath of abjuration, which if they refuse to take, from thenceforth the privileges granted them be taken off'.[96] However, later that year the corporation saw fit to rescind this order.

93 Ó Tuama, Seán, *Filí faoi sceimhle*, Baile Átha Cliath 1978, 136. Translation: /Forsake your native land, /make tracks for London /and avoid the oath of affliction /that put your country in mourning. /Put your unerring hope /in Christ, your dear Lord: /do not trade for the good things of life /the eternity that awaits you.   94 Nary, Cornelius, op. cit., 118.   95 Wall, Maureen, *Catholic Ireland in the eighteenth century*, Dublin 1989, 66.   96 Caulfield, Richard, *The council book of the corporation of the city of Cork*, Guildford 1876, quoted in M. Wall, op. cit., 180.

3

The Laws Have Slept

Since the movement by some catholics for an oath of allegiance to the British monarch had its origin among English catholics, it is appropriate that we should give some consideration to events in England at this point, more particularly as what happened in England was soon to be mirrored in Ireland. With the coming of George I to the throne in 1714, some English catholics felt that the best course for them was to accept the reality of the Hanoverian succession by an oath of allegiance to George and thereby hopefully obtain a bettter deal on toleration. Their expectations in this regard were increased by George's record of rather favourable treatment of catholics in Hanover. The two leading lights in this campaign for an oath for catholics, from about 1717 onwards, were Thomas Strickland and John Stonor.

Thomas Strickland (c.1679–1740) was born in Westmoreland but was brought up in France at the Stuart court-in-exile at St Germain near Paris whither his Jacobite parents had fled. Following his education in the English College at Douai in north-east France and ordination as a priest, he returned to England in 1712. He was soon after proposed as a coadjutor to Bishop Giffard, vicar apostolic of the London district, but was turned down because he was regarded as too young. In 1727 he was appointed bishop of Namur in the Austrian Netherlands but he does not appear to have attended too diligently to his episcopal duties, preferring instead a life of diplomacy and intrigue.[1]

John Stonor (1680–1756) had links with the English aristocracy in that his mother was a daughter of the eleventh earl of Shrewsbury. He was thus a nephew of Charles, duke of Shrewsbury, a convert to the established church who was lord lieutenant of Ireland from 1713 to 1714. Stonor like Strickland was educated in the English College at Douai and was ordained a priest in France in 1709. He was assigned to the English mission in 1714 and two years later was appointed a bishop and vicar apostolic of the Midland district. Shortly after, there was a move, in which Strickland was involved, to have him appoint-

1 Dictionary of national biography.

ed vicar apostolic of the London district in place of the ageing Giffard, but nothing came of this, and he was to remain in the Midland district until his death in 1756.[2]

Of these two, Strickland was regarded as the ring-leader in the campaign for a catholic oath. Fr Lewis Ineese, formerly chaplain to Mary of Modena, James II's queen, in a letter dated Paris, 1 January 1720 to James Stuart, who a year before had taken up residence in a papal palace in Rome, stated that 'it hath been no secret here no more than in England that Dr Strickland for these two or three years past hath been doing his utmost *per fas et per nefas* [by right and by wrong] to get the Catholics of England to own the present usurper, and to submit to him by an oath as Lawful King'. During the summer of 1719, Ineese claimed, Strickland had been twice to Hanover and as often at London for that purpose, and about October 1719 'he [Strickland] valued himself upon the success of his negotiations, and said that he had now gained his point, and that it was resolved by the English ministry that the Catholics who should comply by taking the oath should have a kynd of toleration for their religion, and be discharged of double taxes; and that they who should refuse the oath, should upon that lose the two-thirds of their estates, have all Penal Laws executed upon them and in a word be utterly ruined'.[3]

It was long suspected, Ineese claimed, that Stonor was 'at bottom' of the same mind as Strickland, although Stonor had been careful not to vent his thoughts openly, but in the course of 1719 Stonor had come out publicly in favour of Strickland's proposals. Stonor was regarded as much more dangerous than Strickand because he showed a great deal more judgement and his character gave him more weight and credit. In the autumn of 1719, Ineese went on, Strickland and Stonor had discussed their scheme with Internuncio Santini in Brussels and had claimed afterwards that the internuncio was entirely of their sentiments.[4]

In December 1719, Ineese continued, Stonor sent a letter (with a request that it be translated into Latin or Italian and handed to papal Secretary of State Paolucci) to Laurence Mays, for many years agent in Rome for the English vicars apostolic. In this letter Stonor stated that, the English parliament being now resolved to make a difference between such catholics as would give proofs of their fidelity to the present government and such as would not, it was thought fit to hold a meeting of the chief lay catholics of England and to propose to them what was required of them by the government. Present at this meeting were the dukes of Norfolk and Powis, Lords Stafford and Montaigue and eight or ten more of the chief nobility and gentry. Instead of attending the meeting as expected, Giffard, vicar apostolic of the London district, went on purpose out of town, and there appears to have been no vicar apostolic

2 Ibid.   3 Fagan, Patrick (ed.), *Ireland in the Stuart papers*, vol. 1, 17–18.   4 Ibid., 18.

present except Stonor. It was proposed to the meeting, as the sentiment of the government, that a petition should be drawn up and sent from the catholics to the pope, desiring the following:

1 that the pope should publish a decree declaring it lawful for the English catholics to take the oath of allegiance to King George as lawful king;
2 that the pope should remove Cardinal Gualterio from his position as protector of England and from having anything to do with the catholics of England;
3 that the pope should revoke and annul the indult formerly given to the king (James II) for nominating the bishops of Ireland;
4 that in case any bishop or missioner in England should oppose or not comply with these articles, the pope should take away the faculties of such persons and call them out of the mission.

All the nobility and gentry present at the meeting agreed that what was proposed was very lawful for them to comply with, but at the same time they all refused to sign or send any such petition to the pope. Stonor, Ineese claimed, was adamant that what was proposed was lawful and that the petition should be sent.[5]

Ineese was of the opinion that it would prove the greatest scandal to religion that ever happened in England if the pope were to suffer the catholic bishops and priests to perjure themselves by taking oaths to renounce their only lawful catholic sovereign, while so many protestant ministers suffered themselves to be turned out of their livings and reduced to beggary rather than, by taking these oaths, own a protestant usurper. Besides, warned Ineese, if the pope did not check immediately these proceedings, they would infallibly form such a division and schism among the catholics in Britain and Ireland, that it would not be afterwards in the pope's power 'to make it up'.[6]

No information has been uncovered as to any immediate response from Rome to Stonor's letter. However, when Stonor suggested to Propaganda the following year that English catholics might render temporal obedience to George I, Propaganda warned him that he should behave cautiously.[7]

It has to be said that numerically English catholics at this time were of little importance as compared with Irish catholics. According to contemporary estimates there were about 90,000 English catholics at the beginning of the eighteenth century and this figure had declined to about 63,000 by 1780.[8] This

---

5 Ibid., 18–19. Ineese stated he had seen Stonor's letter and was here giving the contents of that letter from memory. 6 Ibid., 19–20. 7 Fenning, Hugh, 'The three kingdoms: England, Ireland, Scotland' in J. Metzler (ed.) *Sacrae Congregationis de Propaganda Fide Memoria Rerum*, Rome 1974, vol. 2, p. 622. 8 A letter to the pope in 1704 stated that there were 100,000 catholics in England, but in 1706 Dr Betham

compares with a catholic population in Ireland which was approaching two millions by the 1720s.[9] Any importance English catholics had at this time lay in
their being top-heavy with nobility and gentry.

The question of an oath for English catholics again became a live issue in
1728 in the context of arrangements for the Congress of Soissons which started in June of that year. It will be seen later that at that point the campaign for
a catholic oath in Ireland and in England became interlocked.

Attempts by Jacobites to invade Britain and indeed the discovery of plots
for such invasions were invariably followed by repressive measures against
catholics by the Irish administration, with the aim of nipping in the bud any
involvement by Irish catholics in such plots. There were quite elaborate plans
for a Jacobite rising in England in the spring of 1722, and, while nothing much
came of these plans, one of the leaders, barrister Christopher Layer, was arrested, put on trial in November 1722 and executed at Tyburn in May 1723.[10]

When he prorogued the Irish parliament in 1722 it is not surprising, then,
that the lord lieutenant, the duke of Grafton, enjoined the members, when they
returned to their constituencies, to keep a watchful eye on the papists, and that
the same members, when they reassembled in the autumn of 1723, were in a
mood to pass a number of resolutions directed against catholics.[11] On the basis
of these resolutions a bill was prepared which provided *inter alia* that all unregistered priests should depart the kingdom before 25 March 1724; priests found
in the country after that date were to be adjudged guilty of high treason, with
the exception of those who had taken the oath of abjuration before 14 November
1723 and had filed in court a certificate to that effect before 25 March 1724.
It was also provided that every popish archbishop, bishop, vicar general, dean,
jesuit, monk, friar etc. should depart the kingdom before 25 March 1724 on
pain of high treason. Among the other sections of the bill was one providing
that any person found guilty of concealing catholic clergy should be adjudged
'a felon without benefit of clergy and suffer death and lose and forfeit as in the

estimated the catholic population at 80,000. (See Basil Hemphil, *The early vicars apostolic in England*, London 1953, 102.) Taking the mean of these figures we get 90,000.
Similarly, there are two figures for 1780 – 56,000 (Hemphil) and 69,316 (*New Catholic
Encyclopedia*), giving a mean of 63,000.   9 K.H. Connell in *The population of Ireland
1750–1845* (Oxford 1950), Table 1, estimated that the population in 1732 was 3.018m.
as against the estimate of 2m. for 1732 in *Abstract of protestant and popish families* (Dublin
1736) which was based on Hearth Money returns for 1732–33. Connell's estimate was
based on the proposition that the Hearth Money returns were deficient to the extent
of 50 per cent. This view has been challenged by more recent writers, but it would
seem prudent to allow for a 20 per cent deficiency, giving a revised estimated population of 2.4m., composed of about 1.9m catholics and 0.5m. protestants.   10 Daiches,
David, *Charles Edward Stuart. The life and times of Bonnie Prince Charlie*, London 1973,
88.   11 Wright, Thomas, *History of Ireland from the earliest period to the present time*,
London 1854, vol. 3, 309.

case of one attainted of felony'. It was also provided that any person convicted of being a Popish tutor or schoolmaster 'shall suffer as a felon without benefit of clergy'. There was also a prohibition on nunneries setting up boarding schools for girls or guest houses for women.[12]

These measures had to be approved by the English privy council before they could become law and, as was usual on such occasions, there was a scramble by the catholic lobby to organise a campaign to have the measures negatived in London. The Brussels nuncio was alerted and he in turn brought the measures to the attention of the pope who interceded with the various catholic powers to come to the defence of the Irish as resolutely and as speedily as possible.[13] The Franciscan, Sylvester Lloyd, brought news of the bill to France, where the Spanish diplomat, Sir Patrick Lawless, an Irishman from Kilkenny, claimed that he was instrumental in having the bill dropped through the intervention of another Spanish diplomat, Marquis de Pozzobueno.[14] Vatican sources, on the other hand, gave much of the credit for the dropping of the bill to the intervention of de Fleury, first minister of France and later cardinal, with Horace Walpole, English minister at the court of France and brother of Robert Walpole, the British prime minister.[15] At home Fr Cornelius Nary wrote in 1724 a pamphlet against the bill entitled *The Case of the Roman Catholics of Ireland*, a trenchant, expertly argued piece of polemical writing, extracts from which have already been quoted.

The rejection or non-acceptance of the bill by London must also have been greeted with relief by a significant number of the members of the Irish parliament, for the indications are that support for the bill was far from unanimous in either house. How else can one explain how, when Edward Synge, prebendary of St Patrick's, preached a sermon on 23 October 1725 to members of the house of Commons advocating a degree of toleration for catholics, his audience was so pleased with what they heard that they congratulated Synge on an excellent sermon and ordered it to be printed?[16] Or how else can one explain the resolution of the house of lords on 3 December 1725 that 'the most probable way of restraining popish priests and regulars coming into this kingdom, will be to allow a competent number of secular priests to exercise their functions under such rules and limitations as may be for the security of the civil state'?[17]

Some prominent people such as Archbishop William King of Dublin[18] and Archbishop Edward Synge of Tuam (father of the Edward Synge already men-

---

12 The bill can be read in W.P. Burke, *The Irish priests in the penal times*, 455–60. 13 Giblin, Cathaldus, 'Catalogue of material of Irish interest in the collection Nunziatura di Fiandra, Vatican Archives' in *Collectanea Hibernica*, no. 14 (1971), 38. 14 Fagan, P. (ed.), op. cit., vol. 1, 43. 15 Giblin, C., op. cit., 39. 16 Synge, Edward, *Sermon preached in St Andrew's church, Dublin on 23 October, 1725*, Dublin 1725, passim. 17 *Lords Journal Ireland*, vol. 2, 830. 18 National Library of Ireland MS 2056, Abp. King to Edward Southwell 3 December 1723.

tioned), are on record as opposed to the bill. Indeed, in 1722, shortly before the bill was mooted, Edward Synge, *père*, who in his capacity as archbishop of Tuam was a member of the house of lords, was already making moves towards the formulation of a special oath for catholics which would be more acceptable than the oath of abjuration. In a letter dated 22 June 1722 to Archbishop Wake of Canterbury he put forward proposals for such an oath:

> Some Papists, with whom I have discoursed, affirm that they are ready in the strongest terms to swear allegiance to King George and to renounce the Pretender, which (say they) is as great a security as can be given to the civil power. But, (say they) to renounce the Pope's authority or jurisdiction in matters purely spiritual, is against a known principle of our religion. And to swear that the Pretender has not any right to the crown, is to swear to the truth of doctrine, which ought not to be made the matter of an oath. Or to swear that we believe he has no right, is to take an oath concerning a thing of which we are not capable of forming a judgment. The distinction between a king *de jure* and *de facto* having not only been received by men of learning, but also into some of the English Acts of Parliament.[19]

Synge goes on to express the belief that there were as many catholic bishops and priests in the country as at any time for the previous sixty years, and continues:

> And some there are who think it hard to require an oath from them, which even an honest Papist, who desires to be faithful to the present Government, cannot in conscience take ... To obviate all these pretences, and for the relief of all Papists that are sincere and honest, and the detection of those that are not so, I have often thought that an oath might be framed against which they can have no manner of pretence, except they will openly profess themselves not to be subjects to King George, but to the Pretender and the Pope ... A Papist, whose interest as well as duty obliges him to be faithful to the King, positively told me that if I could draw up the form of an Oath of Fidelity, that should be free from those objections which he made, and I have above mentioned, he would propose it to as many of his persuasion as he could; and was content that all who refused it should be treated as rebels.

Later in the same letter he set out the form of oath he had in mind.[20]

The son of a bishop of Cork, Edward Synge, *père*, was born in 1659 at Inishannon near Cork city. Following his appointment as bishop of Raphoe in

---

19 Gilbert Library, Dublin MS 28, p. 174.   20 The text of Synge's proposed oath was as follows: 'I, A.B., do promise, testify and declare before God that I am, and will continue a true and faithful subject unto our Sovereign Lord King George; and that I will bear faith and allegiance to him as a good subject ought to do.

1714, we find him in April 1715 writing to Archbishop Tennison of Canterbury about the best way to rid the country of popery. Appointed archbishop of Tuam in 1716, he soon after that had unsavoury dealings with the renegade priest-hunter, Garzia. However, by 1722 he had undergone a sea-change in his attitude to catholics. He was engaging in dialogue with them and, as we have seen, proposing a special oath of allegiance for them. Around the same time he was in correspondence with Fr Francis Martin of Louvain about the pope's deposing and dispensing powers, and about the possibility of Christian unity, which he encouraged Martin to explore more fully. Later in the 1720s and 1730s he

'I do also profess, testify and declare before God, that I hold myself bound in conscience to pay all that duty and allegiance unto our Sovereign Lord King George, which according to the laws of God, and the present constitutions of this realm now in force, is due to the King of Great Britain and Ireland in all matters and things which concern the lives, liberties and properties of the subjects of this land.

'I do also promise and swear, that I will not at any time, directly or indirectly, by word or deed, encourage or assist any person or persons whatsoever in any design to deprive our Sovereign Lord King George of the crown or Supreme Authority which he now enjoys within the Kingdoms of Great Britain and Ireland, or either of them, or to set up a right or title to the same in any other person whatsoever; and that I will immediately discover every such design that is, or shall hereafter come to my knowledge; so as that the same may, to the best of my power, be prevented, and the promoters thereof brought to punishment according to the laws now in force within this realm.

'I do also profess and swear, that I do not believe the Pope, or Bishop of Rome, or any Council or Assembly of Bishops, or Ecclesiastical Persons, has or have any lawful power, in any case whatsoever, to depose Kings or Princes, or to deprive them of their authority, or any part of it; or to absolve their subjects from their allegiance; Neither do I believe that either he or they or any of them, have power to absolve me from that allegiance which I have now sworn to our Sovereign Lord King George, or to dispense with any part of the Oath which I now take: Neither have I already taken, nor ever will accept of any such Dispensation.

'I do also promise and swear that I will not either directly or indirectly, by word or deed, attempt or endeavour to hinder or alter the Succession of the Crown of Great Britain or Ireland, as the same stands now limited to the heirs of the late Illustrious Sophia, Electress and Duchess Dowager of Hanover; but will to my power maintain and defend the same against all persons whatsoever, and particularly against the person pretending in the life of the late King James to be Prince of Wales, and since his death pretends to be King of England and Ireland, or of Great Britain by the name of James the Third, or of Scotland by the name of James the Eighth. And if I shall at any time know of any attempt or endeavour to defeat or alter the said Succession, I will with all speed make such discovery of the same, as that to the best of my power such attempt or endeavour may be rendered ineffectual, and the authors and promoters thereof punished according to the laws now in force.

'And all this I do sincerely and faithfully profess, promise and swear, according to the ordinary sense of the words now read unto me, in the true faith of a Christian, without any secret collusion, equivocation, or mental reservation; and will in like manner honestly and sincerely to the best of my power perform what I have now sworn, and every part thereof; so help me God.'

engaged in a prolonged controversy with Fr Cornelius Nary on religious top-
ics and it is evident that he and Nary were on friendly terms although neither
pulled any punches when it came to debating doctrinal issues. He was to remain
archbishop of Tuam until his death in July 1741, aged eighty-two years.[21]

In the special form of oath he proposed, Synge appears to have made some
effort towards accommodating the views and susceptibilities of catholics. It will
be seen that there is no requirement for the swearer of the Synge oath to believe
in his conscience that James Stuart had not any right or title whatsoever to the
crown of Britain and Ireland. Instead there is something much less demanding, to wit, a promise to defend the protestant succession against all persons
whatsoever and in particular against James Stuart. It is true that Synge's oath
contains a rejection of the papal deposing and dispensing powers, a requirement not included in the oath of abjuration as set out originally in an English
act and as subsumed into Irish acts of 1704, 1707 and 1709, but as pointed out
in chapter I there were many catholics who would have had no difficulty with
this requirement.

We do not know the reaction of Archbishop Wake to Synge's oath. If he
put his views in writing, they do not appear to have survived. In any event the
proposal appears to have remained dormant for a few years. In the light of the
anti-catholic measures in the 1723 popery bill, Synge may have considered that
the time was not ripe to proceed with such a relatively liberal measure as a
special oath for catholics.

In the event it was left to Synge's son, also named Edward, to take up the
cudgels in regard to an oath for catholics. Edward Synge, *fils*, was born in Cork
in 1691. He took an MA degree in Trinity college, Dublin in 1712, and, following appointments as chancellor of St Patrick's cathedral and chaplain to the
lord lieutenant, he was appointed bishop of Clonfert in 1730. The following year
he was translated to Cloyne and two years later to Ferns. He was translated to
Elphin in 1740 and held that post until his death in 1762. He showed a degree
of sympathy for catholics throughout his life as witness his involvement in a
special oath for them in the 1720s and again, as will be seen, in the 1750s.[22]

In October 1725 in the course of a sermon, already briefly referred to, in
Saint Andrew's church, Dublin, before members of the Irish house of commons,
Synge, *fils*, argued that a toleration might be granted to catholics under certain
conditions. This was a sermon given annually to commemorate the alleged
massacre of protestants during the 1641 rebellion, and was preached by Synge
fils in his capacity as chaplain to the lord lieutenant. In view of his position as
chaplain and of the audience he was preaching to, Synge no doubt put forward
his proposals in the knowledge that there would be considerable support for
them at establishment level.

21 *Dictionary of national biography.*   22 Ibid.

He argued that neither the governors of the Christian church nor the civil magistrates had a right to use force 'to restrict or punish any opinions or practices in religion'. He drew 'the very important conclusion that all persons in a society, whose principles of religion have no tendency to hurt the public, have a right to a toleration'. By toleration he meant 'a liberty to worship God according to their consciences, without any encouragement from the civil government on the one hand, or fear of infliction of punishment on the other'. He went on: 'And the reason why all men whose religious principles do not hurt the public, have a right to a toleration is this, because by the supposition they are guilty of no offence against the state, and it has been proved that the Magistrate has no right to use force against them on any other account.'[23] With regard to the papal deposing and dispensing powers, he stated:

> Though the Church of Rome does, as I have shown, maintain or countenance these wicked doctrines, yet all the members of it do not. The Church of France has ... declared fully against the deposing powers; a late noted professor at Louvain, a native of this kingdom [Fr Francis Martin], has not long since written freely against it, and the design of his book is to prove it to be the duty of the Romanists of both kingdoms to renounce this doctrine, and not only so, but to swear and to pay all dutiful allegiance to his Majesty and to abjure the Pretender. And all of this, if I am rightly informed, many of them declare they are ready to do. They do indeed make one objection to the Oath of Abjuration, as it now stands, which possibly may be obviated without lessening the binding force of the oath itself, but as to the other doctrines mentioned, they say they do not own them and are ready in the most solemn manner to renounce and disclaim them.[24]

He goes on to argue that such people 'ought at least to be allowed some benefit of a toleration'. As regards people who are not prepared to swear allegiance to King George, he claims that '' 'tis evident they could not justly complain though they were at once banished out of the society'.

Following an attack on these proposals by Stephen Radcliffe, vicar of Naas, County Kildare, Synge, *fils*, published early in 1726 a vindication of the proposals in which he had this to say about catholic objections to the oath of abjuration:

> Whoever takes the Oath of Abjuration swears among other things that he does not believe in his conscience that the Pretender has any right or title whatsoever to the crown of this realm. Now this, they say, they cannot with a safe conscience take: for though his Majesty, King George, has a legal

23 Synge, Edward, op. cit. in note 16, p. 30.   24 Ibid., 49.

right, which they say they are willing and ready to acknowledge, yet they cannot say nor swear that the Pretender hath not any right or title whatsoever, because it is possible that according to the constitution of some or all of the Dominions annexed to the crown of Great Britain, this person, if supposed the son of James II, may have an hereditary right which no laws can deprive him of. ... The Papists in fact do generally refuse to take this Oath; is it then better to leave them at liberty, and take no security at all for their allegiance to his Majesty, or to contrive some other Oath of equal force to bind their consciences, which yet may not be liable to this exception? Suppose for instance an Oath of Allegiance and Abjuration to be taken by Papists, and them only ... were conceived in the following terms.[25]

The oath which Synge *fils* put forward at this point differed in a few minor points from Synge *père*'s original draft oath, as set out at note 20. It was part of the package that the country would be served by 500 secular priests but by no regulars. He had no plans for revoking any of the penal laws against catholics, but he pointed out that the consequence of their not being able to purchase land was that they turned mostly to trade and 'have their wealth chiefly in money, which is not so sure a pledge for their quiet and peaceable behaviour as an estate of land, and may much more quickly and effectively be applied to carry on an enterprise against the Government'.[26]

In putting forward his proposals Synge *fils* had, as one might expect, the active support of his father as witness the following extract from a letter written by Bishop Nicolson of Derry to Archbishop Wake of Canterbury early in 1726:

The archbishop of Tuam said he had met with a great many Popish priests, who profess their readiness to abjure all manner of power in the Pope to absolve them from their allegiance; which they were ready to swear in the most binding and solemn manner to King George. But they pointed to an expression or two in the oath of Abjuration which they thought might be omitted without hazard to the Government. And his Grace [of Tuam] seemed to intimate his own intention shortly to give the House [of lords] his reasons for agreeing in the same opinion.[27]

Parliament was prorogued on 8 March 1726 and no record can be found of Synge *père*'s having raised this matter in the house of lords. His claim to have had discussions with catholic priests is not surprising, since his letter of June 1722 to Archbishop Wake mentioned discussions he had with catholics before that date. There must have been renewed and more intensive discussions with

25 Synge, Edward, *A vindication of sermon preached ... on 23rd October 1725*, Dublin 1726, 74.   26 Ibid., 78.   27 Gilbert Library MS 27, p. 380.

catholics from late in 1724 or early in 1725 for a letter from Fr Sylvester Lloyd in the Stuart Papers speaks of 'overtures made to bring Catholics of this Kingdom to take a certain Oath of Allegiance to the present Government' around that time.[28]

Synge *fils*' 'vindication' was followed by a lengthy reply from Radcliffe in which he again argued vigorously against Synge's toleration proposals.[29] Much of Radcliffe's spleen against catholics appears to have derived from his campaign to have the parish priest of Naas, Fr John Power, prosecuted for baptising the children of mixed marriages, a campaign in which Radcliffe was thwarted by the unwillingness of the local magistrate to take any action against Fr Power.

If a ballad published in 1726 is anything to go by, the proposal of the Synges for a special oath for catholics met with some raised eyebrows among their peers in the establishment. Here is an extract:

Now, who will not say you are for the Pretender,
When yo'oppose the true Faith, and the Faith's true defender?
    For you open a door
    For Babylon's whore,
And for all sects that are in the World, and much more:
O S—nge thou had'st better have died in thy youth,
Than thus to be plagued for opposing the Truth.

and this variation on the refrain:

O S—nge, thou had'st better been hanged in a rope
Than thus to turn stickler for Rome and the Pope.[30]

However, it has to be said that Synge *fils*' involvement in the oath did not detrimentally affect his prospects of promotion in the church for, as we have seen, he was appointed bishop of Clonfert shortly after in 1730.

The foregoing developments have to be viewed against the background of rumours throughout the year 1726 of a European war in which Britain would be engaged and which the Jacobite plotters would see as another opportunity of striking a blow for the restoration of the Stuarts. There was still a great deal of support for the Jacobite cause in Ireland, and it was presumably to mollify such sympathisers that the judges in their circuits in the spring of 1726 recommended moderation to the magistrates 'as they did in the most earnest manner

28 Fagan, P. (ed.), op cit., vol. 1, 95.   29 Radcliffe, Stephen, *A reply to Revd. Edward Synge ... wherein his sermon preached in St Andrew's Church Dublin is further considered*, Dublin 1726, 71.   30 Trinity College Dublin, Early Printed Books, Press A.7.4. no. 22.

good behaviour and fidelity to the Catholics'. However, riots in Dublin following the celebration of the Pretender's birthday in June 1726, rumours of a catholic plot in Dublin to murder protestants, the discovery of men enlisting in the service of the Pretender and the gung-ho attitude of the Jacobite supporters to the possibility of a war in Europe, all conspired to change the mood of the authorities with regard to some rapprochement with catholics.[31] This does not mean that there was any general or indiscriminate persecution of catholics, for Stephen MacEgan, then bishop of Clonmacnoise and later bishop of Meath, could claim: 'the opening of letters in the Post Office here [Dublin] has been much practised these four months, but as I never traffic in politics, was safe.'[32] But hostilities in Europe did not materialise apart from some trouble for a few months in Spain when the Spaniards laid siege to Gibraltar early in 1727. With the fading prospects of a European war, Jacobite hopes for an invasion of Britain or Ireland also faded.

The Synges at this stage may have grown disillusioned with the prospects for an oath for a catholic body, a large segment of which was prepared to swear allegiance to no one except James Stuart. The latter's view of an oath of allegiance by catholics to George I, as conveyed by his secretary of state, John Hay, was predictable:

> The only answer which can be made to Mr Lloyd's long letter ... is that the King [James Stuart] never can give his consent to his subjects in Ireland taking any oaths which can hinder them from coming to his assistance and taking a forward part in his service when we shall have occasion to call upon them.[33]

It is time to turn our attention now to the three main catholic players in this drama, two of them, Fr Cornelius Nary and Thomas Nugent, earl of Westmeath, very much in favour of an oath for catholics and one of them, Fr Sylvester Lloyd, quite virulently opposed to such an oath.

Nary was born near Naas, County Kildare, about 1658 and was educated at Paris where he took a doctorate in civil and canon law at the university there. Returning to Ireland about 1698, he was appointed parish priest of St Michan's, Dublin, where he was to remain for the rest of his life. His work as a controversialist and his friendship with Archbishop Synge have already been touched upon. It will be seen from the extracts from *The case of the Roman Catholics of Ireland*, quoted in Chapter 2, that, while he had no problem with an oath of allegiance to the British monarch, he could not accept the oath of abjuration

---

31 For further information on these events see Patrick Fagan, *An Irish bishop in penal times: the chequered career of Sylvester Lloyd OFM 1680–1747*, 80–4.   32 Fagan, P., op. cit. in note 3, 83.   33 Ibid., 78.

as set out in the 1709 and earlier acts. While it is almost certain that he was one of the priests with whom Archbishop Synge had discussions on the form of an oath, it is remarkable how little documentary evidence has survived on his part in that question. The form of an oath Nary eventually produced has survived only because Charles O'Conor of Belanagare printed it in no less than three of his pamphlets many years later. An anonymous intervention published in 1727 in the controversy between Synge, *fils*, and Stephen Radcliffe is believed to have been the work of Nary in collaboration with a catholic lawyer.[34] There is much of interest in this pamphlet, but we are here concerned only with how it impinges on the question of an oath for catholics. The readiness of the majority of catholics to be loyal to King George is emphasised:

> Now I dare answer for all the Catholics of Ireland and am sure that if the same toleration or liberty of conscience were given to them, and the same privileges in their civil rights and in the fruits of their industry, which Catholics under Protestant princes enjoy in Germany and the States of Holland, they would be as zealous for their present Government and as true to it as either Germans or Dutchmen are to their respective Protestant princes. Nay, and would fight tomorrow against the Pope himself should he come at the head of an army with a design to invade their country or their civil rights.[35]

With regard to the pope's dispensing powers the authors comment:

> If I believe the Pope can dispense me to take all the oaths which the laws prescribe, and by which I am qualified to bear any civil or military employment, am I not a very great fool for not enjoying the liberty to enjoy such benefits of life as might render me easy in my circumstances in this world, when I might easily obtain such a dispensation had it been practised, or had it been part of my belief? And is this not the case of all the Catholics of Ireland? Of whom you will not doubt many are capable by their merits and parts to discharge offices of profit and advantage. Whereas by not taking such oaths, neither our gentlemen, nor lawyers, nor merchants, nor dealers, nor even tradesmen do now partake of the liberties or advantages, which the rest of their fellow subjects enjoy. Is it not then plain that we do not believe that the Pope, nor any power on earth, can dispense with or make it lawful to take any oath, but what we intend and resolve to perform?[36]

---

34 Anon, *A letter to Revd Stephen Radcliffe MA, vicar of Naas, on the subject of his letter and reply to Mr Synge's sermon and vindication*, Dublin 1727. For an examination of the authorship of this pamphlet see Patrick Fagan, *Dublin's turbulent priest; Cornelius Nary 1658–1738*, 163–6. Nary's involvement is further emphasised by part 2 of this pamphlet, recently discovered by Fr H. Fenning in Russell Library, Maynooth.
35 Ibid., 13.   36 Ibid., 36.

Thomas Nugent, earl of Westmeath, but generally known as Lord Delvin, was one of the colonels of the Jacobite army present at Limerick at the time of the capitulation and as such was in a position to claim the benefits of the Articles of Limerick. An absentee in England at this time, he was not a rich man, credited with an income of only £400 in the list of absentees published in 1729.[37] His part in the address to the king in 1727 and his subsequent conduct of affairs in London and in France is well documented and will be noted later. He died in 1752, aged ninety-six years.

Fr Sylvester Lloyd was a Franciscan who was born a protestant but who converted to catholicism as a youth. Possessed of all of the proverbial zeal of the convert, he had an extravagant devotion to both pope and Pretender. This devotion paid off in his appointment as bishop of Killaloe in 1728 and as bishop of Waterford in 1739. He emerges as a kind of Pimpernel figure, gravely in cahoots with the Jacobite plotters on the Continent and plying them continually with intelligence reports on the current scene as he flits restlessly between Ireland, Britain and the Continent. Hunted out of Ireland in the persecution of 1744, he died in Paris in 1747.[38] The fact that he carried on a regular correspondence with the Stuart court-in-exile, mainly through Col. Daniel O'Brien, the Jacobite agent in Paris, means that his part in opposing the oath and the address to the king is well documented, although it is most unfortunate that neither his letter of *c.* August 1725 nor his 'long letter' in the spring of 1726 have survived in the Stuart papers, since it seems they would have shed some much-needed light on the movement for an oath for catholics at this time and in particular on the advocates of such an oath on the catholic side.[39] It is possible that these letters found their way into the Vatican archives and that they may still be there.

George I died suddenly in June 1727. His successor, George II, had already, before coming to the throne, acquired a reputation for liberality and toleration where catholics were concerned. It was to capitalise on this reputation that Lord Delvin, who, as we have seen was an absentee living in London, returned to Dublin towards the end of June 1727 and organised a meeting on 8 July 1727 of some of the principal catholics in and about Dublin at the Lyon in Werburgh Street. At this meeting he presented the text of an address of loyalty to the new king which he had prepared. He also informed the meeting that the proposed address had the blessing and support of Cardinal Fleury, first minister of France. When those present had been well primed with drink, Delvin arranged for them to put their signatures to the address, but on more sober reflection, it was claimed, many came back the following morning and insisted on their names being erased from the document.[40]

37 [Prior, Thomas], *A list of the absentees of Ireland*, Dublin 1729, 2.   38 Fagan, P. op. cit., in note 31, *passim*.   39 For references to the existence of these letters see P. Fagan, op. cit. in note 3, pp. 78 & 95.   40 Giblin, C., op. cit., no. 5 (1962), 121.

The address was worded as follows:

To the King's Most Excellent Majesty,
The most humble Address of the Roman Catholics of the Kingdom of Ireland.

Most Gracious Sovereign,
We, your Majesty's most loyal and dutiful subjects, the Roman Catholics of your Kingdom of Ireland, are truly grieved for the unspeakable loss that this nation, as well as your Majesty's other Dominions, has sustained by the decease of our late most Gracious Sovereign, Your Royal Father, the goodness and lenity of whose Government we are deeply sensible of, which emboldens us thus in a most humble manner to approach Your Majesty's Most Sacred Person, to congratulate Your Majesty's happy accession to the Throne, and to crave leave to assure Your Majesty of our steady allegiance and most humble duty to Your Majesty's Person and Government. And we most humbly beseech Your Majesty to give us leave to affirm that our resolution of an inviolable duty and allegiance to Your Majesty proceeds not only from our inclination and the sincerity of our hearts, but also from a firm belief of its being a religious duty, which no power on earth can dispense with.[41]

Lord Delvin then returned to London where he delivered the address to the lord lieutenant, Lord Carteret, who presented it to the king. Contemporary reports say that the address was graciously received by his Majesty.[42] Sylvester Lloyd in a letter dated 15 July 1727 to Col. Daniel O'Brien, tells us that the address was signed by the earls of Carlingford, Westmeath and Fingal, Lord Trimleston, another lord whose name (in Lloyd's letter) is illegible and about twenty 'of the chief of the commons' in and about Dublin.[43] However, Bishop Stephen MacEgan, in a letter to the Stuart court, states that the address was signed by 'not above sixty or a few more'.[44] According to Lloyd 'no clergyman' was consulted in regard to the address and we can conclude from this

---

41 This version of the address is taken from the *Dublin Journal* of 25–7 July 1727. It can be accepted as the official version since it was sent to that newspaper with a covering letter from the authors of the address. It differs in some minor respects from other published versions.   42 *Dublin Journal* 5–8 August 1727.   43 Fagan, P. (ed.), op. cit. in note 3, 96. The name after Trimleston is a short name and it is probably Delvin. The practice of referring to the earl of Westmeath as Lord Delvin, when the latter title was properly the courtesy title of the earl's eldest son, must have led to confusion at times. However, in the case of the address, if, as appears likely, both father and son signed it, one would expect that they used their proper titles. The earl's eldest son was Christopher Nugent, who in fact was to predecease his father and never succeeded to the earldom.   44 Fagan, P. (ed.), op. cit. in note 3, 101.

that it was not signed by any of the catholic clergy. Lloyd also states 'it is incredible with what passion it is carried on by the laity',[45] indicating that the vast majority of the catholic laity of Dublin favoured the address, thus marking a divide between the clergy and laity in the matter of similar addresses and proposed oaths which was to be repeated many times throughout the century.

Lloyd lost no time in organising very effective opposition to the address. A contemporary source tells us that Lloyd 'did by writing as well as by declaiming against it awaken the loyalty of your [James Stuart's] faithful subjects, and not only prevented many from following their [Addressers'] wicked example laid before them, but in some measure rendered the whole project abortive'.[46] The writer went on to claim that Lloyd's behaviour in this affair had made him many powerful enemies and that there was reason to believe that they had stirred up some even of the most eminent of the clergy against him, 'who perhaps conscious of their own omission of duty, might be ready to misrepresent him abroad for their private ends'. The 'most eminent of the clergy' apparently included the archbishop of Dublin of the time, Edmund Murphy, for another correspondent of the Stuart court, Ambrose O'Callaghan, later implied that Murphy and his successor, Luke Fagan, were in favour of an oath for catholics, when he stated that 'we had two here [Dublin] of late, one after t'other, and a shadow on the wall would frighten the stoutest of 'em. They were both of [Thomas] Strickland's calling', Strickland being, as we have seen, one of the principal advocates of an oath for catholics in England.[47]

The campaign against the address included the publication of a list of thirteen Queries,[48] or, in other words, statements in the form of rhetorical questions, severely critical of the address. These questioned whether twenty or thirty lords and gentlemen could in any sense be understood to be the Roman Catholics of Ireland. They stigmatised the signing of the address as 'precipitate, passionate and presumptious'. They claimed that 'arguments were made use of to terrify the weak, or catch the unwary, contrary to the fundamental laws of these realms and injurious to the sentiments of the church and dishonourable to the most renowned fidelity of an Irishman.' They claimed that certain obsequious language in the address 'wiped away our tears without removing the cause' and they characterised them as 'vile and nauseous flattery'.

---

45 Ibid., 96.   46 Ibid., 108–9. Letter dated 9 March 1728 from Fr Francis Stuart, provincial of the Irish Franciscans, later bishop of Down & Connor, to the Stuart court. 47 Ibid., 193. Letter dated 16 February 1734 from Ambrose O'Callaghan, bishop of Ferns to James Edgar.   48 The Queries were published as an appendix to Edward Synge's sermon, preached in Christ Church on 23 October 1731. They were also published independently in the same year, together with a copy of the 1727 address to the king – see copy in TCD library, early printed books section. Synge stated in the course of his sermon 'they had never, that [he] could hear, been made public' at that stage. However, the Queries may have been printed for private circulation among catholics in 1727. The congress referred to in Quare XIII was that of Soissons.

The rejection in the address of the papal power to dispense oaths of allegiance, they describe as 'making a new creed for the Roman Catholics of Ireland and arrogantly deciding of a question of right, which no conscience can affirm, because no understanding can reach'. They ask why did not the junto [Lord Delvin and his friends] go generously and take the Oath of Abjuration for all the Roman Catholics of Ireland 'and so save Lord Delvin the trouble of going for England'. Query IX reads as follows:

> Though allegiance to the Lord's annointed may be perhaps a religious duty, with which no power on earth can dispense, yet since it is evident from our history that there may be kings *de facto* and since Coke and other of our great lawyers say that allegiance is due to kings *de jure* in their natural capacities; and since allegiance does in our language and laws signify something more than mere fidelity, which is reciprocal to mere protection, (we mean as the Flemings swear to their successive Governors, Spaniards, Germans, French, Dutch or English). Whether then, and in every such case, allegiance be a religious duty equally due to all kings *de facto*, as well as *de jure*, and finally, in all cases, whether the Parliament of Great Britain be not a power on earth actually existing, that often has, and still can dispense with such duty.

In the remaining queries they ask whether such of the subscribers as were hurried into this affair should withdraw their names and acknowledge they were imposed upon; whether the Junto were not obliged to answer these and other queries before they presumed to present their address in the name of the whole Kingdom; whether the address would better be entitled 'The humble address of us the Subscribers'; and, lastly, whether 'an humble petition to the king and a remonstrance of our grievances, notwithstanding the public faith given at Limerick and our peaceable behaviour ever since that time, would not be much more proper on this critical occasion and contribute more to our relief at a future Congress'.

But it appears that those who opposed the Address were far from agreed on the line to be taken. Bishop Stephen MacEgan, in a letter to the Stuart court, stated that the address was opposed 'by a vast many as soon as they heard of it, judging a remonstrance of grievances with assurances of fidelity [to George II] to be more proper'.[49] It seems certain that Sylvester Lloyd and his fellow Jacobites would have been strongly opposed to giving any assurances of fidelity to George II, and it is significant that Lloyd in forwarding the Queries above to the Stuart court omitted the last one, which mentions 'a humble petition to the king', presumably because he did not agree with it.

---

49 Fagan, P., op. cit. in note 3, 101. Letter dated 10 November 1727 from Stephen MacEgan, then bishop of Clonmacnoise, to the Stuart court.

Meanwhile the address had been brought to the attention of the Brussels nunciature. In a dispatch to Cardinal Secretary of State Lercari dated 29 August 1727 Nuncio Spinelli maintained that this was the first time since the reign of Henry VIII that the catholics of England, Ireland and Scotland had given recognition in a formal manner to a non-catholic king; and even though many catholics thought they should swear an oath of loyalty to the monarch who preceded the present one, provided they were granted freedom of conscience, none of them considered that it was permitted to them to swear at the same time, as the court desired, that they were of opinion that the pope had no authority over the temporal jurisdiction of princes, an opinion which was to be found in the address in a somewhat mitigated form.[50]

Nuncio Spinelli went on to maintain that, while such an address might be of advantage to the person responsible for it (Lord Delvin), it would certainly do great harm to catholics generally and that it could create scandal and schism among them; that, in so far as the government was concerned, the joy it would experience in seeing that only twenty catholics signed this new oath of fidelity, would not be nearly so great as its sorrow on considering that the other catholics refused to put their signatures to it; and that, finally, the references made in the address to the moderation of the last government would provide the 'heretics' with a satisfactory answer, should they wish to reply to the catholic powers, whenever the latter speak in favour of the British and Irish catholics, or try, by some other means, to keep the non-catholics of Germany and France (?) from abusing their power.

It will be seen, then, from the foregoing that the Vatican establishment still held rigidly to the doctrine of the pope's power to depose princes. It will be seen also that the address was blown out of all proportion by describing it as an oath of fidelity. This was the aspect which the secretary of state concentrated on when on 11 October 1727 he intimated to the nuncio that he was not yet in a position to give a precise answer to the 'oath taken by the Irish Catholics to the present king of England'; that the pope had referred the matter to the Holy Office for detailed examination, after which he would decide what should be done.[51]

The accession of George II to the throne entailed a general election to the Irish house of commons in 1727. Catholic freeholders, freemen etc, subject to their swearing the oath of abjuration under section 24 of the 1704 act (2 Anne c. 6), still had the vote and it appears that their support went largely to Tory candidates, that is, in respect of those seats (only about 25 per cent of the total of 300) for which there was any real contest. But any hopes catholics may have had of securing relief from the new parliament were to be dashed for, Lloyd tells us, a petition from them 'for leave to take long leases, mortgages and

50 Giblin, C., op. cit., no. 5 (1962), 121–2.   51 Ibid. no. 14 (1971), 40.

perhaps lands etc was at last reading not only rejected but to their great confusion hissed with indignation out of the house'.[52]

Back in London Lord Delvin continued his efforts to promote, according
to his lights, the catholic cause. Fr Sylvester Lloyd tells us in a letter dated
Douai, 1 June 1728 that Delvin was very obsequious to the English court, that
he had been introduced to the 'Elector' (George II) and his Lady by the duke
of Richmond and had been received very graciously. Lloyd claimed that Delvin
intended to submit a petition to the king in the name of the Irish catholics begging that they might have leave to purchase lands and to take long leases, inasmuch as their behaviour to the government had always been peaceable, and
that besides their late address they were ready to give the governnment all such
further security for their fidelity and allegiance as should be thought necessary.
Lloyd considered such a petition extremely injurious because it not only confirmed the late address but tacitly surrendered the Articles of Limerick, 'our
sheet anchor', and left catholics absolutely at the discretion of the government
for such oaths and tests as the authorities should think proper. Lloyd claimed
that none but the 'Addressers' had given in to this new scheme, that Delvin had
been very busy and had received remittances from his party in Ireland for carrying on the affair. Lloyd went on to say that it had been whispered to him by
one of Delvin's intimates that a copy of the proposed petition had been sent
to Paris with a view to having it recommended by Cardinal Fleury to the French
government. Finally, Lloyd claimed that Delvin was 'despised and avoided by
all honest men in London'.[53]

From a chronological point of view it is appropriate to give some consideration at this point to the form of oath attributed to Fr Cornelius Nary, for it
appears he finalised this oath some time after the accession of George II, since
that monarch is mentioned in it. I have failed to discover in what circumstances
or for what purpose Nary formulated this oath. It may be that Lord Delvin
commissioned him to draft it for the purpose of Delvin's schemes and negotiations as outlined above. As we shall see, this oath was to enjoy a new lease
of life when a registration of priests bill was before the Irish house of lords in
1756, and as far as can be ascertained, it was first printed in 1756, long after
Nary's death. Charles O'Conor of Belanagare was to make this comment on it
in a letter to John Curry dated 9 December 1767:

Were our masters in earnest, a test oath would not be difficult. King William
required of our people no more than a simple oath of allegiance; and did
the wisest men now in the Kingdom club hands to frame a test against per-

---

52 Fagan, P., op. cit. in note 3, 107. Letter dated 9 March 1728 from Fr Sylvester Lloyd
to the Stuart court.   53 Ibid., 110–111. Letter dated 1 June 1728 from Fr Sylvester
Lloyd to Col. Daniel O'Brien.

jury, duplicity etc, they could not produce one more full to every point than Doctor Nary's, which is annexed to the *Vindication*, etc., Appendix No. 2.[54]

Nary's oath can be read at note 55 below.[55] The declaration in that oath that 'it is no article of my faith that any person whatsoever has power to absolve me from my obligation to this oath or that the Pope hath power to depose princes' is in line with a similar declaration in the Synge oath. The declaration of allegiance to George II and the promise 'to make known all treasons, traitorous conspiracies and plots against his person, crown or dignity' is likewise on a par with a similar promise, though in different language, in the Synge oath. However, while the Synge oath contains a promise not to hinder or alter the Hanoverian Succession and to maintain and defend the same against all persons whatsoever, in particular the person pretending to be James III, Nary's oath is silent on this point.

The possibility of an outbreak of war in Europe during 1726 and 1727 concentrated the minds of statesmen on the need to provide a forum within which the nations of Europe could discuss and, hopefully, settle differences. Such was the aim of the European Congress which opened at Soissons, an old cathedral town on the Aisne in north-east France, in June 1728. Because of the possibility that religious toleration might be one of the subjects on the agenda of the congress, there were consultations in Ireland and in England as to how the case of English and Irish catholics should be presented. It is evident from the Stuart papers that Bernard Dunne, bishop of Kildare, was selected by Primate MacMahon to represent the Irish catholic interest at the congress. Dunne had spent many years in France before being appointed to Kildare and so was an obvious choice for such an assignment, but he declined to make any move

---

54 Ward, Robert E. et al., *Letters of Charles O'Conor of Belanagare*, Washington D.C. 1988, 211.   55 Nary's form of oath was worded as follows: 'I, A.B., do promise and swear to bear true faith and allegiance to his Majesty King George the Second, his heirs and successors, and that I will make known all treasons, traitorous conspiracies and plots, against his Person, Crown or Dignity, if any such shall come to my knowledge. I also profess that I detest and abhor from my heart as impious, scandalous and abominable to believe that it is lawful to murder or destroy, any Person or Persons whatsoever, for, or under pretence of being heretics; and also that base, unchristian principle that no faith is to be kept with heretics. I further declare that it is no Article of my Faith, that any person whatsoever has power to absolve me from my obligation to this Oath, or that the Pope hath power to depose Princes: And therefore I do promise and swear that I will not teach, preach, hold, maintain or abet any such doctrines or tenets, and that I will not accept of any Absolutions or Dispensations whatsoever with regard to this Oath, or any Part thereof.

'And all this I promise and swear upon the Faith of a Christian freely, readily and willingly, in the plain and ordinary sense of the words now read unto me, without any secret Collusion, Equivocation, Evasion or Mental Reservation whatsoever. So help me God.'

pending the agreement of the 'Pretender'.[56] Fr Sylvester Lloyd was selected by the Irish regular clergy to represent them at the congress and, unlike Dunne, he had no hesitation in doing so. In early summer 1728 he was in England consulting with English catholics on the line to be taken. Highly articulate, plausible and well-informed, Lloyd made such an impression on the English catholics that they chose him, along with the Englishman, Fr Charles Fell, to represent the catholic interest at the congress. He was to find, however, to his considerable dismay, that the duke of Norfolk and other chief catholics of England did not expect any relief from the penal laws without being obliged to take the oath of allegiance at least as a test of their fidelity, and that these English catholics were inclined to take such an oath, 'if not perhaps something more', if required.[57]

When he moved to Flanders at the end of May 1728, Lloyd briefed the nuncio in Brussels on the intentions of certain Irish and English catholics in regard to an oath to the king. The nuncio lost no time in bringing the matter to the attention of the Vatican, for Cardinal Spinola, in a dispatch dated 24 July 1728 to the nuncio, pointed out that these intentions had been subjected to serious examination in Rome and it had been decided that the nuncio should make certain that the catholics in question refrained from doing anything impetuous, as this could result in more harm than good for themselves and their religion; they were rather to direct their petitions to Cardinal Fleury whose assistance, and that of all the other catholic powers, the pope would endeavour to procure for them. Finally, Spinola warned that, if Spinelli learned that the catholic clergy, presumably in Ireland or England, intended to take some kind of oath to the 'duke of Hanover', he was to see to it that no decision was taken by them until the matter had been examined at Rome and precise directions issued by the Holy See.[58] Nary's proposed oath has to be viewed in the light of this warning. It surely must have had the effect of stopping him and others of like mind in their tracks as far as further progress with an oath of allegiance was concerned.

However, efforts to put the religious question on the agenda of the Soissons congress met with little support even from the Vatican, whose temporising attitude stemmed in part from the fear that any concessions achieved by Irish and English catholics would have to be counterbalanced by an oath involving not only allegiance to George II but also renunciation of the pope's deposing and dispensing powers. There was also the consideration that any concessions gained for Irish and English catholics would almost certainly have to be matched by similar concessions for persecuted protestants in France and Poland. The open-

56 Fagan, P. (ed), op. cit. in note 3, 103 (Bp Dunne to Stuart court, 3 December 1727) and 160 (same to same, 12 May 1730).   57 Ibid., 111, Letter dated 1 June 1728 from Fr Sylvester Lloyd to Col. Daniel O'Brien.   58 Giblin, C., op. cit., No. 14 (1971), 41.

ing, then, of the can of worms of religious toleration could have a net overall result unfavourable to catholicism from the Vatican's global view-point. As for the English catholics it appears that Prime Minister Walpole, somewhat out of the blue, sent them express orders at their peril not to make any application to the congress or to any foreign power whatsoever.[59]

So catholic interest in the Congress of Soissons ended, although its deliberations were to drag on into 1731. Sylvester Lloyd returned to Ireland and soon afterwards was appointed bishop of Killaloe. As for Lord Delvin, Lloyd reported in July 1728 that he had disappeared from his home in London about ten days before and was said to be gone to Soissons 'to pursue his old game'.[60] Lloyd cautioned that it was proper to keep a sharp eye after him for 'his restless spirit will not stop at small things'. Early in August Fr Thomas Southcote reported from Paris that Lord Delvin was, he thought, still there, 'and finds too many of his own scandalous principles'. But Southcote hoped he had defeated Delvin's designs by preparing a memorial for the information of the Paris nuncio exposing the consequences and tendencies of Delvin's endeavours.[61] This is the last we hear of Lord Delvin as far as an oath of allegiance is concerned. Presumably he too soon realised that there was nothing to be gained from toting his proposals in the precincts of the congress.

Southcote also mentions that Thomas Strickland, lately appointed bishop of Namur, was active in the Soissons area at this time. It will be recalled that Strickland was one of the original champions of an oath for catholics in England. With Lord Delvin and Strickland strongly advocating the oath for catholics and Lloyd and his Jacobite friends completely opposed to such a move, the catholic body in Ireland and England was irretrievably split. Southcote remarked that catholics were 'so divided that it is impossible to do them any good'.[62]

The extent and venom of catholic opposition to the address to the king and to the idea of an oath of allegiance, must have had the effect of alienating many of those protestants who were favourably disposed to toleration for catholics. Edward Synge, *fils*, purported to be greatly dismayed by the degree of opposition to the address to the king when, in the course of a sermon in Christ Church cathedral, Dublin on 23 October 1731, he thundered:

And would to God that it had really been what 'tis most artfully styled 'the most humble address of the Roman Catholics of Ireland'. We might then hope that the deadly venom of Popish Principles was at last destroyed: and that notwithstanding their gross errors in religion, they were now disposed

59 Fagan, P. (ed.), op. cit. in note 3, 119, letter dated 23 July 1728 from Fr Sylvester Lloyd to Stuart court.   60 Ibid., 122, letter dated 1 August 1728 from Fr Sylvester Lloyd to Col. Daniel O'Brien.   61 Ibid., 123, letter dated 3 August 1728 from Fr Thomas Southcote to Stuart court.   62 Ibid., 123, same to same.

to be and continue good subjects. But the truth is, and 'tis fit it should be known, that neither the body of the Roman Catholics of Ireland, nor the major part of them concurred in or approved of this address. No! They were generally displeased at it: And of those who were displeased, some had not the prudence to conceal their dislike, but drew up and dispersed a most remarkable set of Queries, in which the address itself and the promoters of it are very freely censured, particularly, the former clause just now mentioned is called 'vile and nauseous flattery', and the latter is said to be 'making a New Creed for the Roman Catholics of Ireland'.[63]

Synge goes on to claim that, though the address might be a fair proof of the good affection of the particular persons who joined in it, it was no proof at all that the catholic body generally were in a more loyal disposition to the king and the government, or less attached to the interest of the Pretender or less influenced by the 'pernicious doctrines of the Romish Church'. Since, Synge argued, the catholics of Ireland had never renounced the pope's deposing and dispensing power, and since in these Queries they had declared against renouncing it, 'they may and ought to be considered as enemies to our present Happy Establishment'.[64]

But he had not forgotten the ideas on toleration for catholics which he had previously put forward, for he still conceded:

> The clearest principles of right reason and the Christian Religion establish this as an everlasting truth, that all subjects that have the misfortune to differ from the Established Religion, ought to be treated with as much lenity on account of their religious errors, whatever they be, as is consistent with the welfare and security of the Government.[65]

In a valuable note to this sermon, as printed in 1732, Synge reviewed briefly the various acts from 1697 onwards in relation to the catholic clergy and came to the conclusion that it was never the intention of the legislature 'entirely to deprive the Papists of priests to officiate among them'. It was the intention of the 1704 act for registering catholic clergy that secular priests might live and officiate unmolested; the requirement in the 1709 act for these priests to take the oath of abjuration was, he claimed, necessary for the security of the state. He looked upon the 1704 act as a provision made for a certain time 'at the

63 Synge, Edward, *Sermon preached in Christ Church cathedral, Dublin on Saturday 23 October 1731 ... by Edward, Lord Bishop of Clonfert*, Dublin 1732, 14–15. The 'former clause' was the sentence in the address 'and we most humbly beseech your Majesty ... the sincerity of our hearts'. The 'latter [clause]' was the words of the address 'but also from a firm belief ... on earth can dispense'. 64 Ibid., 15. 65 Ibid., 17 (*recte* 21).

expiration of which the legislature might come to a further resolution', but no such resolution had yet (1732) been taken. The priests registered in 1704 were then, he wrote, nearly all dead and others had come into their places. 'The laws in being have slept', he wrote, 'as it were by a general consent of all orders and degrees of men: and the legislature has not yet made any new ones.' He ends by characterising the resolution ('designed as a foundation of a law') of the Irish house of lords in December 1725, already mentioned, as 'a plain proof that their lordships did not at that time think it proper or necessary entirely to deprive the Papists of Ireland of their Parish Priests'.[66]

Nevertheless, a worsening climate in regard to toleration culminated in 1731 in the promotion in the Irish parliament of five bills, all inimical to catholic interests, viz. (a) a bill closing loopholes in the law on the holding of arms by catholics, (b) an amendment of the law in relation to popish solicitors, (c) a bill for registering the popish clergy, (d) a bill for better putting in execution the laws for banishing popish regulars etc. and (e) a bill to annul and make void marriages between protestants and papists celebrated by popish priests and friars.

We need concern ourselves here only with the bill for registering catholic clergy. A bill, described by Primate Boulter as partly for the registration of popish priests and partly for driving out the regulars, had been before the 1729–30 session of parliament, but Boulter counselled against proceeding with it at that time, stating that 'I must own it is better letting them [catholics] alone, whatever may otherwise be proper, till after the Congress at Soissons is over'.[67] The bill agreed in the lords in the 1731–32 session provided for the registration of secular priests. As to the progress of this bill through the lords, Primate Boulter presented the heads of the bill on 7 December 1731 when it was given its first and second reading. On 8 December 1731 the primate reported that a committee of the house had gone through the heads and had agreed them with several amendments. On 9 December the heads of the bill were read a third time and it was ordered that his Grace (the primate) attend his Grace the lord lieutenant with the heads of the bill and desire him to transmit the same to Great Britain in due form.[68]

I have failed to find a copy of the heads of this bill and so we are in the dark as to the terms of the oath, contained therein, to be taken by catholic clergy.

---

66 Ibid., 17 (*recte* 21).   67 Boulter, Hugh, *Letters*, Dublin 1769, vol. 1, 344. No heads of bill for registering popish priests are mentioned in the *Lords Journal* for the time in question. What Boulter appears to have had in mind was a bill 'for better securing the Protestant interest of this Kingdom against the further attempts of the Papists', the heads of which were presented to the house by Ralph Lambert, bishop of Meath, on 30 December 1729, when they were read a first and second time and committed to a committee of the whole house. They were considered in committee on 2 January 1730, but no further action was taken; the index to the journals states that they were 'not reported'.   68 *Lords Journal Ireland*, vol. 3, 173–6.

However, one source states that any priest registering under the bill was required to take an oath of abjuration and loyalty.[69]

There are two contemporary comments on the proposed oath which are worth noting. Bernard Dunne, bishop of Kildare, in a letter dated 24 April 1732 to the Stuart Court remarked about it:

> Had matters succeeded with them [the Irish lords and commons] there was an oath to be tendered to those of my cloth which none but men void of both honour and conscience could swallow. Twas the second part of the same tune with the A—— [the catholic address to the king] and could not miss to meet with the same fate among men of untainted principles.[70]

The second contemporary reference to this oath is in a letter of 16 January 1732 from Fr Ignatius Kelly of the Irish Jesuit house at Poitiers in France to the General of the Jesuits in Rome:

> Yesterday I received from Ireland from our Fathers Thomas Hennessy and Michael Murphy letters full of lamentation and affliction because of the very cruel acts recently passed in Parliament against the Holy Catholic Religion which must go into exile from that unhappy kingdom if those wicked acts are confirmed by George II. ... As regards ecclesiastics whether secular or regular, whoever of them is found in Ireland after March the 25th next will be hanged on the gallows unless before the said date he takes the detestable and heretical Oath of Abjuration against the power of the Supreme Pontiff, against the authority of the Holy See; a reward of £50 is granted the discoverer in the said case as in the others.

Fr Kelly goes on to claim that still more dreadful measures were contained in the 'said acts against the Catholic religion in defiance of the public faith and agreements publicly signed by William III at the Siege of Limerick but afterwards and especially now violated'. He asks the Jesuit General to bring the matter to the attention of the pope so that 'he may deign to recommend seriously and immediately this urgent business to his nuncios with the Catholic powers that by their representation they may try to avert this storm'. He concludes by stating that Fr Michael Murphy had written to him on the instructions of 'their Lordships the Bishops now at Dublin'.[71]

As to the nature of the oath in the proposed bill, Fr Kelly's description of it as 'an oath of abjuration against the power of the Supreme Pontiff, against

69 Giblin, C., op. cit., no. 9 (1966), 28.   70 Fagan, P. (ed.), op. cit. in note 3, 174, letter dated 24 April 1732 from Bernard Dunne, bishop of Kildare to Stuart court. 71 Finnegan, Francis, 'The Jesuits of Dublin 1660–1760' in *Reportorium Novum*, vol. 4, no. 1, 76–7.

the authority of the Holy See' has to be seriously questioned. That kind of oath would be akin to the oath of supremacy and could not be taken by anyone calling himself a catholic; it is scarcely credible that the authorities would have required such an oath from a catholic priest as a condition of registration, more particularly having regard to Synge *fils*' interpretation at this time of the laws in regard to the catholic secular clergy set out above.

It will be noted that Bishop Dunne's comments on the bill are couched in much less strident tones than Fr Kelly's, for the reason, one presumes, that the sole objection of a committed Jacobite such as Dunne would be the requirement to abjure the Stuarts. Since Dunne was well known to be tainted with Gallican principles, he should have had no objection to renouncing the pope's deposing and dispensing powers if that were a requirement of the oath in the bill.

It seems likely, then, that this oath, like the 1709 oath, required the abjuration of no one other than James Stuart. Whether it took any cognisance of the Synge oath or indeed of the Nary oath is another matter for speculation, although it is probable that, unlike the 1709 oath, it contained a renunciation of the papal deposing and dispensing powers, which was a feature of both the Synge and Nary oaths. Such a renunciation would be anathema to a Jesuit like Fr Kelly, since the Jesuits were the great upholders of papal authority and prerogative, and this may well be what he found 'detestable and heretical' and 'against the power of the Supreme Pontiff'.

In the event the bill, like those at (d) and (e) in the list above, was not approved by the English privy council. In anticipation of anti-catholic measures in the forthcoming parliamentary session, Ambrose O'Callaghan, newly appointed bishop of Ferns, had undertaken in July–August 1731 a mission to the Austrian court and persuaded the Emperor to order his ambassador in London, Count Kinski, to take appropriate action.[72] The intention was that Kinski would consult with the duke of Dorset, the new lord lieutenant, before the latter proceeded to Ireland to open the 1731 session of parliament. But Kinski's representations, if indeed made, had no effect in forestalling the designs of the Irish house of lords which proceeded to approve the heads of the five bills listed above. It is probable that when the heads were sent to London for approval Kinski continued to exert pressure on the privy council to negative them, although the official reason given by the privy council for not approving the registration of clergy bill and the bills at (d) and (e) above was that they were of an extraordinary nature and very different from the laws of England against papists.[73]

---

72 Fagan, P. (ed.), op. cit. in note 3, 168–9.   73 N.L.I. microfilm Pos. 3651, f. 74.

4

The Axe Laid to the Root

For the remainder of the 1730s and throughout the 1740s an anti-catholic majority continued to dominate both houses of the Irish parliament, but as always there were many members sympathetic to catholics, for example the Synges and Bishops Clayton and Berkeley. The latter's *The Querist*, published in 1735, contained much that was sympathetic and favourable to catholics and understanding of their situation. As regards an oath for catholics, he asked rhetorically:

> Whether an oath testifying allegiance to the king, and disclaiming the Pope's authority in temporals, may not be justly required of Roman Catholics? and whether in common prudence or policy, any priest should be tolerated who refuseth to take it?[1]

The voices of moderation, however, tended to be drowned by a rabid and vocal majority.

But against all the odds the catholic church continued to progress and to consolidate itself. Bishops were appointed to vacant sees and went about their usual duties, albeit discreetly. Quite decent chapels, indeed some quite imposing ones as in Cork and Waterford, made their appearance in the cities and larger towns, and registers of births, deaths and marriages were initiated in many parishes. The catholic laity continued to prosper as merchants, and in the various trades and crafts and there were some who made their mark in the medical profession. On the land many catholics grew rich as graziers, the thirty-one year limit on leases for catholics virtually confining them to that type of agriculture to the great detriment of tillage. This insuppressible nature of the catholic resurgence, the experience of having anti-catholic bills rejected by the English privy council in 1732 and earlier, the relative failure of the charter schools and the constant spectre of the 'Pretender' always ready, with his

1 Johnston, Joseph, *Bishop Berkeley's Querist in historical perspective*, Dundalk 1970, 147. See also Berkeley's pamphlet *A word to the wise*, Dublin 1749.

supporters on the Continent as well as at home, to take advantage of Britain's difficulties, all these combined to instil in the majority in parliament a feeling of great fear and distrust of catholics.

An information sworn by Fr John Hennessy, parish priest of Doneraile, County Cork in January 1732 that money was being collected by the catholic clergy for the use of the 'Pretender', led to a witch-hunt by the authorities, involving Archbishop Butler of Cashel, Bishops Lloyd of Killaloe, O'Keeffe of Limerick and MacCarthy of Cork. Government investigations disclosed that the money was in fact being collected for the purpose of financing a lobby in London against the five anti-catholic bills already mentioned; whereupon the lords committee examining the matter had to discard the allegations of money being collected for the 'Pretender' and came to the conclusion that 'there was a Popish ecclesiastical jurisdiction exercised in this Kingdom by Popish archbishops, bishops and vicars general in open violation of the laws of the land', and they recommended that the lord lieutenant should issue a proclamation to all magistrates to put the laws against popery in execution.[2] This proclamation heralded a persecution of catholic clergy in the first half of 1734 which was most keenly felt in Munster.[3]

In the same year the bill against catholic solicitors,[4] which had been approved by the English privy council in 1732, became law. The effect of the Solicitors Acts 1698 and 1707 was that no solicitor could practise in Ireland unless he had first taken the oath of allegiance, the new oath of supremacy, the oath of abjuration and had made the declaration against Transubstantiation; but there was a saver in respect of any solicitor entitled to the benefit of the Articles of Limerick who had practised as a solicitor in the courts in Charles II's reign and had taken the oath of abjuration before 1 July 1707. Barristers, if they wished to practise, were subject to the same conditions under the act to prevent the further growth of popery 1704, but with the added requirement that they should receive the Sacrament according to the usage of the church of Ireland. No saver in respect of the Articles of Limerick applied in the case of barristers.

One would have thought that the acts of 1698 and 1707, not to mention a further act in 1727, were sufficiently copper-fastened to prevent catholic solicitors, apart from those covered by the Articles of Limerick, from practising but apparently loopholes were found, as was pointed out in the preamble to the Solicitors Act 1734:

Whereas the laws now in force against Popish solicitors have been found ineffectual by reason of the difficulty of convicting such solicitors, and the

---

2 *A report from the committee to inspect the original papers seized in the houses of MacCarthy alias Rabah, a reputed popish titular bishop, and Joseph Nagle, a reputed popish solicitor,* Dublin 1734, 4. 3 Fagan, Patrick, *An Irish bishop in penal times: The chequered career of Sylvester Lloyd OFM 1680–1747,* Dublin 1993, 135–6. 4 7 George II c. 5.

mischiefs thereby intended to be remedied remain, to the great prejudice of the Protestant interest of this kingdom: and whereas by means of such Popish solicitors the acts against the growth of popery have been and daily are greatly eluded and evaded: for remedy whereof and for preventing obscure and ignorant persons from practising as attorneys and solicitors, be it enacted ...

Under the 1734 act (section 4), therefore, barristers, attorneys, solicitors and certain court officers and functionaries were required, in order to be licensed under the act, to take a further oath that they would not willingly or knowingly suffer any disqualified barrister, attorney, solicitor etc. to act or practise in their name in any suit, cause or matter in any court of law or equity in the kingdom; and that they would not knowingly take as an apprentice or employ as a clerk or solicitor any person of the Popish religion.

There was in section 10 an Articles of Limerick saver on the same terms as before but, since a solicitor claiming benefit would need to have been practising nearly fifty years before in Charles II's time, there were obviously very few who would qualify. Section 18 was of interest to catholic solicitors in that it excluded from the scope of the act 'any suits or prosecutions for any crimes whatsoever, which by the laws of this Kingdom are to be punished by death'.

In the 1739–40 session of parliament further measures were taken against catholics. Bishop Lloyd of Killaloe reported 'a terrible stroke against us' by parliament which had driven many of the catholic gentry into England. What was involved was an act for disarming papists,[5] and for preventing protestant servants, employed in the houses of papists, from bearing arms. Justices of the peace were required to tender the oath of abjuration to such persons as were brought before them charged with offences under the act. Again there was a saver in respect of those covered by the Articles of Limerick but subject to their taking the oath of allegiance only to King George II.

In February 1744, with war between France and England threatening and the possibility of an invasion by a Jacobite force, the greatest persecution since the days of Queen Anne was initiated with a proclamation ordering that the laws against popery be put in execution.[6] The proclamation continued to be enforced in greater or lesser degree throughout 1744. The summer of 1745 brought the Jacobite rising in Scotland and, left to its own devices, the Dublin parliament at its new session commencing in the autumn of that year would in all probability have introduced even harsher measures against catholics. But the British government had other ideas as to how Jacobite support in Ireland might be contained; they decided that that end might best be achieved by

5 13 George II c. 6.   6 Brady, John, *Catholics and catholicism in the eighteenth century press*, Maynooth 1965, 65.

conciliation and they sent over Lord Chesterfield as lord lieutenant with orders
to implement such a policy. Chesterfield's short term as viceroy was later viewed
as a watershed in the treatment of Irish catholics, whose inaction during the
Jacobite rising was not forgotten by the authorities. Some made generous
acknowledgment of how the catholics had behaved themselves, like Prime
Serjeant Eaton Stannard, MP for Midleton, Co. Cork, when he stated:

> We had the comfort and satisfaction to see that all was quiet here [during
> the 'forty five']; and to the honour of Roman Catholics be it remembered
> not a man of them moved tongue, pen or sword either during the late wicked
> rebellion in Scotland or on the then occasion [the Lucas agitation]. And for
> my part, while they behave with duty and allegiance to the present estab-
> lishment, I shall hold them as men in equal esteem with others in every
> point but one: And while their private opinion interferes not with public
> tranquility, I think their industry and allegiance ought to be encouraged.[7]

Never again was there to be any general attempt to reactivate the religious provisions of the penal laws, although there would be the odd case of harassment
of individual clerics.

Chesterfield's impression of the Irish parliament during his period as lord
lieutenant can be gleaned from the following comment:

> I have with much difficulty quieted the fears [of protestants] here, which
> were at first very strong, partly by contagion from England and partly from
> old prejudices, which my good subjects are far from being above. They are
> in general still at the year 1689, and have not shook off any religious or
> political prejudice that prevailed at that time.[8]

On the occasion of Hamilton's first bill in the 1755–6 parliamentary session for
the registering of popish priests, Chesterfield remarked that he had thought of
such a bill when he was in Ireland during 1745–6 but soon found that it would
be impossible to carry it through the house of commons in any decent shape.

---

7 [Charles O'Conor], *A vindication of the political principles of Roman Catholics*, Dublin
1760?, 21–2. As to Charles O'Conor's authorship of this pamphlet, see article by C.J.
Woods in *Eighteenth Century Ireland*, vol. 7, 147–8. The date 1741 on the pamphlet is
manifestly incorrect, and Dr Woods, having regard to internal evidence, states that it
could not have been published before 1760. He favoured 1761 as the likely date on the
basis that the year MDCCXLI shown on the pamphlet was a careless error for MDCCLXI.
However, Fr H. Fenning tells me that the date 1760 appears on the bookseller's advertisement for the pamphlet. I have therefore taken 1760 to be the year of publication,
although the likelihood is that there was a further edition in 1761.   8 Bradshaw, John
(ed.), *The letters of Philip Dormer Stanhope, earl of Chesterfield*, London 1892, vol. 2, 790.

It can be assumed, therefore, that Chesterfield was the driving force behind the heads of a bill to explain and amend the 1704 act for registering the popish clergy which was before the 1745–6 session of the Irish house of commons. On 20 December 1745 leave was given to bring in the heads of such a bill and James Cuffe (County Mayo), William Carr (Cashel City) and William Gore (Kilkenny City) were ordered to prepare and bring in the same. On 13 January 1746 James Cuffe presented the heads of the bill, which were received and read and committed to a committee of the whole house. On 1 February 1746, the order of the day being read for setting up a committee of the whole house to consider the heads of the bill, it was resolved that the house would on 1 May following resolve itself into such a committee. However, the last sitting of that session was on 11 April 1746 and parliament was prorogued on 20 May.[9]

Although nothing further was heard of this Registry of Priests bill, introduced in the 1745–6 session, the subject was kept alive in a very interesting, anonymous pamphlet entitled *The ax laid to the root or reasons humbly offered for putting the Popish clergy in Ireland under some better regulations.* There were three editions of this pamphlet, all in 1749, indicating a considerable, if short-lived, public interest in the subject matter.[10]

Although the proposals in the pamphlet were only suggestions for legislation which never went any further than suggestions, nevertheless the pamphlet is important as a barometer of protestant public opinion on the catholic question at that time. Furthermore, it must have had an influence on the proposals on the same subject which emerged in the 1750s. It also gives a good deal of factual information on what the administration were pleased to call 'the state of popery' in the 1740s.

In a lengthy preamble to the main proposals in the pamphlet the author dwells at some length on the situation which had emerged over the years in relation to popery. The laws against popery, he says, have had very little effect; popish priests swarmed all over the kingdom and the resort to the mass-houses was as public and unrestrained as to churches of the established church. The designs of the charter schools had been traversed and obstructed by popish priests who terrified poor parents from yielding up their children to be educated in such schools, choosing rather to abandon them to idleness and beggary than to have them brought up industrious protestants. (p. 1) Popish bishops residing in the kingdom were more numerous than the bishops of the established church, and, holding their visitations and exercising their jurisdiction with little caution or restraint, the hierarchy of the church of Rome was as effectually maintained in Ireland to all spiritual purposes, as if it were established by law. (p. 3) There was a chain of command stretching from pope to archbishops to bishops to

9 *Commons Journal Ireland*, vol. 4, pp. 477, 480 & 491. I have failed to discover a copy of these heads of bill. 10 I am indebted to Fr H. Fenning for this information.

priests to laity. The religious orders of monks, friars, jesuits and nuns had their nests in many places and were perfectly known in the vicinity. From hence issued those strolling mendicants who were the instruments of clandestine marriages. (pp. 3–4)

The author claims that the Gavelling Act has had some considerable effect in influencing catholics to convert to the established church, but the effect had been upon the laity only and that merely external; it had not gone to the root, its only effect being upon men of estates in land who hardly ever were seen at protestant services, and whose wives, children and dependents generally were open papists. They themselves commonly sent for the priest in their extremity. (p. 4)

He goes on to claim that the laws against popery were little more than dead letters. The 1745 uprising in Scotland showed how vulnerable the protestants were. 'And will not our terrors and dangers return upon such an emergency? When we are well assured that we are every moment in danger from an enemy within our bowels, who lies in wait for our estates and our blood?' (p. 5)

The charter schools were expected to lay a good foundation for the conversion of the common people, but progress must naturally be slow and insensible for a generation yet to come. In the meantime measures must be taken to reduce the number of priests by registering a sufficient number and 'cashiering' the remainder. (p. 5–6) It would lie in the wisdom of the legislature to frame a law for this purpose, but previous thereto the following hints were humbly offered for their consideration by the author. (pp. 7–11)

1 That it is agreeable to reason that papists giving good security for their fidelity to the government should be tolerated
2 That a sufficient number of priests be allowed.
3 That all such priests be registered under such terms and conditions as an honest papist can consistently with his religion and conscience submit to; for otherwise the best men among them would be excluded and the worst retained.
4 That every popish priest at the time of being registered should show his letters of orders, take the Oath of Fidelity to his Majesty and the following:

I, A.B., do from my heart abhor, detest and abjure as impious and heretical that damnable doctrine that &c [*sic*][11] and I do declare upon my conscience that neither the pope nor any authority upon earth, can absolve

---

11 How much of the proposed oath is left to the imagination at this point is difficult to say. The words which usually follow 'damnable doctrine' in such oaths are 'that no faith is to be kept with heretics and that princes excommunicated or deprived by the pope may be deposed or murdered by their subjects'.

me from my Oath of Fidelity to his Majesty King George the Second and his successors and that I will accept of no such absolution.

5 That upon the death or removal of such priest, another may succeed under the same qualifications.

6 That every registered priest shall wear some particular decent habit to be approved by the Government and Council and if he shall be found above one meaasured mile from the house of his usual residence without the same, he shall for the first offence forfeit and pay to the informer five shillings, and ten shillings for every other offence. [It will be very useful, the author of the pamphlet states, to have every popish priest known and distinguished, for want of which he will do mischief and pervert under the disguise of a lay habit.]

7 The number of priests to be registered shall be limited by counties at the discretion of the Government and Council and no more admitted to be registered but upon oath made of a vacancy.

8 Every county to be divided into particular districts consisting of one or more parishes and one priest registered for each district who shall officiate in no other district unless during a vacancy or unless the neighbouring priest should be disabled by sickness or infirmities.

9 That at the time of registering, such priest shall bring two papists of known and sufficient ability to be bound in a bond of £100 for his good and quiet behaviour during his residence.

10 That after the 25th of March 1751 every popish priest, who is not registered and every person officiating as such by performing any clerical office or ceremonies that are peculiar to the Church of Rome either in public or in private, shall for the first offence be fined in the sum of £50 and be imprisoned for the space of one year and for the second offence be fined in the sum of £100 and be imprisoned during life.

11 That one bishop of the Romish Communion shall be allowed by the Government and Council to reside and exercise his function in each of the three provinces of Leinster, Munster and Connacht under certain regulations and large security and to be registered as the priests are, taking the oaths as above. That every such bishop shall confer Holy Orders upon none but natives of the kingdom of Ireland and shall be himself a native. That he shall confer orders at four stated times of the year only, to be fixed by law. And that every candidate shall three days at least before his ordination repair to some justice of the county where such candidate resides and there take and subscribe the following oath, annexing his name with the place of his residence:

I, A. B. do swear in the presence of God who will judge me the Last Day that since the first day of May last past I have not received any education or instruction in any Popish university, college, seminary or school without this kingdom of Ireland and that I will not hereafter study or take any degree in any such university, college, seminary or school, so help me God.

Such justice of the peace to be required to certify under his hand and seal the names of all such candidates together with the oath taken by them and to give a copy thereof with his certificate to one of the candidates which shall be sufficient authority to the bishop for ordaining them and without which he shall not confer orders. The original to be returned to the Quarter Sessions that it might remain on record and a penalty on any bishop who ordained without such certificate.

Such Justice of the Peace shall not issue a certificate until the candidate who requests it shall bring to him the name and place of the registered priest whose vacancy he is nominated to supply, certified by the minister and one or both of the church wardens of the parish where the vacancy happened. [This precaution is necessary, the author explains, in order to prevent the needless multiplication of idle popish priests who are a heavy burden on the poor people.]

12 That two seminaries be tolerated under proper regulations for the instruction of such young men as are intended for popish orders; the masters or tutors to be natives of Ireland and after a certain time no person to be ordained who had received foreign education.

13 That upon the vacancy of a registered bishop the two remainig be allowed to consecrate another who shall be a native of Ireland and who had been a registered priest.

14 That every person who shall perform any office or function peculiar to a popish bishop, but not registered to that end, shall for his first offence be fined in the sum of £500 and be imprisoned for the space of one year and until he has paid such fine; and for the second offence be fined in the sum of £1,000 and be imprisoned for life, which will be a punishment much more dreadful to them than transportation.

15 That every papist of any religious order being convicted thereof shall be fined in the sum of £100 and be imprisoned for life.

In the remainder of the pamphlet the author elaborates on these proposals, offers further reasons therefor and makes some suggestions and remarks on other aspects of the treatment of catholics.

He remarks that the true question is whether it will not be better to have three popish bishops, who shall be amenable to government and put under such strict ties and restraints, than forty dispersed through the kingdom in disguise to work all the mischief in their power behind the curtain without any

restraints and who are the instruments of secret correspondence with our enemies abroad in times of public danger; and whether it will not be safer to let
in a thousand priests at the public gate and mark them as they enter than to
suffer five times that number to steal in unknown at the postern and by that
means swarm over the whole nation without measure. (p. 11)

He emphasises that the proposed scheme, by exempting a limited number
of bishops and priests from the penalties they were liable to as the law then
stood and this under certain limitations and restrictions, could in no sense be
called an Establishment. (p. 11) He asks whether it would not be safer to make
those bishops and priests friends of the government by granting them protection, than to continue them enemies 'within our very bowels'. They would ever
be so as long as the penal laws hung idly over their heads without any execution. (p. 12)

He claims that the catholic clergy were 'the chief instruments and intelli-
gencies with our enemies abroad' and that protestants would feel securer 'by
cashiering four parts in five of them'. The nation must ever remain poor and
unthriving 'while this swarm of locusts preys upon our vitals'. Poor tenants
while they paid at least double tithes [to both catholic and protestant clergy]
must always remain beggars (pp. 12–13). If the popish clergy were once made
amenable to the law, the poor people might easily be brought to labour on holy-
days; he makes a calculation of the monetary benefit of such an eventuality to
the country as a whole. The present was the most opportune time for the
scheme proposed since Britain was then at peace with the catholic powers. (pp.
13–14)

He refers to an attack made on the home of Mr Mills, a justice of the peace
in County Galway. Government caution about making moves against the
catholics involved might have been due to the possibility of reprisals against
protestants in France, but this should not have been a consideration since
protestants in France were already severely persecuted. (p. 14)

If catholics were ever to gain the upper hand again, he prophesises that 'not
a protestant, if his life were spared, would remain possessed of one foot of land
in the kingdom', and 'if the Chevalier ['Pretender'] had gained the victory at
Culloden we should presently have seen the papists [of Ireland] in arms and
all Ireland a field of blood'. (p. 16–17)

He makes 'two momenteous points relating to the [catholic] laity'. Firstly,
it would be good policy to allow papists to purchase, or take mortgages of, such
lands as were forfeited in the rebellions of 1641 and 1688, market towns always
excepted. While there was the objection that this might strengthen the hands
of catholics since 'power will always attend property', there was the more
weighty consideration that an estate of land or a registered mortgage in catholic
hands would be a strong pledge of fidelity by such catholics to the government.
Furthermore, the chief buyers of lands and acquirers of mortgages would be

popish merchants; these had 'jockeyed out the protestant merchants, who were treated with less favour in popish countries' and were a danger to the state because of their intimacy and correspondence with enemies abroad. However, if a popish merchant 'buys an estate of land, he becomes another person' since his interest then attaches him to the government. (pp. 17–18) Secondly, leases possessed by papists would gavel after their decease and, being a personal estate, would in the space of six months go in equal distribution between the children of both sexes who should within that time become protestants. (p. 20)

The author sums up: 'Popery is forbidden by law but allowed in practice; it is dead by law but alive and flourishing in fact.... Must popery go on quietly and gain more strength?.... To roar against popery till men burst their lungs, will avail nothing.... This monster is not to be afrighted by mere noise.' (pp. 20–21)

He ends on a warning note: 'If popery were a system of doctrines merely spiritual, I should not quarrel with our Papists.... But while popery continues to be a complicated system, mixed up with many doctrines of a political nature, that are dangerous to civil governments and societies; whilst it avows the lawfulness of breaking faith and the solemnest oaths made to Protestant princes and makes a merit of dethroning them and murdering their innocent subjects, it becomes all Protestants to look about them and to guard their lives and fortunes against a body of such insidious enemies, till they shall publicly disavow principles and tenets so dangerous to all civil societies, which I fear they will never do.' (p. 22)

As regards the proposals in this pamphlet, the central theme that there should be a register of catholic secular priests was not, of course, new. The act of 1704 provided for such a register and the act of 1709 required registered priests to take the oath of abjuration. As we have seen heads of bills were brought into the lords in the 1731–2 session and into the commons in the 1745–6 session to amend the 1704 act. With regard to the oath proposed in the pamphlet to be taken by priests on being registered, the most notable feature was that it contained no abjuration of the Pretender, and we can only speculate whether this was simply an oversight or whether it was considered that such an abjuration would constitute, in the pamphlet's own words, 'such a condition as an honest papist could not consistently with his religion and conscience submit to'.

There was nothing new either about the proposal that three catholic bishops be allowed – one each for Leinster, Munster and Connacht. Theophilus Bolton, successively bishop of Elphin and archbishop of Cashel, had proposed in 1726 that there should be an establishment of 600 catholic priests with one bishop living constantly in the country to ensure a succession. Bolton did not propose catholic seminaries for the education of priests as in the pamphlet, but he did propose that facilities for such education should be provided in Trinity

College, Dublin.[12] The additional oath which the author of the pamphlet would require of ordinands apparently derived from the fear and suspicion of the kind of education imparted in the Irish colleges abroad. A certain degree of apprehension in regard to the colleges operated by the Jesuits in Spain and Rome was to be expected. As for the Irish colleges in France, because of France's role as Britain's traditional enemy and as a hotbed of Jacobitism for many years, an education acquired by Irish clerics there would, despite the anti-papal proclivities of the French church, be bound to be suspect. We find the same antipathy to the foreign education of Irish catholics surfacing again when the education act of 1782 was being debated.

Turning to the other remarks and suggestions in the pamphlet, the proposal that catholics be allowed to purchase lands and take mortgages had previously been raised by, among others, Bishop Synge in a pamphlet published in 1726 (already mentioned in Chapter 3),[13] but it would not have been much of an advantage to catholics to purchase lands, if on their deaths, as stated in the pamphlet, their property would gavel to such of their children as became protestants.

It is a bit grotesque that the author should complain about the payment of dues by catholic tenants to their priests, even if there were too many of them, but apparently sees nothing at all peculiar in their paying tithes to protestant ministers who provided them with no service whatsoever.

The author's final broadside against papal deposing and dispensing claims is largely unanswerable – the matter has been gone into at some length in Chapter 1. Irish catholics of the time were required to bear two quite unnecessary burdens – the outmoded papal claims and the Stuart claim to the throne which, although it had right on its side, was becoming more of a lost cause with every year that passed.

As far as can be discovered, the identity of the author of this pamphlet has never been revealed. One very interesting aspect of the pamphlet is the extent to which some of the proposals compare with those of the earl of Chesterfield in his letter to Bishop Chenevix in January 1755 – see next chapter – even to the extent of being couched in almost identical language. Chesterfield's proposal that all penalties of death be changed into imprisonment for a term of years, or in some cases for life is to be found in the pamphlet. Likewise Chesterfield's view that he 'would require the priests to take the oath of allegiance simply and not the subsequent oaths which in my opinion no real Papist can take; the consequence of which would be that the least conscientious priests would be registered and the most conscientious ones excluded' is also to be found in the pamphlet. Chesterfield's proposal that papists should be allowed to buy land,

---

12 Gilbert Library, Dublin, MS 27, 380. 13 Synge, Edward, *A vindication of a sermon preached ... on Saturday 23rd of October 1725*, Dublin 1726, 78.

let and take leases, but subject to the Gavel Act, is repeated in the pamphlet, as also the effect of such a proposal in attaching such papists to the government interest. It seems unlikely that Chesterfield borrowed these ideas from the pamphlet and then trotted them out as if they were his own, without attribution.

Taking into account that the pamphlet was published a few years after heads of a bill for registering the Popish clergy had been introduced in the commons in January 1746, it would not be surprising if the author of the pamphlet borrowed some of his ideas from those heads. Since, as already indicated, Chesterfield was the driving force behind that bill, it seems likely that he would have put his views in writing to the three members, Cuffe, Carr and Gore, charged with preparing the heads of the bill. This may point to one of these three as the author of the pamphlet, on the supposition that otherwise Chesterfield's views could not have been so faithfully reproduced in the pamphlet. Of these three James Cuffe would be more likely than the other two since it was he who presented the heads to the house on 13 January 1746, indicating that he was more actively involved. Cuffe was the grandson of a planter, also named James Cuffe, who in 1666 was made a grant of the town and lands of Ballinrobe, County Mayo together with extensive estates in Mayo and Galway. Cuffe represented the county of Mayo in parliament and died in 1762.[14] The concern expressed in the pamphlet about an attack by catholics on a neighbouring County Galway magistrate, Mills, may also be a pointer in the direction of Cuffe as the author.

It may be asked, however, if the foregoing speculation is correct, why Cuffe, or the other two mentioned, had apparently no part a few years later in the registry of priests bills 1756 and 1757. But it could be asked with equal pertinence why, following their part in the abortive 1746 registry of priests bill, the same persons were not to the fore in the 1756 and 1757 bills, and the answer to both questions is that the heads of the latter bills were processed in the lords, and accordingly members of the commons, like Cuffe, Carr and Gore, could not be involved until a later stage. Nevertheless, it is conceded that the foregoing speculation about the authorship of the pamphlet may be wide of the mark. Other possible authors are William Henry and John Brett, both of whom figure in the next chapter.

14 Archdall, Mervyn, revision of John Lodge's *Peerage of Ireland*, London 1786, vol. 3, 379.

5

The Registry of Priests Bills, 1756
and 1757

As will be apparent from previous chapters, there had been for decades in Ireland a *de facto* toleration of the catholic religion 'by connivance' as it was called. In other words the laws against that religion and against catholic education were simply not operated except in special circumstances as, for example, when a Jacobite invasion threatened or when war broke out between Britain and France and there was the all too real possibility of a French invasion of Britain and/or Ireland. But toleration by connivance was an unregulated form of toleration which resulted in a situation where there were, in the government's view, far too many priests, both of the secular and regular variety, and in particular of the latter whom the administration regarded as a menace to themselves as well as a burden on the poor. As had been advocated by several people for two or three decades, what was needed was a system under which a reasonable number of priests would be registered subject to certain conditions, and the remainder required to leave the country.

We have seen in Chapter 4 that from the time he had been lord lieutenant in 1745–6, the earl of Chesterfield had in mind just such a form of regulation of the catholic clergy. He retained a deep interest in Irish affairs for many years after his departure from the country, and he was to unburden his opinions to his former chaplain, Richard Chenevix, for whom he had secured, during his term as lord lieutenant, first the bishopric of Killaloe and afterwards the more lucrative bishopric of Waterford and Lismore, where Chenevix was to remain until his death in 1779. Chenevix was an Englishman and we cannot say whether he had any real interest in Irish catholic affairs other than as Chesterfield's creature and as the conduit for his opinions.[1]

A man with similar views to Chesterfield, James Hamilton, Viscount Limerick and later earl of Clanbrassill, had the name of being well-disposed to his catholic neighbours. His family controlled a Dundalk borough seat in the Irish house of commons and as a young man in his twenties he had taken that

1 *Dictionary of national biography* (*DNB*), London 1895.

seat in the 1715 general election. He had to vacate it on becoming a viscount in 1718 but he was later from 1732 on to sit for English constituencies in the British house of commons.[2] He was thus a man of considerable parliamentary experience who would have been over sixty years when he began to interest himself in the idea of a registry of priests bill. How long his plans for such a bill had been in gestation we do not know but his first draft of the heads of a bill must have been available by 1754 for Chesterfield's comments on them are dated 29 January 1755.

Heads of a bill could be processed either in the Irish house of lords or in the commons; but when they were returned approved by the English privy council, it was then required that they be passed in both houses. Since Hamilton was a member of the Irish house of lords it was of course natural that the heads of his bill should be introduced, discussed and put through the various stages in that house. In addition to Bishop Chenevix his most prominent supporters in the lords were Bishops Edward Synge of Elphin and Robert Clayton of Clogher.

Bishop Synge we have already encountered in connection with efforts to formulate an oath for catholics in the 1720s and 1730s. Robert Clayton was born in Dublin where his father, an Englishman, was rector of the parish of St Michan's. Robert was educated at Trinity College, Dublin and was ordained in the established church. He was appointed bishop of Clogher in 1745 on Chesterfield's recommendation, having previously been bishop of Killala from 1730 and of Cork from 1735. He was a rich and generous man who had inherited family estates in England. As a bishop he was out of step with his colleagues on the bench on several points of doctrine. His views on the Athanasian and Nicene Creeds were to cost him advancement to the archbishopric of Tuam. He was preparing to go before the other bishops to defend his criticism of the Thirty-nine Articles when he fell ill and died in February 1758.[3]

George Stone, the primate, was another figure on the protestant side who played an important role, not so much in his capacity as primate but as one of the lords justices. These latter were the effective government of the country in the absence of the lord lieutenant, who lived in Ireland only during parliamentary sessions, which lasted for at most eight months every two years. Stone was an Englishman who, following his appointment as archbishop of Armagh, was first appointed a lord justice in 1746. He was regularly re-appointed as such until his death in 1764 and was regarded as the most influential man in Ireland during that period. Stone's first concern was the protection of the English interest, as distinct from the protestant Anglo–Irish interest, in Ireland. His attitude to the registry bill and to catholics in general will be examined at the appropriate point.[4]

2 Lodge, John, *The peerage of Ireland*, London 1789.   3 *DNB.*   4 *DNB.*

On the catholic side those most prominently involved were Charles O'Conor of Belanagare, Lord Trimleston, Michael O'Reilly, archbishop of Armagh and three Dublin churchmen, Richard Lincoln, Patrick Fitzsimons and John Clinch.

Charles O'Conor was descended from the O'Connor kings of Connacht. Although his family lost a substantial portion of their estates in the seventeenth century, they managed to hold on as tenants to about 700 acres around Belanagare in County Roscommon. He was a self-taught man whose formal education ended when he was aged fifteen. Although he wrote extensively on the history of Ireland, we are here concerned only with his political writings and activities. His many pamphlets on Irish catholic affairs, several of them published anonymously, were a major contribution to the struggle to secure an amelioration of conditions for catholics from the 1750s right through to the 1780s. He was a formidable and plausible controversialist, who enjoyed the friendship and trust of many prominent people on the protestant as well as on the catholic side.[5]

Robert Barnewall, Baron Trimleston of Trimblestown Castle near Trim, County Meath, had succeeded to the title in 1746 and was one of a dwindling band of catholic nobles. In addition to being a land-owner, he was also a physician who had qualified in France and had an extensive practice in Dublin and Meath. He was to remain prominent in catholic affairs until his death in 1779. He was a difficult, temperamental person with an exaggerated idea of his own importance.[6]

Michael O'Reilly, the primate, had the reputation of being a great, reforming prelate. As vicar-general, in the absence of a bishop, of the diocese of Kilmore he succeeded during the 1720s in eradicating abuses in that diocese and turned it into one of the best regulated in the country. On the appointment of a bishop to Kilmore in 1728, the primate, Hugh MacMahon, brought O'Reilly to Armagh as vicar-general. He was appointed bishop of Derry in 1739 and archbishop of Armagh in 1749. In his later years he allowed himself to come too much under the influence of Lord Trimleston with, as we shall see, unfortunate repercussions.[7]

Until the consecration of Richard Lincoln as coadjutor archbishop of Dublin in January 1756, that diocese, due to the increasing senility of Archbishop Linegar, had been for some years effectively managed by three of the senior clergy, Patrick Fitzsimons and John Clinch, the vicars-general and Richard Lincoln, archdeacon of Glendalough. A fourth, Canon John Murphy, had also been part of this junto until his death in July 1753. However, once Lincoln, a Dublin merchant's son, took over as coadjutor early in 1756, he naturally assumed total control and proved to be a single-minded, contentious, quarrel-

5 *DNB.*   6 Lodge, J., op. cit.   7 Fagan, Patrick (ed.), *Ireland in the Stuart papers*, Dublin 1995, vol. 2, 97.

some archbishop who brooked no opposition, particularly from the regular clergy.[8] The divisions between the catholic hierarchy and the laity, which had been evident at the time of the catholic address to the king in 1727, were to manifest themselves again during his time as archbishop. Having been nominated by James Stuart, like all the other catholic bishops of the time, he was obliged to walk a tight-rope of loyalty to that personage while at the same time trying to keep on the right side of the government at home, a balancing act rendered all the more difficult by the fact that the Seven Years War, with Britain and France once again on opposing sides, virtually coincided with his term as archbishop. A *laissez faire* policy seemed to him the only sensible one, for the clergy at any rate, and this was to bring him into conflict with Charles O'Conor, Dr John Curry, Lord Trimleston and other catholic laymen who were trying to effect some movement at government level on the catholic question.

So much for the main characters involved. In addition, the earl of Chesterfield had a preliminary, but important, offstage participation through his correspondence with Bishop Chenevix of Waterford. It would appear that Hamilton's registration proposals had been conveyed by Chenevix to Chesterfield towards the end of 1754. In letter dated 29 January 1755 to Chenevix, Chesterfield made the following comments on the proposals.

I have carefully read over Lord Limerick's [Hamilton's] bill and approve of the principle. I had thought of such a one when I was in Ireland but soon found it would be impossible to carry it through the House of Commons in any decent shape; but should Lord Limerick think proper to push it this session I would recommend a few alterations. I would only require the priests to take the oath of allegiance simply, and not the subsequent oaths which, in my opinion, no real papist can take; the consequence of which would be that the least conscientious priests would be registered and the most conscientious ones excluded. Besides that, where one oath will not bind, three will not; and the pope's dispensation from the oath of allegiance will not be more prevalent, nor more easily granted than his dispensation from that oath by which his own power is abjured. But then I would make the oath of allegiance more full and solemn, as for instance:

I, A.B., duly considering the sacred nature of an oath and the horrible crime of perjury which by all the religions in the world is justly abhorred as a most damnable sin, do most sincerely promise and swear that I will be faithful and bear true allegiance to his Majesty King George the Second. So help me that great and eternal God who knows my inmost thoughts and whom I now most solemnly call upon to attest the truth of them.

8 Fenning, Hugh, *The undoing of the friars of Ireland*, Louvain 1972, passim.

The person taking this oath should be obliged to recite it distinctly and deliberately and not be allowed to mutter it over in that indecent and slovenly manner in which oaths are generally taken. I will venture to add those who will not observe this oath taken in this manner, will still less observe any abjuration of the pope's dispensing power, since such abjuration is by all Papists looked upon as a nullity. I would also advise that all penalties of death which in these cases must end in impunity, should be changed into close imprisonment for a term of years or for life. Then there would be perhaps detections and prosecutions, but in case of death there will be none. For who will go and hang a poor devil only for being a regular, or an enthusiast?[9]

It is also convenient and appropriate to note here some general remarks which Chesterfield made two years later in a letter to Chenevix dated 22 November 1757:

Some time or other (tho' God knows when) it will be found out in Ireland that the Popish religion cannot be subdued by force, but may be undermined and destroyed by art. Allow the Papists to buy land, let and take leases equally with the Protestants, but subject to the Gavel Act which will always have its effect upon their posterity at least. Tie them down to the government by the tender but strong bonds of landed property, which the pope will have much ado to dissolve, notwithstanding his power of loosening and binding. Use them who come over to you, though perhaps only seemingly at first, well and kindly, instead of looking for their cloven feet and their tails, as you do now. Increase both your number and your care of the Protestant Charter Schools. Make your Penal Laws extremely mild and then put them strictly in execution. *Hae tibi erunt artes.* This will do in time and nothing else will, nor ought. I would as soon murder a man for his estate, as prosecute him for his religious and speculative errors.[10]

Hamilton had consultations on his proposals, albeit belatedly, about November 1755 with the Dublin clergy in the persons of Richard Lincoln, Patrick Fitzsimons and John Clinch. James O'Keeffe, bishop of Kildare and Leighlin, in a letter to Cardinal Corsini, gives an account of these proceedings.[11] Following a brief account of the provisions of the proposed bill, he says that the lords let it be understood that they were influenced to bring in this bill,

9 Burke, W.P., *The Irish priests in the penal times*, Shannon 1969, 204.   10 Bradshaw, John (ed.), *The letters of Philip Dormer Stanhope, earl of Chesterfield*, London 1892, vol. 3, 1193.   11 Archives of Propaganda Fide (APF), SC Irlanda 10, ff. 519–20, National Library of Ireland (NLI) microfilm Pos. 5372. The original of this letter is in Latin.

not because of any hatred for catholics as such, but solely because of the mendicant orders whose numbers presented a danger of the utmost gravity to the government as well as to the people generally. O'Keeffe then refers to rumours put about by the regulars throughout Dublin city that the provisions in the bill (which included the banishment of the regulars from the country) had been solicited from the government by the secular clergy. To this 'infamous calumny', O'Keeffe says, a subsequent occurrence supplied a handle. Around the end of the previous year (1755) it was signified to the vicars general of Dublin and Archdeacon Lincoln that a certain noble (Hamilton) wished to confer with them about a certain matter. In the course of the subsequent meeting Hamilton indicated that parliament had in mind to confer certain reliefs and immunities on catholics but on condition that they would agree to a test of loyalty acceptable to parliament. He enquired what kind of test they wished to give and the clergy replied that they considered that no test ought to be refused which was consonant with their religion and a right conscience. But they could not agree to a formula off their own bat and they asked to be allowed to consult the other clergy and the laity in the matter. They then made a full disclosure to both the secular and regular clergy and sent letters to all the bishops so that they could indicate what should be done in circumstances of this kind. However, without waiting for a reply, Hamilton went ahead with the bill which, O'Keeffe claimed, turned out to be no less deadly to the seculars themselves as to the regulars. O'Keeffe said he was transmitting this report to Corsini so that the regulars might not continue 'to defame us among our superiors and equally among those under us'.

With regard to consultation between Hamilton and the catholic laity, it appears from a letter dated 6 January 1755 from Charles O'Conor to his son, Denis, that the laity had not been consulted at that stage.[12] He reports attending 'clubs and associations', presumably in Dublin, which 'break up without coming to any resolutions, while our enemies act in concert to bring their schemes to bear'. At one of these meetings he proposed 'that we should make a tender of our loyalty to the king; give him a test of political orthodoxy and petition for the repeal of the penal and punitive laws'. However, O'Conor in a further letter dated 7 February 1756 to his son, Denis, states that he 'was indeed during the late debates employed by both parties as far as a person of my little consequence might be employed for the good of both'. He goes on to mention an hour-long conversation he just had with Bishop Clayton who gave him a commission, which he says he executed as well as he could. Presumably the commission had something to do with Hamilton's bill which had just been printed.

---

12 Ward, Robert E. et al. (eds.), *Letters of Charles O'Conor of Belanagare*, Washington D.C. 1988, 8.

O'Conor was not, therefore, very forthcoming at that stage as to the nature of his discussions with the promoters of the projected legislation. When, however, some months later, he published his pamphlet *The principles of Roman Catholics exhibited*, he revealed the text of an oath which 'they [Roman Catholics] are ready to give the government, when called upon'. He again in 1761 printed the same form of oath in his *The danger of Popery to the present government examined*, prefixed by the following: 'We think it proper in this place to subjoin the test of Fidelity offered by the Roman Catholics some years since, to the Government, when heads of a bill relative to their case, was brought into the House of Lords.' He printed the same form of oath for a third time in his *A vindication of Lord Taaffe's civil principles*, written in 1767 but published in 1768, with the heading: 'A test of Fidelity offered by the Roman Catholics of Ireland in 1756, when the heads of a bill relative to their case was brought into the House of Lords.' But it was only in a letter dated 9 December 1767 to John Curry that he revealed that the form of oath which appeared in the three pamphlets mentioned was one prepared by Fr Cornelius Nary back in the 1720s or possibly the 1730s. The relevant extract from this letter is included in Chapter 3 where the text of Nary's oath is also given and discussed. We can conclude from all this that the catholic side in 1756 resurrected Nary's oath and submitted it to the promoters of the bill with a view to its substitution for the oath included in the heads of bill.

On the progress of the bill through the house of lords, the *Lords Journal* tells us that at their sitting on Friday, 2 January 1756 the house was adjourned during pleasure and put into a committee to take into consideration the state of popery and that after some time spent therein the house was resumed.[13] However, it later emerges that the only resolutions arrived at that day had to do with preventing Irish-born officers in the French service from returning to Ireland and with prohibiting his Majesty's (Irish) subjects from being seduced into that service.

The house met again on Monday, 5 January and was again put into committee to take into further consideration the state of popery. When the house was resumed Lord Massereene reported that the committee had come to several resolutions. These were later agreed as follows:

1 That the number of popish priests, monks and friars has of late years greatly increased in this Kingdom to the manifest prejudice of the Protestant religion, of his Majesty's Government and the peace and welfare of the Kingdom

2 That the allowing a competent number of Popish secular priests to exercise their functions, under proper rules and restrictions, with a due execution of the laws against Regulars and persons exercising ecclesiastical

13 *Lords Journal Ireland*, vol. 4, 36.

jurisdiction, would tend to deliver this Kingdom from the great number of monks and friars that at present infest it.[14]

The house then adjourned until the following day.

Such are the bare bones of the proceedings in the lords on the dates mentioned, as reported in the *Lords Journal*. We are indebted to one William Henry for a more detailed report, a résumé of which is given below, of the discussions which took place at these two sittings of the house in committee.[15] Henry, who was dean of Killaloe, had a vogue as a preacher and he was also the author of a number of pamphlets on religious subjects. Charles O'Conor described him as 'a little, prattling, public orator' whose father, a presbyterian minister, had lived near O'Conor.

Henry tells us that when the house met in committee on Friday 2 January 1756 there were present three archbishops, twelve bishops and twenty lay lords. The speaker and all the house of commons came in to hear the business 'and there was a crowd of others ... among whom your servant [Henry] attended closely'. Lord Limerick (Hamilton) began the business by laying before the house in a long and well-prepared speech the present unhappy state of the protestant interest here. He identified two evils – Jacobitism and the popish clergy 'all under the strongest oaths of allegiance to the Pretender'. To remedy the first, Irishmen who entered the French service must be prevented from re-entering the country. With regard to the second, some method should be found 'to untwist the cord of Popery and Jacobitism'.

There were at least 1.5 million papists in the country,[16] Lord Limerick continued, and these could not be excluded from their religious worship. He referred to the toleration of popery by a 'universal connivance', to 'pompous mass-houses' and to an 'inundation of the regular orders'. He estimated that there were at least 12,000 secular and regular clergy in the country.[17] He proposed as a solution that they should tolerate a competent number of secular priests under proper restrictions and regulations.

He then offered the committee the following resolutions:

1 The great numbers of French officers, natives of the Kingdom, who had lately come over thither tended to endanger his Majesty's government and the peace of the kingdom.

14 Ibid., 37.   15 NLI microfilm Pos, 989 of British Library MS 35,838.   16 The estimate of 1.5 million papists is quite inaccurate. It is now estimated that there were around 3.0 million people in the country in the 1750s and of these about 2.3 million were catholics. K.H. Connell in *The population of Ireland 1750–1845*, p. 25 gives an estimate of 3.2m. for 1754 but subsequent writers on the subject have found Connell's estimates to be somewhat inflated.   17 The figure of 12,000 catholic clergy in the country at this time is very wide of the mark. The actual figure was about 2,100 – see note 9, Chapter 1.

2 Some effectual law should be provided to prevent such persons as had entered the French service from ever returning thither.

3 The great increase in Popish priests, jesuits, monks and friars threatened much danger to his Majesty's government and the Protestant religion.

4 Tolerating a competent number of secular priests for the service of the Papists, under proper restrictions and regulations, would tend to drive away the great number of monks, friars and the regulars now among us.

All agreed to the first two of these resolutions. As regards no. 3 the archbishop of Dublin objected that before such an assertion was made, there should be an enquiry, and the bishops of Kildare and Down agreed. The bishop of Elphin (Synge) referred to the enquiry into the state of popery in 1731 and he showed how amazingly popery had increased since then. The whole kingdom was swarming with popish schoolmasters. Every common papist who had three or four sons devoted one of them to the church. This son would be a deacon at seventeen years and in another year he would be ordained priest by a particular dispensation allowed to Irish bishops. He would then be sent abroad to travel and beg through all the popish countries and at twenty-four years, being entered into some order, he returned to this country.

Such persons swarmed in all parts of the country, doing incredible mischief not only in alienating the people from the government and eating their (word illegible), but also in destroying all sense of virtue and modesty among the populace by their drunkenness and immodesty. It was common for these regulars to marry all the common people promiscuously; and the next week for a shilling more to re-marry the very same people to others. By this course the whole populace of the papists was debauched, and as he reckoned, 20,000 men who might have been useful at the plough, lived idle lives devouring all the industry of others.

The third resolution, Henry states, was then agreed to, some other lords and bishops having supported it. Lord Limerick was a bit annoyed at the objections of some bishops to this resolution, and said that, if he were a bishop, he would think it his duty to know minutely the state of religion in his diocese and to 'watch against such wolves'. As it was then late, consideration of the fourth resolution was put off until Monday the 4th (*recte* 5th) when the house was full and all the commons were present.

The Lord Primate (Stone) got up and made a speech of more than an hour, 'the fullest, clearest, easiest, strongest and most properly delivered which I have ever heard in that house'. He made two main points – (a) he disagreed with the cavils made at the previous sitting against the (protestant) clergy, as if the continued strength of popery was due to some neglect in them, and (b) he doubted the expediency at this time of the oath proposed for popish clergy.

The primate reflected on the different origins and progress of the Reformation in Ireland and in England. In England it arose from the desire of the people and the great grants of monastery lands to the nobility made it the latter's temporal interest. In Ireland, on the other hand, the Reformation was quite opposite to the inclinations of the natives who, during the reign of Elizabeth, were generally in rebellion against the crown. This 'prejudice' continued invincible during the reigns of James I and Charles I until it broke out in the great rebellion of 1641. The plantation of Ulster appeared a step in the right direction but the planters turned out to be mostly dissenters and the resulting contentions between protestants gave great encouragement to papists.

The protestant religion, the primate claimed, could never be said to be well-established in Ireland until the Revolution of 1688. Since that time the bishops and clergy had done everything they could and had succeeded in part. But the number of established clergy was inadequate (only 800 as against 12,000 popish clergy), parishes were too poor and in many cases tithes had been alienated by certain great families. As to the expediency of registering the Popish clergy, he could not think it prudent. In general, he, in conversation, had often liked well some such expedient, but he owned that as it drew nigh the greatness of the object terrified him. He owned that courage in such vast attempts failed him especially when many difficulties started up.

As to these difficulties, firstly, it was very probable that after all their pains, they might end in giving some kind of sanction to popery, without getting rid of those swarms of regulars against whom none would inform. Secondly, it was far from being improbable that scarce one popish priest would be found who would take the oaths, make the renunciations and give the security required, especially as they were all already under oaths to the pope and the Pretender. In such a case the laws would be nugatory or followed by a persecution which would inflame things at home and stir up foreign popish princes to interpose strongly. All princes in such cases would naturally apply and yield to one another and here he gave (as an extreme example) the history of Cromwell's bargain with Cardinal Mazarin to tolerate the papists in Ireland. In the present case he believed they were begining at the wrong end. It would be better to give aid and encouragement to the protestant religion than to give a legal right to popish priests to execute the offices of their religion. To this purpose he had prepared some resolutions which he would later offer to the house.[18]

The bishop of Elphin then stood up to support the resolution and made a long speech. He agreed with most of what the primate had to say. He

18 At its meeting on 6 January 1756 the house of lords passed a number of resolutions in regard to the reform and reorganisation of the established church in Ireland. These were seen as a means of stemming the growth of popery and were concerned with an increase in the number of ministers, the revival of parishes by the rebuilding of old churches and the settling of resident ministers in such parishes. (*Lords Journal Ireland* vol. 4, 38)

proceeded to give an account of the state of popery in his diocese, which was mostly in the counties of Roscommon and Sligo but it also included a small part of Galway. He had conducted a census of the diocese and he produced to the house figures to show that catholics vastly out-numbered protestants there. The bishop of Raphoe referred to the difficulties in converting papists, who were so much subject to the anathemas of the friars. The bishops of Down and Clogher 'also spoke well on this point but [I] shall not repeat their arguments'.

Lord Limerick then answered some of the exceptions made, but Henry did not expand further on this. When the bill was read, Limerick claimed, it would obviate all these exceptions. The Primate then proposed an amendment: 'That it was the opinion of the committee that the tolerating a competent number of secular priests, together with a due execution of the laws against all the other popish ecclesiastics might be a means etc. [*sic*]' and in this form it was passed.

'This day [6 January 1756]', Henry concluded, 'Lord Limerick brought in the heads of his bill which is pretty much the same as in the act of the 2nd of 2 Anne but better guarded and better care taken to have it executed.[19] It is ordered at his own desire to be printed and it seems agreed on that it shall lie over unto another session.'

The heads of the bill as printed consisted of 48 pages of text, devoid of numbered sections.[20] It first of all refers to the 1704 act for registering catholic clergy as well as the amending acts of 1705 and 1709. It goes on to refer in particular to the regular clergy, who are described as having 'strongly imbibed the most envenomed principles of popery, having always been incendiaries and avowed enemies to his Majesty's person and government and to the Protestant interest of this kingdom, and ready at all critical junctures to exert their credit and influence to foment sedition and rebellion and at all times to procure many of his Majesty's subjects to enlist in the service of the Pretender and of foreign Popish princes, and that their great numbers tend to the impoverishing of many of his Majesty's subjects of the Popish persuasion who are forced to maintain and support them'.

The bill goes on to claim that all those priests who were registered in 1704 were dead[21] and that a new register of a sufficient number of secular priests would contribute to the more vigorous execution of the laws against regulars. It was proposed that the grand juries of Dublin city and county at the

19 The act intended here is 2 Anne c. 7 (the act for registering the Popish clergy 1704). While the 1756 bill had the same general aim as the 1704 act, that of registering the catholic clergy, there was a great difference in the detail of the measures proposed in each case. It is of interest that even at this early stage it was expected that the 1756 bill would be carried over to the next session. 20 Royal Irish Academy, Haliday Pamphlet no. 261 of 1756. 21 The claim that all the priests registered under the 1704 act were then dead was not correct. The promoters of the bill would not have had to travel very far to find a priest registered in 1704 and still alive, in the person of John Linegar, archbishop of Dublin, and there were no doubt others like him. In the revived 1757 bill all the priests registered in 1704 were 'presumed to be dead'.

general quarter sessions and the grand juries of the other counties and cities at the general assizes should after 1 January 1757 nominate one secular priest for each [civil] parish in the said counties and cities for which a priest was registered under the 1704 act. Every priest applying to be so nominated was required to state his name, place of abode, age, time and place of receiving holy orders and the parish or parishes for which he desired to be nominated. He was also required to produce a certificate of good behaviour signed by two or more principal popish inhabitants, to enter into recognisances, with two sureties of £50, to be of good behaviour and not to remove out of the county where his place of abode lay. Every priest, prior to nomination, was required to take in open court the following oath:

I, A.B., do promise and swear to bear true faith and allegiance to his Majesty King George the Second his heirs and successors according as the succession to the crown of Great Britain and Ireland stands now limited to the heirs of the Illustrious Sophia, Electress and Duchess Dowager of Hanover. And that I will make known all treasons, treasonable conspiracies or plots against his person, crown and dignity, if any such shall come to my knowledge. I also profess that I do detest and abhor from my heart as impious, scandalous and abominable to believe that it is lawful to murder or destroy any person or persons whatsoever, for or under the pretence of being heretics, and also that base, unchristian principle that no faith is to be kept with heretics. I further declare that it is no article of my faith that any person whatsoever has power to absolve me from the obligation of this oath or that the Pope hath power to depose princes. And therefore I do promise and swear that I will not teach, preach, hold, maintain or abet any such doctrines or tenets. And all this I promise and swear upon the faith of a Christian and of a priest, freely, readily and willingly in the plain and ordinary sense of the words now read unto me without any secret collusion, equivocation, evasion or mental reservation whatsoever. So help me God.

Justices of the peace and the 'going' judges of assize were to be empowered to administer this oath. Lists were to be made, of priests who had taken the oath, for placing before the lord lieutenant and privy council 'to the intent that they may, if they see cause, examine any or all the said lists, and disapprove of any or all the nominations, as to them in their discretion shall seem meet'. A list of parishes for which there were no nominations was to be submitted to the lord lieutenant who could appoint priests for those parishes, but the total number of priests was not to exceed the number registered in 1704. In the case of large parishes the lord lieutenant and privy council might appoint one, two or more additional priests but the number of such additional priests was not to exceed 100 for the whole kingdom. In the case of vacancies through death, a priest from another parish might be assigned temporarily to the vacancy until such time as a new secular priest was appointed by the procedure above.

All priests appointed parish priests were to be exempt from all pains, penalties and forfeitures to which they might have been subject as popish priests prior to appointment, and each was required to nominate the place, or at most two places in his parish, where Mass was to be celebrated, but justices of the peace might approve a change of place due to a change of circumstances. A priest was prohibited from appearing outside his mass-house in his habit or from attempting any procession at funerals etc., 'it being the true intent and meaning of this act that every priest and the deluded people, in compassion to whom, till such time as by God's Blessing they may be converted, this Indulgence is designed, should on all and every occasion of their superstitious worship, behave themselves with that privacy and modesty which becomes persons in their circumstances'.

Provision was made for dismissal, by order of the lord lieutenat and privy council, of any priest, who after appointment promoted sedition or attempted to pervert any protestant to the popish religion, or admitted any protestant to a recantation of the protestant religion, or attempted to inveigle or seduce any of his Majesty's subjects into the service of the Pretender, or any foreign prince or state. Appointment of another priest to replace such priest was provided for.

Every priest, on pain of dismissal, was required at each service in his mass-house to exhort the people in Irish and English to pray for his Majesty King George II and the royal family. Updated lists of registered priests were to be maintained for the different counties and such lists were to be read in open court on the first day of every assize, or general quarter sessions in the case of Dublin, and to be ready for inspection by anyone wishing to see them.

It was provided that 'all and every Popish Ecclesiastic of whatever kind or denomination he or they may be, whether secular or regular, and every person exercising the office or function of a Popish priest, who shall be and remain in the Kingdom, or hereafter come into it, other than and except such priests whose names and descriptions shall from time to time appear and be found in some one of the said lists, shall be and continue subject to all pains, penalties and forfeitures to which all Papists exercising ecclesiastical jurisdiction, and all regulars of the Popish clergy and all unregistered Popish priests are subject to by any law or statute now in force against popery, particularly by an act passed in the ninth year of his Majesty King William the Third, of glorious memory, entitled an act for banishing all Papists exercising any ecclesiastical jurisdiction, and all regulars of the Popish clergy out of the Kingdom, and shall be liable to be sued and prosecuted and punished in such manner as by the said acts or any of them is directed and prescribed'.

The high sheriff of each city and county was required to compile a list of all unregistered priests living in their areas. Such priests were to be 'presented'

to the grand juries and required to surrender themselves within thirty days to
a justice of the peace and be committed to gaol until they were brought to trial.
Priests who did not surrender themselves and who were afterwards apprehended were to be committed to gaol, there to remain without bail or main-
prize until they were transported out of his Majesty's dominions. If persons so
transported returned into the Kingdom, they would be guilty of a felony, without benefit of clergy. Penalties were prescribed for persons 'concealing, aiding,
abetting or succouring' unregistered priests; there was to be a reward of £100
for any person discovering an unregistered priest.

The foregoing is a broad outline of the provisions of the bill. The first point
to be observed is that there was no mention at all of bishops, but it was scarcely expected that they would, without demur, pack up and leave the country.
There had been a *de facto* toleration of bishops for decades and a sudden rever-
sal of that situation, involving the arrest of bishops, imprisoning them and
eventually transporting them, could not have been achieved without great unrest
among the catholic community and it is extremely doubtful if the administration had the political will to face up to that situation. The more likely development was that, if the bill had become law, bishops would proceed to have
themselves registered as parish priests for their mensal parishes and continue
discreetly to exercise their episcopal functions, as John Dempsey, bishop of
Kildare, had done in the case of the 1704 registration of priests act.[22]

Although, then, the bishops had no role in the selection of parish priests,
no doubt, if the bill had become law, bishops and vicars general would have
continued to try to exercise their authority so as to ensure that no priest applied
for registration but those who were suitable. But since bishops were eventually
in no position to enforce their authority, there was ample scope for unsuitable
priests to cause trouble by applying to the assizes and quarter sessions for registration and by satisfying the conditions laid down in the bill, which had little
to do with their suitability for priestly duties.

The form of oath proposed was similar in all material respects to the form
attributed to Fr Nary, which, Charles O'Conor tells us, was proffered by the
catholic side when the bill was brought into the house. It appears, then, that
Hamilton was ready to accommodate the catholics on this crucial point. Nary's
oath was probably resurrected by Fr Patrick Fitzsimons (later archbishop), who,
as a young priest, would have known Nary and indeed had been appointed
parish priest of Nary's old parish of St Michan in 1744.

As regards the lord lieutenant's role in appointing priests to parishes for
which no priest had been nominated, or to larger parishes which required more
than one priest, the bill was silent as to how the lord lieutenant was to be
apprized of the names of such priests, considering this was a subject about

22 See *A list of the names of popish parish priests*, Dublin 1705.

which he was likely to be totally ignorant. With regard to the filling of future vacancies for parish priests, there was no indication as to where the new priests were to come from nor as to who, if anyone, was to select them from the catholic side.

The compiling of lists of unregistered priests by high sheriffs and 'presenting' such priests to grand juries with a view to prosecution and transportation was a procedure which had failed lamentably in the case of the abjuration oath of 1709 (see Chapter 2) and there could be little expectation that it would be any more successful in the 1750s.

As regards the further progress of the bill, Hamilton commented that 'a considerable number of the lay lords approved of it, but all the bishops except three [presumably Synge, Clayton and Chenevix] opposed the carrying of it into execution at this juncture'.[23] On 29 January 1756 a proposal in the lords to give the bill a third reading in three months time was carried by 18 votes to 16 but, apparently because by that date parliament would normally be prorogued or near to prorogation, this was regarded as a defeat of the bill. 'Deferred to a distant day' was the expression in use in such cases. Present in the house on 29 January 1756 were the earls of Kildare, Antrim, Westmeath, Cavan, Inchiquin, Ross, Grandison and Bessborough; viscounts Mountgarrett, Masserene, Doneraile, Castlecomer, Boyne, Limerick, Powerscourt and Bellfield; the archbishops of Armagh, Dublin and Cashel; the bishops of Clogher, Derry, Elphin, Cork, Raphoe, Waterford & Lismore, Killaloe, Killala, Down, Ferns, Cloyne and Limerick and Lords Athenry, Howth, Tullamore, Desart and Rawdon. In the event parliament had not been prorogued when the three month period had elapsed in April 1756; at that stage (29 April) it was resolved that the third reading be adjourned to that day month, no doubt in the knowledge that prorogation was imminent. The house on 29 April was rather 'thin' with only the earls of Westmeath and Carrick; Viscounts Doneraile, Boyne and Lanesborough; the archbishop of Dublin; the bishops of Elphin, Raphoe, Waterford & Lismore, Killala, Down, Ferns, Clonfert and Ossory and Lord Tullamore present. The last sitting of that (1755–6) session was on 8 May 1756 when parliament was prorogued by the lord lieutenant.[24]

Charles O'Conor's comments on the form of oath included in the heads of bill are of considerable interest:[25]

> In the debates on this bill, some persons disapproving of the test first proposed, altered it in the second printed heads [i.e. those published in January 1756]; and in this respect they deserve the thanks of every true lover of his

23 Brady, John, 'Proposals to register Irish priests 1756–7' in *Irish Ecclesiastical Record*, January–June 1962, 209–22. 24 *Lords Journal Ireland*, vol. 4, 29 January 1756.
25 O'Conor, Charles, *The principles of Roman Catholics exhibited*, Dublin 1756, 88. This pamphlet was advertised in *Dublin Journal* of 6 July 1756.

country. Some Roman Catholics did indeed object to one clause in the oath; others did not; but both meant well. Those who scrupled ... thought it the more constitutional form to swear allegiance to his Majesty and his successors simply (according to Bishop Berkeley's proposal), than to swear that they will unconditionally maintain a conditional law.... This being the case of those honest men, who objected to one clause in the second printed test, it is but reasonable to let the public know what people they have to deal with, and to show the whole world the strong test they are ready to give the government when called upon. [Here follows the text of the oath later attributed to Cornelius Nary] This they think a test equal to the importance of the object of it; and they conceive it strictly constitutional, as it *in fact* excludes all *indefeasible* hereditary right; and as it cannot clash with any future test, which the legislature may find expedient to impose: For, though it is certain that the legislature have an unlimited power to repeal their own laws; yet it is equally certain, that they cannot, with the same ease, repeal the oaths *antecedently* taken by others, where oaths are unconditional, and no reservation made for a future dispensation.

Later, writing to Curry on 28 July 1756 O'Conor questioned whether the acceptance of an oath by catholics had necessarily to be seen as *a quid pro quo* for some relief from the penal laws:

They [some catholics] reason as if our Test and relief from Penal Laws should go hand in hand. Right. But should not some previous steps be taken? May not the suspension or repeal of those laws be brought to arise in some degree from a voluntary test even in our present condition.

The majority of catholics hailed the defeat of the bill as a major triumph and the proposers of the bill in the lords found themselves generally denigrated although they would no doubt protest that they had been acting in a benign manner towards catholics. Paradoxically, those lords who opposed the bill, no matter what their reasons were for so doing, were regarded as the catholics' friends. The regular clergy in particular were jubilant since the reference in the bill to the banishment provisions of the 1697 act, meant that those provisions, which they had come to regard as a dead letter, would be revived with full force if the bill had passed. In the course of a letter dated Dublin, 5 February 1756 to the Stuart court, the Augustinian, Fr James MacKenna reported in coded language:

Our youngster [lord lieutenant] on the late occasion in the change [parliament] hath been very passifick. There were 18 of the buyers in the change for us and 16 against us. The overseer [bishop] of Elphin [Synge] proposed all the mischief, whilst the good Inglese overseer of Armagh [Primate Stone] stood strenuously for us and overruled all machinations de Irlandese whilst the rest of our native buyers and overseers were opponents.[26]

Primate Stone's motives in opposing the bill have been a matter of debate even among his contemporaries. Fr MacKenna's view above that he opposed it in favour of the catholic clergy, was one which was supported by Dr John Curry. Charles O'Conor, on the other hand, was quite unequivocal in his view that 'the Primate opposed that bill on the principle of persecution, that he represented it not as an indulgence only but as a toleration of popery by law, what he thought should never be admitted'.[27] Stone also opposed the revised 1757 version of the bill both in the lords and in the Irish privy council – in the latter place in opposition to the lord lieutenant himself.[28] William Henry's report of Stone's speech in the lords in January 1756 shows that he was, with some hesitancy, concerned about the bill giving a legal right to popish priests to execute the offices of their religion. On another occasion he claimed he opposed the bill because it was 'repugnant to the laws of England'.[29] Nevertheless, he had the reputation of being quite well-disposed towards catholics. Charles O'Conor, never a model of consistency, was to say of Stone a few years later that he was 'doubtless a most worthy person, and were men of his temper at the head of the protestant cause for two hundred years past, we should not have the history of Christendom disgraced by dissensions and those concommitant evils'.[30] Fr John Creagh, dean of Limerick, claimed that Stone was very well disposed to catholics and would do the impossible to help them.[31]

It should be emphasised that the bill was concerned specifically with the catholic clergy; it impinged little on the catholic laity whose main concern continued to be the detrimental effects of the property provisions of the penal laws. It is not surprising, then, that during the period the bill was in preparation and before parliament (i.e. 1754–58) Charles O'Conor and Dr John Curry were busy following an independent, if parallel, course in regard to the catholic question with an improvement of the position of the laity as their primary aim. O'Conor's *The case of the Roman Catholics of Ireland*, published about June

26 Fagan, P. (ed.), op. cit., vol. 2, 192.   27 Ward, R.E. et al.(eds.), op. cit., 51. 28 James, Francis G., *Ireland in the Empire 1688–1770*, Cambridge, Mass. 1973, p. 256. 29 Brady, J., art. cit., 209–22.   30 Ward, R.E. et al. (eds.), 97.   31 APF, S C Irlanda 10, f. 584, NLI microfilm Pos. 5373. I am indebted to Fr Hugh Fenning OP for a translation of this letter from the Italian. This letter, further reference to which will be made later, is dated London 26 December 1757 and is addressed to Cardinal Protector Corsini. It is unsigned but from internal evidence it is clear that it was written by Fr John Creagh, dean of Limerick. Creagh was in London at the time probably as part of a team to lobby the privy council in the expectation that the registry of priests bill would shortly be coming before the council for approval.

1755, stressed the economic advantages of a relaxation of the penal laws on property owned by catholics. In tandem with this he advocated that catholics should show their loyalty to the government by a special oath of allegiance to the king.[32] A copy of this pamphlet was presented to the lord lieutenant, the marquis of Hartington, when he arrived in Dublin in the summer of 1755.[33] O'Conor gave these matters a further airing about June 1756 in his *The principles of Roman Catholics exhibited*, mentioned above,[34] while his *Maxims relative to the present state of Ireland*, published in 1757 in the style and form of Bishop Berkeley's *The Querist*, further stressed the economic advantages of a relaxation of the property laws.[35]

Meanwhile in April 1756 an incident occurred which may have had an influence on future events. Archbishop O'Reilly of Armagh had called some of his clergy together at Dundalk for the purpose of distributing the holy oils. There was also some business concerning the retrenchment of feast-days, which led to an altercation – nothing new to the Armagh clergy, among whom fighting and squabbling was endemic throughout the eighteenth century. The altercation, however, evolved into something really serious when someone swore an information that O'Reilly and his clergy were engaged in collecting funds for the Pretender, a very serious charge more particularly as Britain and France were on the brink of war and there were reports of preparations at French ports for an invasion of Britain and Ireland. O'Reilly and some of his clergy were arrested and brought before Hamilton in the latter's capacity as a local magistrate. They were soon released on the instructions of the lord lieutenant, but not before they had been thoroughly examined by Hamilton.[36] While Hamilton treated O'Reilly with great civility throughout the examination, there must, in the light of subsequent events, be a question as to what exactly passed between them.

In a letter dated 20 August 1756 to Dr John Curry, O'Conor makes a number of important points.[37] Firstly, the present men in the administration or in parliament imposed no bondage on catholics, though their predecessors did. Secondly, he believed that none could be more indulgent (to catholics) than the present administration. O'Conor here appears to be referring to the lord lieutenant, Lord Hartington, who in fact had gone to England at this time and was not to return. Thirdly, the penal laws were ruining the country economically because the catholics, who made up the bulk of the tenants, were necessitated, through the operation of the thirty-one year leases applicable to them, to graze their farms rather than till them. Fourthly, O'Conor declares his support for

32 O'Conor, Charles, *The case of the Roman Catholics of Ireland*, Dublin 1755.   33 Wall, Maureen, *Catholic Ireland in the eighteenth century*, Dublin 1989, 95.   34 O'Conor, Charles, *The principles of Roman catholics exhibited*, Dublin 1756.   35 O'Conor, Charles, *Maxims relative to the present state of Ireland*, Dublin 1757.   36 Fenning, Hugh, *The Irish Dominican province 1698–1797*, Dublin 1990, 269–70.   37 Ward, R.E. et al. (eds.), op. cit., 19–22.

the doctrine that 'no act of the Roman Court, no spiritual power of the Roman see can dispense with legal obligations to legal government', thus rejecting the papal deposing and dispensing powers. Fifthly, he castigates the catholic clergy inasmuch as their 'personal ambition, foreign connections, subservient maxims and future prospects prevail over the true interests of our party'. [In other words, loyalty to James Stuart and to outmoded papal claims were in the nature of a millstone around the necks of the catholic clergy, inhibiting any desire to improve the catholic position]. Therefore, O'Conor explains in a further letter to Curry dated 22 September 1756, 'the weight of this affair lies properly on the shoulders of the catholic laity, on the persons acquainted well with the state of the case before us, and who have no foreign connections, nor any measures to keep with foreigners'. He is particularly dismissive and scornful of Archbishop Lincoln of Dublin, the 'Hyper Doctor', as he calls him, interposing 'with his authoritative gag and his foreign whip'.[38]

A new lord lieutenant, the duke of Bedford, took up duty in September 1757. Hamilton had in the meantime revived and revised his registry of priests bill and in correspondence with Bedford in July 1757 he had argued that, if catholic parish priests were given official status, they would become 'as good subjects of the King of Great Britain as German priests in the Electorate are to the Elector of Hanover', the king of Great Britain and the Elector of Hanover being of course one and the same person.[39] It appears that Hamilton had consultations with Lord Trimleston on this occasion but not with Charles O'Conor or John Curry. O'Conor remarks in a letter dated 2 November 1757 to Curry:

> We would rejoice in silence at seeing the subject taken out of our hands by abler men. Since this has not been done, nay, since it has not been attempted in any tolerable compass, men of less capacity may be allowed the merit of a good intention and of discharging their conscience in giving the best idea they can of a subject in which the bondage of a million of persons is involved. The fault is theirs, not ours.[40]

Hamilton's new bill differed in the following points from the previous one.[41] Firstly, the condemnation of the regulars in the preamble was removed completely, as was the claim that a new register of secular priests 'would con-

---

38 Ibid., 24.   39 Bedford Correspondence, vol. 2, 264 quoted in F.G. James op. cit., 256–7.   40 Ward, R.E. et al. (eds.), op. cit., 41.   41 The heads of the bill introduced on 12 October 1757 were little more than a draft with several gaps for number of priests, amount of fines and awards, commencement dates, extent of prison sentences. These gaps were filled in in the subsequent discussion in the house and other amendments were made, most notably in the wording of the oath to be taken. It is these amended heads which are here compared with the 1756 heads of bill. For the heads of the 1757 bill as amended see NLI microfilm Pos. 5373, ff. 592–3.

tribute to the more vigorous execution of the laws against regulars'. As regards this apparent softening in the administration's approach to the regulars, it may have been brought to their attention that the pope had already pre-empted them in the matter of bringing the Irish regular clergy to heel with the papal decree of 1751. However, the new bill still provided that all unregistered and regular clergy must quit the country by January 1759.

Secondly, it was made clear in the 1757 bill that each existing parish priest would apply personally to the grand jury or the general quarter sessions for registration, an additional item of information to be furnished being the length of time he had officiated as a parish priest. Under the 1757 bill lists of registered priests were required to be sent to the clerk of the privy council and not to the lord lieutenant as in the previous bill. The power in the 1756 bill of the lord lieutenant and council to disapprove of priests on the list was dropped in the 1757 bill. The total number of additional priests who could be approved for larger parishes was increased from 100 to 200.

Thirdly, the most striking change of all was in the oath to be taken by priests on registration. Where previously there had been a fairly lengthy oath with a renunciation of the papal deposing and dispensing powers and the belief that no faith should be kept with heretics or that it was lawful to murder anyone on the pretext of his being a heretic, there was now a very simple oath viz.[42]

I, A. B., duly considering the sacred nature of an oath and sincerely detesting the horrible crime of wilful and deliberate perjury do promise and swear that I will be faithful and bear true allegiance to his Majesty King George the Second, his heirs and successors, and that I will make known all treasons, traitorous conspiracies or plots against his person, crown and dignity, if any such shall come to my knowledge, and this I promise and swear upon the faith of a Christian and a priest in the plain and ordinary sense of the words now read unto me without any secret collusion, equivocation, evasion or mental reservation whatsoever. So help me God.

It should be noted that the oath in the new bill as originally published in October 1757 was practically the same as that in the 1756 bill, but that this was amended to the version above in the course of debate in the house.[43] The new oath was in line with Chesterfield's view that priests should be required to take the oath of allegiance simply, and it is difficult to see how it could be objected to by anyone but the most dyed-in-the-wool Jacobite.

---

42 NLI microfilm Pos. 5373, ff. 592–3.   43 The version of this oath, in effect the Nary oath, given by W.P. Burke in *The Irish priests in the penal times*, p. 205–6 is taken from the heads as introduced on 12 October 1757 and so is not the form of oath as later amended in the house.

Fourthly, there was in the 1757 bill an entirely new provision in respect of chaplains for persons of rank and property. According to the bill there were several such persons in the kingdom 'who continue addicted to the superstitious worship of the Church of Rome' and it was provided that the lord lieutenant, at his discretion, could grant to such a person permission to keep a domestic secular priest who would officiate as a popish priest and celebrate Mass within his mansion house. Among other conditions it was provided that the person of rank should take the same oath as the priest but with the words 'and of a priest' deleted. There was a limit of fifty on the number of such chaplains for the whole country. This provision was probably made at the suggestion of Lord Trimleston.

Fifthly, another new feature of the 1757 bill was 'the proper provision for a succession' of priests mentioned in the preamble and provided for later in the bill. In the case of a vacancy for a priest due to death, retiral, dismissal etc., the lord lieutenant might be petitioned that a secular priest be permitted to come into the kingdom to supply the vacancy and that a passport be granted for that purpose. The petition was required to be signed by five priests on the list of registered priests. The priest coming into the country was required to make a declaration that he was a secular priest and not a regular. It might appear at first sight that this provision conflicted with the function of bishops to ordain priests, but in fact it affected that function only marginally and indeed amounted to more or less what was happening anyway. The tradition had been for secular priests to be ordained at home and then to go to colleges abroad for further education, although there was a minority of such priests who entered those colleges as youths and were ordained there. Thus the priests who under the bill would return from abroad to fill vacancies would in the great majority of cases have been ordained by a bishop at home before proceeding to a college abroad.

Sixthly, there is no mention at all of bishops in the course of either bill. The possibility, already mentioned in our examination of the 1756 bill, that bishops could have themselves registered as parish priests for their mensal parishes appears even more valid in the case of the 1757 bill, considering that the reference to the act for banishing all papists exercising any ecclesiastical jurisdiction has been dropped in the 1757 bill. The probability that there was a tacit understanding, between Hamilton and the catholics whom he consulted in regard to the 1757 bill, that bishops would remain in the country, register themselves as parish priests and continue to function discreetly as before, becomes even more likely.

Given that the 1757 bill was generally much more liberal than the previous one, it is difficult to understand the rather petty, niggling and complicated provisions introduced into the 1757 bill in the course of debate in the house during October/November 1757 in regard to the prosecution of persons found to be concealing, aiding, abetting or succouring unregistered priests or attending at Masses celebrated by such priests. On the other hand, the provision in the 1756 bill that priests who returned to Ireland after transportation would be guilty of a felony without benefit of clergy (that is, a capital offence), was altered in the 1757 bill to close imprisonment of such priests during their natural lives – admittedly a very severe punishment, but at least it was not capital.

But the fact that the bill did not openly address the question of providing a cadre of bishops was seen as a serious defect by some catholic, and at least one protestant, commentators. A Dublin protestant divine, John Brett, in a dedication to Hamilton dated 4 November 1757 of a printed version of his sermon to celebrate the alleged massacre of protestants in 1641, had this to say:

> Allowing them a succession of priests and not allowing at the same time bishops, a competent number to keep up the succession, may be thought a hardship and perhaps a defect in the bill: Because it is of the essence of their religion and the want of them may put them under inconveniences intolerable in their way; having no seminaries here for the education of priests, the supplies must come from abroad and may, it is true, be ordained there; but as they are precluded from coming until the vacancy happens, where the distance is so great, the intermission by delay may be longer than is reasonable. Whether public wisdom may think fit to alter this, I cannot say ...

As to the general reaction of protestants to the bill, Brett stated:

> People I find in opinion that the indulgence granted to the Roman Catholics by this bill is too great: It is, in their sense, not only a legal toleration, but in a manner a kind of civil establishment of the Popish religion, and this they are afraid will make them more insolent, and less obedient to the laws than they were before.[44]

On the catholic side it appears there had been expectations with regard to the revised bill which were not realised. A pamphlet had been published in Dublin about August 1757 with, it was confidently said, Hamilton's approbation, dealing with the regulation of the catholic clergy in Holland. What was involved was a full toleration for catholics in that mainly protestant country and included was a provision that the secular magistrates should approve of the person presented for a particular parish by his ordinary, whether bishop, metropolitan or nuncio. An oath or declaration of fidelity to the government was required. The expectation was that the government had in mind a similar system for Ireland and there were many catholics who would welcome such a system. For

44 Brett, John, *A friendly call to the people of the Roman catholic religion in Ireland*, Dublin 1757, 2.

instance, Charles O'Conor expressed the view that 'if the catholics of other countries submitted to these ordinances, what should hinder a similar submission on our part'.[45]

When, however, the actual provisions of the bill became known, O'Conor was foremost in denouncing it.

> Nothing can be better known than that our spiritual economy cannot be exercised a moment without the spiritual jurisdiction of bishops. This is not only virtually but effectually forbidden by the bill. What more do we want with regard to the true intent of it? No more is, in truth, necessary. Take away episcopal authority from among the Papists, and Popery in a few years is laid in its grave.[46]

In a subsequent letter of 27 November 1757 O'Conor castigated the bill as 'the destruction of popery by popery itself'.[47] He advocated in the same letter that the chief clergy and laity of Dublin should come together with a view to setting forth their grievances and 'hint the consequences of the bill were it to pass into law'.[48] O'Conor also refers to consultations which had been going on between certain catholics and Hamilton:

> As to the physician [Lord Trimleston?], I think it is impossible he should have any instructions from his principals to give assurances of their being satisfied with the bill in its present form. He might indeed declare their satisfaction as to the general tenor of it, but express their anguish at the part which struck at the fundamentals of our hierarchy, and that an alteration of the bill on that head would render it palatable to the whole party. Such, I presume, was his commission.[49]

Archbishop O'Reilly, in a letter dated 4 December 1757 to the Brussels nuncio, claimed that the selection of parish priests had been put in the hands of the viceroy. Certainly, this would be true in the long run, since, according as existing priests quitted the scene through death or whatever, they would be replaced by priests from abroad, selected by petitioning the lord lieutenant in the manner already outlined, and eventually all parish priests would have been appointed in this manner. But it should not be forgotten that the great majority of priests so appointed would have been ordained by Irish bishops before they left Ireland to attend colleges on the continent for further education. Indeed, O'Reilly points out in the same letter that if bishops had been more vigilant in the selection of ordinands, 'the crop of these scandals' would be lessened.

45 Ward, R.E. et al. (eds.), op. cit., 41–2.   46 Ibid., 45–6.   47 Ibid., 47.   48 Ibid., 48.
49 Ibid., 49.

He also complains about the danger, under the projected regime, that un-worthy priests might intrude themselves into parishes and about the way in which episcopal authority generally might be undermined. But, although he mentions in his letter that regular clergy, found in the country after January 1759, would be imprisoned, there is no mention of a similar treatment of bish-ops and there is an underlying assumption in his letter that they would not be disturbed.[50]

As regards the progress of this revised bill through the house, on 12 October 1757 Hamilton, who the previous day had been introduced to the house in his new capacity as earl of Clanbrassill and had taken his place at the lower end of the earls' bench, presented the heads of the bill, which were received and read a first time.[51] On 2 November the heads were read a second time and it was agreed to take them in committee on 9 November. It was ordered that all lords in and about the town be summoned to attend the service of the house upon that day.[52]

The house duly met in committee on 9 November and Lord Jocelyn report-ed that the committee had gone through the heads paragraph by paragraph and had made several amendments thereto. The house met again on 11 November when the amendments made in committee on the 9th were agreed to and the heads of the bill were ordered to be printed as amended.[53] At their sitting on 21 November the house divided 15 to 11 in the affirmative on the bill and it was ordered to be read a third time on 6 December 1757.

At the sitting of the house on 6 December a motion to adjourn the bill to 1 June 1758 was defeated by 21 votes to 19, some proxies being taken into account.[54] This was taken as a final approval of the heads of the bill which were then by order read a third time. It was also ordered that the earl of Clanbrassill (Hamilton) attend the lord lieutenant with the heads of the bill and desire the same might be transmitted to Great Britain in due form.

Fr John Creagh, already mentioned, records that the bill was passed after a debate lasting eight hours and that the archbishops of Armagh and Dublin, and the bishops of Limerick and Down spoke with the greatest warmth against the bill, and that all the other bishops voted with them except four who in any

---

50 APF, Irlanda 10, f. 598, NLI Pos. 5373. The original is in Latin.   51 *Lords Journal Ireland*, vol. 4, 87.   52 Ibid., 93.   53 Ibid., 94. Present in the house on 9 November 1757 were the earls of Kildare, Cavan, Inchiquin, Drogheda, Ross, Shannon, Lanesborough and Clanbrassill; Viscounts Strangford, Castlecomer, Powerscourt and Jocelyn; the archbishops of Armagh and Dublin; the bishops of Clogher, Cork, Waterford & Lismore, Killala, Down, Ferns, Cloyne, Clonfert and Ossory; and Lords Howth, Knapton and Russborough.   54 Ibid., 98. Present on 6 December, in addition to those on 9 November, except the bishop of Ossory, were the earls of Westmeath, Grandison and Belvedere; Viscounts Fane and Loftus; the archbishops of Cashel and Tuam; and the bishops of Elphin, Derry, Dromore, Killaloe, Limerick and Kilmore. The bishop of Ossory was represented by a proxy on 6 December.

case declared themselves against the Catholic party.[55] The bill still had to be approved by the Irish privy council before being sent to London for approval by the English privy council. Normally approval by the Irish privy council would follow almost as a matter of course but on this occasion, quite against expectations, the bill had, according to Fr Creagh, such a stormy reception in the council that, on the first occasion it was before that body, it was under discussion until the small hours of the morning and disagreement among the councillors was such that no agreement was reached on that occasion. However, later it was thrown out by the council at its meeting on 21 January 1758 by 13 votes to 11.[56] Primate Stone, the three other archbishops, the lord chancellor, the chief justice of the king's bench, the lord chief baron joined with the earl of Shannon and others in defeating the bill, even after the lord lieutenant, Bedford, had spoken at length in its favour. Bedford had indeed strongly supported the bill throughout its passage through the lords. Popery, he claimed, was *de facto* established already and all he wanted to do was to control it with favourable result.[57]

Fr John Creagh was of the opinion that the bishops in the house of lords voted against the bill on this occasion because it established a supreme authority and power in the viceroy and his council to reject or approve at their discretion the candidate for any parish whatsoever (without regard to the bishop or the pope); that these were the presbyterian principles which rejected all episcopal jurisdiction; and that the protestant bishops had taken to heart the suppression of the catholic hierarchy in Ireland, fearing that they themselves might soon be attacked.[58]

But it is difficult to see Creagh's views in this matter as other than farfetched and disingenuous. The church of Ireland bishops would never equate themselves with their popish counterparts, nor would it occur to them that they might conceivably one day suffer the same fate. True, they had been suppressed by Cromwell but that was a dim memory and never likely to occur again.

Chesterfield's comment on the ultimate rejection of the bill is also worth recording:

Lord Clanbrazil's bill is thrown out at last, and perhaps never the worse though I approved of it; but it would be so altered and mangled before it had passed the two houses that it would have been worse than none.[59]

Indeed, the parliament was living up to the character he had given it three years before:

55 APF, SC Irlanda 10, f. 584, NLI Pos. 5373.   **56** James, F.G., op. cit., 256–7. **57** Bedford correspondence quoted in F.G. James, op. cit., 256–7.   **58** APF, SC Irlanda 10, f. 584, NLI Pos. 5373.   **59** Maty, M. (ed.), *Miscellaneous works of … the earl of Chesterfield*, London 1778, p. 49.

That assembly is more *peuple* [plebian?] than any I knew in my life. They are still blinded by all the prejudices of sect, animosity and fury, and no bill in which Papists are mentioned can go through that house in a proper form. For (the reverse of bears) they will lick it out of shape.[60]

The truth of the matter was that, if Hamilton and the other supporters of the bill could be described as anti-catholic, then those who opposed it were, with few exceptions, even more anti-catholic, many of them rabidly and uncompromisingly so.

Meanwhile, an event had occurred which was to cause deep divisions among the catholic hierarchy and clergy generally. Lord Trimleston, in his capacity as self-appointed advocate of the catholic cause, as already stated, had consultations with Hamilton on the bill and it is entirely possible that secret deals were made. Trimleston wielded considerable influence over certain members of the hierarchy. He may have been the mysterious layman who gained such an influence over the senile Archbishop Linegar of Dublin in the early 1750s that one of the vicars-general of that diocese,[61] Patrick Fitzsimons, felt compelled to resign temporarily. He certainly acquired an ascendancy over Michael O'Reilly, the primate, who had his headquarters near Drogheda not that far from Trimblestown castle, and over Augustine Cheevers, who was descended from a family of Meath gentry and who had been appointed bishop of Meath in 1756.[62] James O'Keeffe, bishop of Kildare, also appears to have succumbed to Trimleston's spell. On 1 September 1757 the foregoing prelates, together with the bishops of Clogher, Derry and Kilmore assembled at Trimblestown Castle.[63] The only bishop from the Armagh province who was absent was Raphoe and he was represented by the bishop of Derry. The diocese of Ardagh, also in the Armagh province, was vacant at this time. At least two of these bishops were noteworthy for their hostility to the regular clergy. O'Reilly had declared in 1753 that 'nothing makes the catholic name so offensive to the government, and nothing is more prone to excite persecution, than the immoderate number of wandering friars',[64] while O'Keeffe in January 1756 in the course of a letter to Cardinal Corsini beseeched his eminence to do something about the mean and shameful accumulations of these mendicants and claimed that, because of their reputation and way of life, the Irish parliament's hatred of them was such that it would never desist from devising new measures against catholics as long as these mendicants were perceived to be returning to the country in such numbers and loitering quite publicly among the poor.[65]

---

60 Bradshaw, J. op. cit., vol. 3, 1116.   61 APF, SC Irlanda 10, ff. 430–1, NLI Pos. 5373   62 White, James, *Annals of Limerick*, Royal Irish Academy MS 24.D.21, 318–20. 63 Ibid., 318–20.   64 Fenning, Hugh, *The undoing of the friars of Ireland*, Louvain, 1972, 170–71.   65 APF, SC Irlanda 10, ff. 519–20, NLI Pos. 5372.

The purpose of the Trimblestown Castle meeting, which was said to be the brain-child of Lord Trimleston, was to draw up a pastoral letter supportive of government, perhaps in the mistaken belief that the main proposals in the registry of priests bill would be on the lines of the Dutch model in the pamphlet already mentioned. O'Reilly was certainly aware of that pamphlet, for it was he who forwarded a copy of it to Charles O'Conor, apparently in the belief that it had been published in Dublin with Hamilton's approbation.[66] It is entirely possible, too, that O'Reilly had compromised himself in some way when, under arrest, he was interviewed by Hamilton in April 1756, as already noted. In any event, after some days deliberation, the assembled bishops produced the draft of a pastoral which was signed by them all on 5 September 1757, with Derry signing on behalf of the absent Raphoe. The pastoral is set out in full as Appendix no. 1 to this chapter, together with the covering letter (Appendix no. 2) with which O'Reilly sent the pastoral to the other three archbishops.[67] O'Reilly intended that the archbishops would circulate the draft to their suffragans, but from the tone of the covering letter it is clear that he expected that all the bishops would be in agreement with the draft. Incidentally, it will be seen from this covering letter that O'Reilly had a very poor opinion of the usefulness of the pamphlets published by Charles O'Conor around this time.

It is also clear from the covering letter that the purpose of the pastoral was two-fold: firstly, a general purpose of countering the prevalent unjustified protestant prejudice against catholics and protestant misunderstanding of catholic principles; and secondly, a particular purpose in regard to Hamilton's bill which is evident from the passage: 'No time more seasonable for our purpose than the present as the Lords, whose bill miraculously miscarried in the last session, have been ever since smoothing the way, least that, which they are to usher in with redoubled efforts this winter, may meet with any obstruction.'

The lords referred to in this extract were Lord Limerick (i.e. Hamilton), Bishops Synge and Clayton and no doubt others, such as Bishop Chenevix, who supported the bill. It will be noted that Fr James White, the eighteenth century contemporary Limerick annalist, to whom we are indebted for the text of the pastoral presented here, was of the opinion that the purpose of the pastoral was 'to avert the blow' (of the bill). One interpretation, then, of the extract above is that the bishops expected the bill to be carried and that their best gambit was to try to counter its worst effects by rejecting the papal deposing and dispensing claims and by declaring their loyalty to the king, and so, if the worst came to the worst, make it morally difficult for the administration to take action against an anti-papal hierarchy, demonstrably and effusively loyal to the king, and so ensure that the previous *de facto* toleration of the hierarchy would continue. An alternative, and perhaps equally valid interpretation, is that the

---

66 Ward, R.E. et al. (eds.), op. cit., 41–2.   67 White, James, op. cit., 318–20.

issue of a pastoral on the lines of the draft would act as a support for those lords who would be making such an effort in the forthcoming session to push what the catholic bishops expected would be a favourable bill through the house.

Although it was the declarations in the pastoral which were later to be found most objectionable, it has to be said that there was little in these declarations which was new. The first is a straight forward renunciation of the papal deposing and dispensing powers in line with the Gallican Articles of 1682 and with the views of some Irish divines earlier in the century such as Fr Francis Martin of Louvain and Fr Cornelius Nary.[68] The second rejected a barbarism of the past which very few, even among the most ultramontane faithful, would have been prepared to espouse in the mid–eighteenth century. The third follows naturally from the renunciation of the deposing and dispensing powers in the first. The fourth is an enlargement of the renunciation of the papal power of dispensing subjects of monarchs from their oaths of allegiance.

It would also be rewarding to compare the declarations with Fr Nary's oath, offered by the catholic side when the 1756 bill was introduced, or with the oath in the act of 1774 which eventually proved acceptable to all catholics, clergy and laity alike. It has to be asked: is there anything in the declarations which is not in the 1774 oath? Indeed, there is in the 1774 oath an abjuration of the Stuarts which is entirely absent from the declarations. Furthermore, all the pastoral would require of the faithful was that they should pray for King George; there was no mention of swearing an oath of allegiance to him.

It should also be emphasised that the pastoral was only a draft. Although Archbishop O'Reilly did expect that it would be accepted by the other bishops, obviously it could have been amended if the other bishops had a mind to do so. It need hardly be added that this was a pastoral which was never issued to the faithful.

Why then did this draft pastoral meet with so much opposition and why were the signatories treated to such a torrrent of denigration and obloquy? Firstly, the various declarations were invested with too much stridency and a degree of inaccuracy through being prefaced by the words 'it is not and never was a doctrine of the Roman Catholic Church that ... ' In fact the official position was that the various tenets challenged, with the possible exception of the second one (see Appendix 1), were and would be for some decades to come, the official doctrine of the catholic church, notwithstanding the Gallican Articles and the views of certain catholic divines. There was no getting away from the fact that the papal deposing and dispensing powers had been enshrined in the third canon of the Fourth Lateran Council and had never been rescinded.

Secondly, it has to be said that the draft pastoral was given too wide a circulation. The bishops should have kept it to themselves and their closest

68 For details of the Gallican Articles see Chapter 1.

advisers. Above all, it should not have been let next or near the regular clergy, who had been severely wounded by the restrictions on novitiates in the papal decree of 1751 and were now due to get the *coup de grâce* if Hamilton's bill went through. But far from any curb being put on circulation of the pastoral, we find the archbishop of Cashel discussing it with a general meeting of clergy in Limerick.[69] Lincoln in Dublin was more circumspect: he discussed it with a council of eight, but unfortunately included in that eight was at least one regular, Thomas Burke, a Dominican, who, in Lincoln's words, 'was panting for a mitre',[70] and soon was to find one in Ossory. By letting the regulars in on the act Lincoln was in effect discarding the option of having the pastoral amended. Disregarding Lincoln's admonition of silence, Burke wrote on 22 September a denunciation of the pastoral to Fr Charles O'Kelly, a fellow Dominican, who had been recently appointed to the prestigious post of theologian in the Casanatensian Library in Rome. Burke named Trimleston as the prime mover in the affair and dubbed the Augustinian Bishop Cheevers of Meath 'a Judas among the regulars'. He claimed that the Dublin clergy had unanimously rejected the pastoral and that the pastoral paved the way for the success of Hamilton's bill.[71] Fr John Creagh, in his letter already noted, made the point that if in the future catholics were to complain about the bill (presumably on its becoming law), protestants would throw in their faces that their very own primate was the first to promote it, and with the difference that the bill as passed in the lords did not go as far as the declaration in the pastoral in the matter of renouncing certain papal claims, since parliament thought that catholics would judge a renunciation of that extent altogether too severe. Creagh went on to point out that many aspects of the Trimblestown declaration contained in the oath prescribed in the first printed copy of the bill (presumably that of October 1757), were later expunged by order of the house of lords.[72] This is a reference to the fact that, as noted above, the oath originally proposed was later considerably scaled down during the debate in the lords.

Lincoln's somewhat ambivalent role in this affair is traceable to his earlier involvement in the form of an oath. Moreover, his recent appointment as archbishop was brought about with the support of O'Reilly, support which may have been crucial in view of O'Reilly's position as primate. This may have put Lincoln in an invidious position *vis-à-vis* O'Reilly and it is hard to escape the conclusion that initially he was prepared to go some of the way with the draft pastoral, for on 4 October a letter, purporting to come from Lincoln, was read in the Dublin chapels,[73] which had several points of resemblance with the pastoral. In this letter Lincoln exhorted the faithful

69 White, James, op. cit., 318–20.   70 Fenning, Hugh, op. cit in note 36, p. 274. 71 Ibid., 271–2.   72 APF, SC Irlanda 10, f. 584, NLI Pos. 5373.   73 *Dublin Journal* of 4 October 1757. For O'Reilly's part in the promotion of Lincoln see M.J.C. [M.J. Curran], 'The Archbishop Linegar-Lincoln succession' in *Reportorium Novum*, vol. 2, no. 1 (1958), 211–12.

to continue in the same happy and Christian dispositions and thus by degrees you will entirely efface in their [Government's] minds those evil impressions which have been conceived so much to our prejudice, and industriously propagated by our enemies.

Their greatest thankfulness was due, the letter admonished, for the lenity and moderation with which the penal laws were executed ever since the accession of the present royal family (George II). He cautioned them against cursing, swearing and blaspheming, 'to which the poorest sort of our people are most unhappily addicted', and went on:

It is probable that from hence some people have taken occasion to brand us with this infamous calumny, that we need not fear to take false oaths, and consequently to perjure ourselves, as if we believed that any power could authorise such damnable practices, or grant dispensations for this purpose. How unjust and cruel this charge is, you know by our instructions to you, both in public and private, in which we have ever condemned such doctrines as false and impious. Others, likewise may easily know it from the constant behaviour of Roman Catholics, who have given the strongest support of their abhorrence to those tenets, by refusing to take oaths, which, however conducive to their temporal interest, appeared to them entirely repugnant to the principles of their religion.

Lincoln concluded by beseeching God

to direct the counsels of our rulers, to inspire them with sentiments of moderation and compassion towards us. We ought to be more earnest at this juncture in our supplications to Heaven, as some very honourable personages have encouraged us to hope for a mitigation of the Penal Laws. Pray then the Almighty to give a blessing to these their generous designs, and to aid their counsels in such a manner, that whilst they intend to assist us, like kind benefactors, they may not, contrary to their intentions, by mistaking the means, most irretrievably destroy us.

On 4 October the signatories of the pastoral met again at Trimblestown Castle and wrote an explanatory letter to Cardinal Corsini in his capacity as cardinal protector of Ireland. They complained that the text of the pastoral, which would have been published only if all the bishops agreed with it, was now in the public domain and if the bishops were to draw back on what was contained in it, it would confirm protestants in their false opinion of catholicism. They were left with no option but to have the pastoral printed because of the behaviour of indiscreet and calumnious friars. In addition Bishop Cheevers of Meath wrote to the Fr Charles O'Kelly mentioned above explaining and justifying the pastoral.[74]

On 27 October a further letter was issued to the Dublin parish priests for reading at Masses on the following day. The full text was as follows:[75]

> You are ordered to read the following paper to your respective congregations with an audible voice tomorrow without addition or diminution.
> Dear Christians, as you cannot be ignorant of the imminent dangers with which our holy religion is now threatened, we should be wanting to ourselves and to you if we did not exhort you to join your prayers with ours that the Almighty God may avert this evil by inspiring our rulers with such sentiments of moderation and lenity towards us as are compatible with our tenets.
>
> Your past peaceable behaviour gives us the greatest satisfaction and we most earnestly recommend to you a continuation of this conduct upon all occasions. As we shall ever disclaim and detest any scurrilous libel or Grub Street paper which may seem to be written in the name or on behalf of Roman Catholics, so we expect that you will not only by your actions but likewise by your discourses show your just abhorrence to whatsoever may give any the least offence to the government. For the above purpose and your perseverance in those commendable dispositions you [parish priests?] are ordered to read the Litanies publicly every day the ensuing week.

This represents a complete watering down of the letter issued on 4 October and it may be that the latter proved an embarrasment to Lincoln in the light of the furoré created mainly by the regulars and the obvious points of similarity between the letter of 4 October and the Trimblestown pastoral.

Writing to Cardinal Corsini on 13 December 1757 with the benefit of considerable hindsight, Lincoln gave his account of his involvement in this affair.[76] He claimed that as soon as the draft pastoral was transmitted to him for his approbation, he foresaw the blow which menaced the religion of this unfortunate country and for the present caused all his efforts to be stifled at source. He wrote a letter to Lord Trimleston, at whose house the piece was plotted, and in return for a very polite but expostulatory letter, he received only abuse. He asked Archbishop O'Reilly to meet him some miles from Dublin, when he did not fail to represent to him as forcefully as possible, the inconvenience, the danger and the ruin which the new tenets (in the pastoral) would bring to the poor church in Ireland, which up to this despite persecution, had in some measure

---

74 Fenning, H., op. cit in note 36, 272–3.   75 O'Conor/Curry correspondence, Royal Irish Academy MS B.i.1.   76 APF, SC Irlanda 10, f. 596, NLI Pos. 5373. The original is in French.

triumphed over all her enemies. He eventually won his point with O'Reilly who agreed that he (Lincoln) should write to the archbishops of Cashel and Tuam with a view to suppressing entirely the proposed pastoral letter. He did not fail to do so immediately for he knew the scandal which would be the sad result through all the kingdom, if the affair came to be known to the public.

Lincoln went on to say that he believed it necessary in the prevailing circumstances to call together some regulars, together with his vicars and some others of the secular clergy, to inform them of the measures he had taken to stop the publication of the unfortunate piece and to recommend to them a complete silence. It were to have been wished that they had followed his advice and that some, particularly regulars, had shown themselves a bit more discreet, in which event religion would have been better served. The upshot, however, was that the affair became public and they had been unable to screen themselves from the consequences. Lincoln speculates that the regulars had particular aims in view in demonstrating their zeal in this matter to the nuncio, a zeal which he himself had seen only very indiscreet indications of, in regard to an incident which otherwise would have attracted little attention.

Lincoln goes on to fulminate against the regular clergy who had represented him and the secular clergy generally as the promoters of an act of parliament which had just passed the upper house and which amounted to nothing less than the annihilation of the little remains of their Holy Religion. Since the month of July he had implored the protection of the pope towards procuring the mediation in this matter of the catholic ambassadors in London. He had at the same time drawn up a memorandum for the Spanish court and had received a favourable response. He had also made the necessary applications to some very illustrious persons in London and he hoped that the Lord would preserve them from this storm. But all this would not stop the tongues of many regulars; the wounds which he received from these false brothers were still more deadly than those from his enemies. For the present he consoled himself with the witness of his conscience, but when the danger was passed he would not hesitate to punish some of the authors of such an infamous commotion.

However, Rome did not react as Burke and his fellow regulars had hoped.[77] In fact the reply sent by Corsini on behalf of the Congregation de Propaganda Fide to Archbishop O'Reilly was much less severe than might have been expected. The Congregation considered that the whole business of the pastoral was unnecessary and ill-advised and that something on the lines of the letter read in the Dublin chapels would have sufficed; that O'Reilly and his colleagues ought to have foreseen that the text of the pastoral could not be kept secret, that most bishops would find it difficult to accept it and this non-acceptance, publicly known, would expose them to persecution. The Congregation admonished the

77 Fenning, H., op. cit in note 36, p. 274.

signatories against taking any further action, unless to endeavour to repair the harm already done. Why not, Corsini asked, follow the example of Dutch and German catholics who succeeded in living quietly under protestant rulers without ever taking any formal oath of allegiance?

O'Reilly did not long survive the controversy. He 'lost his life miserably', according to Dr Richard Reddy, on 4 February 1758. Reddy claimed that he had been 'set on' [led astray] by a 'lay person of figure' [no doubt Lord Trimleston].[78] He died completely at peace with the church, for previous to his death he had revoked anything he had ever said or done against the Holy See.

As for the other signatories of the pastoral, they were treated to their share of contempt and obloquy. Here is Bishop John O'Brien of Cloyne in a letter to the Stuart court:

The subscribers of the infamous pastoral are now in great confusion, as they should be, but I am sorry that I find that the confusion of some of them proceeds only from a just apprehension that that work will exclude them from a certain succession lately opened by the death of their chief. I should be greatly mortified and surprised that any of them were named for that place because it would be nothing less than a plain approbation of what they had done but I don't fear or apprehend it.[79]

O'Brien was quite right in his prediction that none of the signatories would follow O'Reilly as primate. That honour went to a Connacht man, Anthony Blake, who proved to be a disaster as archbishop of Armagh and eventually had to be removed because of the unsatisfactory performance of his duties.

Archbishop O'Reilly was not the only one of the main players to depart the scene early in 1758. Two of the main protagonists on the protestant side were also soon to die – Bishop Clayton in February and Hamilton in March 1758. The departure of the latter two meant that the bill would not be revived. The remaining promoter of the bill, Bishop Synge, was now aged sixty-six and had lost his zest for parliamentary work. Charles O'Conor commented that two links in the triple chain were broken and that the third was 'almost eaten through by its own rust'. And he asked:

Is not this a good omen? And to lay aside all figure, is it not better we should never have any relaxation of our sufferings than be served in the maner those late friends of ours intended.[80]

78 Fagan, P. (ed.), op. cit., vol. 2, 226.   79 Ibid., 222.   80 Royal Historical Manuscripts Commission, Report no. 8, appendix, 460. Letter dated Good Friday 1758 from Charles O'Conor to John Curry. As a further example of O'Conor's inconsistency he was to say of Synge in October 1759 that he was 'undoubtedly a man of the first abilities in this nation' – see R.E. Ward et al. (eds.), op. cit., 72.

It was to be the last attempt at registering the catholic clergy and at framing an oath for registered priests. Henceforth the emphasis would be on framing an oath of allegiance for catholics, acceptable to both laity and clergy, in return for which catholics might hope for some amelioration of the Penal Laws.

APPENDIX NO. I

The Trimblestown Pastoral September 1757
(taken from Fr James White's *Annals of Limerick*.)

Dr Michael O'Reilly, archbishop of Armagh and some other Roman Catholic bishops, mostly his suffragans, being apprehensive that the Act of Parliament against the Roman Catholic clergy, which was brought into the House of Lords by the Lord Limerick in January 1756 and which then failed of passing into a law, which he again introduced this ensuing session of parliament, imagined they would avert that blow by publishing a general pastoral letter to be subscribed by all the Catholic bishops wherein they would make known their loyalty to the present Government; for this purpose they assembled at Lord Trimblestown's seat on the 5th of September 1757 and planned the following pastoral letter which they sent to all the Catholic bishops of the Kingdom to be signed by them.

A pastoral letter to be signed by the chiefs of the Roman Catholic clergy in Ireland and directed to all the priests serving in parishes throughout the Kingdom

The constant, universal and invariable doctrine of the Roman Catholic Church has perpetually taught submission, obedience and fidelity to the Princes and Powers which the Almighty has placed in the seat of government over [them], his love and charity to all our fellow creatures, sincerity, truth and fidelity in all our dealings [?], engagements and callings be they with persons of our own or any other religion or profession whatsoever without distinction. This doctrine our Divine Master has taught during his temporal life upon earth by his own example and precepts. The apostles preached and followed it. The Church of Christ holds, professes and teaches it, condemns and rejects as abominable and false all contrary doctrines or tenets. You have learned it in the bosom of that Holy Mother and we make no doubt of your having been faithful to your ministry and the sacred trust reposed in you for the salvation of the flock committed to your care and that you have instructed them in these points of the Christian Doctrine. We exhort you and require of you to continue so to do in a most zealous and earnest manner, and as we find with equal concern and astonishment that there are some among our Protestant fellow subjects who notwithstanding our public and private profession of these our principles and our constant disavowal of all tenets contrary to them, do believe or affect to believe that we hold or profess several doctrines and principles obnoxious to the state and our Protestant neighbours, from whence they take occasion both in public and in private to calumniate and misrepresent our principles, misleading and deceiving the public into false notions and bad opinions of those who profess the Roman Catholic religion, against the evidence of their constant loyal submission and good behaviour from the time of the Revolution to this day and very much to the prejudice of the real interests of this Kingdom as they have created indifference and distrust on one side which were productive of circumstances which leave [?] the other, a considerable part of the inhabitants of Ireland, under difficulties and incapacities which restrain their industry and take away from them the satisfaction [?] of contributing so largely as otherwise they might have done, to the improvement, wealth and strength of this Kingdom. Therefore, in order to effectually remove all such suspicions, to put a stop to all future calumnies of that nature, for the honour of our religion, for our justification and as a most solemn, constant and incontestable evidence of our principles and tenets as subjects of King George, as Christians and neighbours with regard to all those with whom we have or may have any connections or dealings, be they of any religious profession or persuasion whatsoever. Anno 1757.

We strictly command on the first Sunday after you shall receive this to read from the altars of your stations with an audible voice before you dismiss your congregation the following declaration and to continue so to do on the first Sunday of every quarter in every year, and we do further command you on every Sunday and Holyday at the end of Mass in your several stations to offer up a prayer to the Almighty God, beseeching his Divine Majesty to bless our good and gracious sovereign, King George and his Royal Family, and that he would be pleased of His infinite goodness to grant them their spiritual and temporal necessities, and to invite the congregation to join with you therein.

In confidence of your obedience and exact performance of these our commands we give you our benediction and beseech the great God to assist you with his divine graces in your labours for the edification and instruction of your flocks and that you and they may walk upright in His sight as good, charitable and moral Christians, peaceable and faithful subjects to the King and that you may love and serve God above all things and your neighbours as yourselves of whatsoever religion or profession they may be.

The Declaration

Not so much for your instruction, Brethren of the Roman Catholic Communion, hoping that there are none among you ignorant of these points, as for the vindication of the doctrine of our Church from aspersions and calumnies, we do declare that it is not and never was a doctrine or tenet of the Roman Catholic church that the Pope or General Councellors [*sic*] have power to depose kings or to absolve their subjects from their allegiance.

On the contrary it is by no means lawful for subjects to oppose or to do violence against their king or his established government or to conspire with his enemies directly or indirectly against him or the state under which they live and by which they are protected; and every subject who should so transgress would become [guilty] of mortal and most serious sin before God, any secret act of Deposition or Absolution notwithstanding.

It is not and never was a doctrine or tenet of the Roman Catholic Church that those of her communion may break faith with, murder, plunder and defraud those of a different communion or religion.

On the contrary such is abominable and damnable doctrine equally repugnant to the law of nature which obliges us to observe the same fidelity, honesty [?] and charity towards those of a different religion as we should to those of our own.

It is not and never was a doctrine or tenet of the Roman Catholic Church that the Pope hath any direct or indirect authority or power over the temporal power and jurisdiction of princes.

On the contrary if the Pope should pretend to dispense of his Majesty's subjects from their allegiance or invade his dominions, we would deem such dispensation null and void and all Roman Catholic subjects bound in conscience to defend their king and country at the hazard of their lives and fortunes.

It is not and never was a doctrine or tenet of the Roman Catholic Church that the Pope or any person on earth can license me to take false oaths, to lie, to forswear or to prejudice themselves on any account whatsoever or to [word missing] their neighbours, cheat or injure them or their native country on pretence of promoting the Catholic religion or for any other purpose whatsoever.

On the contrary such doctrines and tenets are condemned by our church as unchristian, abominable, sinful and wicked and all pardons and dispensations granted or pretended to be granted for any such objects [?] or purposes are null and invalid, adding sacrilege and blasphemy to the above named crimes.

And now, Roman Catholic Brethren, I most earnestly exhort you for the love of our Saviour, Jesus Christ, by your behaviour as good Christian subjects to our king and his government and as good, charitable, moral, honest neighbours to all men that you will on all occasions give proofs to the world of the sincerity of your conformity to this doctrine and of your being convinced that your duty to God, your king and your [country] obliges you so to do. I am yours &c. [*sic*]

We, the undernamed, do hereby declare that in the annexed pastoral letter we find nothing contrary to the Scriptures, tradition or decrees of General Councils [or] to the faith, morals and doctrine of our Holy Mother the Church. We moreover think it highly expedient and necessary in our present circumstances that all our absent brethren, without whose concurrence we would do nothing, should adopt and enforce said pastoral letter in their respective districts in order to wipe off the foul aspersions thrown upon us, and hereunto we most earnestly invite them through the bowels of charity and the compassion they owe to the poor afflicted Roman Catholics under their care. Given under our hands at Trimblestown this 5th day of September 1757.

Michael [O'Reilly] Armagh
Daniel [O'Reilly] Clogherensis
Augustinus [Cheevers] Midensis
Jacobus [O'Keeffe] Kildarensis
Joannes [McColgan] Derrensis
Andreas [Campbell] Kilmorensis
Joannes [McColgan] Derrensis ex commissione Nathaniel [O'Donnell]
    Rapotensis

Copia vera ita testor Jacobus White Notarius Apostolicus

Fr White's MS continues:

Dr Michael O'Reilly, having sent the original pastoral letter signed by the above bishops to Dr James Butler, archbishop of Cashel for him and his sufragans to sign it, Dr Butler thereupon came to Limerick and called together the clergy who were here at hand, our bishop Dr Lacy being then out of town, and after receiving their opinion that it was not lawful to sign it, and that they were sure their bishop Dr Lacy would also think so, which he afterwards ratified, Dr Butler declared that to be his own opinion and therefore he on the spot sent it back to Dr Reily without the signatures of any of the bishops of Munster who all rejected it as we find did the archbishop of Dublin and his suffragans, Dr O'Keeffe of Kildare excepted, and was rejected likewise by the archbishop of Tuam and his suffragans.

APPENDIX NO. 2

(From Cashel archives, NLI microfilm Pos. 5998)

A copy of Dr Michael O'Reilly, Archbishop of Armagh, his letter to another metropolitan

Dr Sr,

As a far greater part of Protestants entertain no other ideas of us and our principles than those received from the Press and Pulpit, it seems surprising

to me, who am grown so old in the Mission, that we have never taken any public method of removing their prejudices, public, I say, for to think that a few
tracts of controversy, writ by Catholic authors, were capable of doing it, is a
very mistaken notion. Not one thousand part of them have thought it worth
their while to peruse [?] them; not one hundred part of them have heard that
any such a thing was published. This ignorance of our tenets may be remarked
by ourselves when we talk to them and more particularly by our Catholic gentlemen of sense who talking sometimes occasionally on the topic of religion
with personages of that Communion and taking withal some pains to disabuse
them, are told that it were to be wished that others of the Profession would
think as they do, in which case they might expect to meet with more indulgence and consideration from the Government. But your priests, say they, by
whom the common people are influenced, instil other sentiments into them.
Now, methinks, there is no method of setting those prejudiced gentlemen right
in regard to this more proper than this public solemn way of addressing our
hearers in the face of the world. Is not this method better calculated for unprej-
udicing them than that of a controversy written by any one individual layman
or ecclesiastic who dares not have it even anonimously advertised in the Gazette.
Let us not therefore be any longer wanting to ourselves or hearers whose welfare in every respect challenges our utmost vigilance and attention. We can
expect no bad consequence from publishing this Pastoral. We shall thereby
gratify the benevolent, humane and charitable part of Protestants who have no
quarrel to us but on account of principles not ours and which we now no less
solemnly than unanimously disown, a disavowal that will undoubtedly very much
mortify others of them who care not what our tenets are, provided they are
such as will disqualify us from being looked upon as sincere and inoffensive
subjects. No time more seasonable for our purpose than the present as the
Lords, whose Bill miraculously miscarried in the last session, have been ever
since smoothing the way, least that, which they are to usher in with redoubled
efforts this Winter, may meet with any obstruction. All our clergy and Laity
of the most distinguished rank and sense here think so, but no time is to be
lost. If you think you may implicitly depend on the compliance of your worthy suffragans, be pleased to let me know without delay; if not, I am confident
you will exert your usual activity in procuring it with the utmost dispatch and
signify it to

Your most affectionate humble servant MR

Trimblestown September the 5th 1757

6

Enter the Mitred Earl

The Seven Years War from 1756 to 1763 was a period of great unease for the British and Irish administrations, with frequent rumours of French preparations for an invasion of Britain or Ireland. It was a period when it behoved Irish catholics to keep on the right side of a nervous parliament and government, and at no time was this more necessary than in the autumn of 1759 when two expeditions, composed of Irish émigré and French soldiers, set sail from France. The one from Brest, under Conflans, was engaged and defeated by the British admiral Hawke. The expedition from Dunkirk under Thurot, after many months at sea and greatly depleted, eventually landed at Carrickfergus, County Antrim in February 1760, but pulled out after a few days.

It is not surprising, then, to find the 'Roman Catholic gentry, merchants and citizens of Dublin' (306 of them) presenting in December 1759 an address of loyalty to the lord lieutenant, the duke of Bedford. They began by offering hearty congratulations on recent successes by sea and land. They acknowledged the lenity extended to them by the then king and by his father and went on: 'Our allegiance is confirmed by affection and gratitude; our religion commands it; and it shall be our invariable rule firmly and inviolably to adhere to it.' They refer to the 'foreign enemy meditating desperate attempts', and they assure the lord lieutenant that 'we are ready and willing, to the utmost of our abilities, to assist in supporting his Majesty's government against all hostile attempts whatsoever'. They most humbly hope that 'means may be devised to render so numerous a body [the Roman Catholics] more useful members to the community, and more strengthening friends to the state, than they could possibly have hitherto been, under the constraints of the many penal laws against them.' They conclude by describing Bedford as 'a viceroy in whom wisdom, moderation and justice are so eminently conspicuous'.[1]

1 The names of the signatories were published in *Dublin Gazette* for 1 December 1759. There were 306 or 307 signatories depending on whether one accepts 'Ma & Ed. Byrne' as one or two signatures. The text of the address was published as Appendix 2 to Nicholas Viscount Taaffe's *Observations on affairs in Ireland from the settlement in 1691*

The address, however, was by no means unanimous. It was not signed by any of the catholic clergy in the city since it was strongly opposed by their archbishop, Lincoln, who was ostensibly of the view that they had no right to address the lord lieutenant since they were 'no people in the eye of the law', and that they ought to express their obedience by letter and not by an address. But Charles O'Conor dismissed this view, claiming that Lincoln had personal points to serve and such as he dare not avow,[2] a reference no doubt to Lincoln's delicate situation *vis-à-vis* James Stuart, to whom he owed his nomination as archbishop. Lincoln also influenced a number of the laity against signing the address; for example, only three of the catholic physicians in the city were among the signatories. This prompted Charles O'Conor to remark that if the influence of some should prevail to 'render' the majority from subscribing to the address, this would not only destroy the good effect of the address, but would revive the odium so long operating, till of late, against catholics in the three kingdoms.[3] In the event the reaction of the lord lieutenant was very favourable and highly complimentary. He ordered the speaker of the commons to call Mr Anthony Dermott, one of the principal catholic merchants in the city, before the house. The speaker told Mr Dermott that the lord lieutenant had received the address most graciously and he handed Mr Dermott a written reply in which the addressees were assured that 'the zeal and attachment which they professed could never be more reasonably manifested than at the present conjuncture, and that so long as they [Roman Catholics] conducted themselves with duty and affection, they could not fail to obtain his Majesty's protection'.[4] There were similar addresses to the lord lieutenant, around the same time and for the same reason, from the catholics of the cities of Cork, Limerick and Waterford.[5]

The same considerations prompted the humble petition and remonstrance of the catholics of Ireland to George III in December 1760, following his accession to the throne. This address had been originally prepared with a view to presenting it to George II, but he died before presentation could be effected.[6] It was signed by six hundred of 'the most considerable catholics in the Kingdom' but once again it was the subject of bitter disagreement among the catholic body, and on this occasion there was a three-way split. The clergy opposed the address in principle for the same reasons as before. A third group, the gentry of Meath and Westmeath, led by Lord Trimleston, disagreed with the wording of the address and submitted their own separately to the king.

to the present time, Dublin 1766. It is a bit strange to find the address harking back to the 'lenity' of George I who died in 1727.   2 Ward, Robert E. et al. (eds), *Letters of Charles O'Conor of Belanagare*, Washington D.C. 1988, 79.   3 Ibid., 79.   4 Wall, Maureen, *Catholic Ireland in the eighteenth century*, Dublin 1989, 105.   5 See *Dublin Gazette* for various dates early in 1760.   6 Brady, John, *Catholics and Catholicism in the eighteenth century press*, Maynooth 1965, 100–1. For the address of the noblemen and gentlemen of Meath and Westmeath see ibid., 99–100.

The main address was rather lengthy for such a document and recalled the promises made to catholics in the Articles of Limerick and how those articles had been systematically infringed by the various penal enactments of the Irish parliament. It dwelled at some length on the activities of discoverers and informers, and complained that 'our profusions of loyalty have been often cruelly misrepresented', and concluded with the hope that 'the continuance of that behaviour, enforced by our religious principles, and of your Majesty's great and inherent goodness towards us ... may at length be the happy means of our deliverance from some part of that burden which we have so long and so patiently endured'.[7] But there was no mention at all of catholics taking an oath of allegiance to the king.

During the early 1760s the central administration in Ireland continued to be well-disposed to catholics but were baulked from making any concessions by a parliament composed predominantly of landed proprietors with a vested interest in maintaining the status quo. The outbreak, under the aegis of the Whiteboy organisation, of agrarian trouble in Munster and South Leinster was grist to the mill of members of parliament and a local magistracy only too eager to represent these outbreaks as Jacobite-inspired. This point of view was not, however, shared by the administration who believed the disturbances were primarily due to bad economic conditions, and who would have had a good deal of sympathy with Lord Chesterfield's view that 'if the military force had killed half as many landlords [as Whiteboys] it would have contributed more effectually to restore quiet', that the poor people in Ireland were used worse than Negroes by their lords and masters, and that 'there is a sentiment in every human breast that asserts man's natural right to liberty and good usage, and that will, and ought to rebel when oppressed and provoked to a certain degree'.[8]

The earl of Halifax replaced the duke of Bedford as lord lieutenant in 1761. William Hamilton was appointed chief secretary and he brought over with him as his private secretary a young Irishman on the threshold of fame, Edmund Burke. Although he occupied only a minor position, it is believed that the pro-catholic Burke had some influence in steering the administration towards a mild and enlightened outlook in the matter of relations with catholics. Charles O'Conor confided to his son, Denis, that 'no viceroy was ever more popular than the present, and none I believe ever deserved to be more so'.[9] In the autumn of 1761 Burke is believed to have been already at work on his never-completed *Tract relative to the laws against Popery in Ireland*. In this pamphlet he deals successively with the penal laws regarding catholic property, education, use of arms and exercise of religion. To the latter he devotes less than a page but,

7 Mitchel, John, *The history of Ireland from the treaty of Limerick to the present time*, London, no date, vol. 1, 84–6.   8 Bradshaw, John (ed.), *The letters of Philip Dormer Stanhope, earl of Chesterfield*, London 1892, vol. 3, 1313.   9 Ward R.E. et al. (eds), op. cit., 122.

since the work was never completed, we cannot say whether this was in any way significant. On the question of the oath to be required from catholics (Chapter 3), he is not at all forthcoming; he mentions that the oath required under the 9th Article of the Treaty of Limerick was the oath of allegiance and no other, but there is no mention of the oath of abjuration nor of any of the oaths proposed later on. In Chapter 4 he points out that the penal laws against property operated to discourage all industry and to prevent the improvement of land because of the short leases of thirty-one years available to catholics.[10]

When Burke called the years 1761–7 'a savage period' for Irish catholics, he probably had in mind the ruthless suppression of the White boys, the sectarian bigotry engendered thereby and the effect of all this on his own catholic relations in Munster. But outside of Munster, while it could not be said that the catholic question had made much advance, neither was there much attempt to enforce the penal laws, if we except the activities of the discoverers. Apart from commissioning the protestant Henry Brooke to write his series of Farmer's Letters on *The case of the Roman Catholics of Ireland*, the Catholic Committee remained particularly quiet during the first seven years of its existence, but this was due largely to Archbishop Lincoln's opposition to the committee – for the same reason that he opposed any semblance, however mild, of catholic agitation – and to the association's own embarrassment with the activities of the Whiteboys. After ten years of pamphleteering, with not much to show for it, Charles O'Conor confessed disillusionment: 'for my part I have done with these affairs' he complained, 'my efforts have only gained me ill-will from many of our own people'.[11] Archbishop Lincoln continued his peculiar stance with, in March 1762, an exhortation read in all the Dublin chapels for the king's success in war and the peace of these kingdoms, as well as for the spiritual and temporal happiness of the Royal Family and of the lord lieutenant.[12]

Lincoln's death in 1763 coincided with the end of the Seven Years War. Said to be the son of a ploughman from Clonsilla, county Dublin, the new archbishop, Patrick Fitzsimons, was more sympathetic to the active pursuit of catholic goals and to the participation therein of the catholic clergy. He was accused, even in reports to the Vatican, of being 'the author of the oath of allegiance',[13] presumably from the part he had played initially in Hamilton's first bill. With the new archbishop of Armagh, Blake, content to cling to his Galway home and only rarely make an appearance in his diocese, primatial authority in Ireland in Fitzsimons's time and for many years thereafter lay virtually with the archbishop of Dublin.

---

10 Burke, Edmund, *The works of Edmund Burke*, London 1812, vol. 6, passim.
11 Ward, R.E. et al. (eds), op. cit., 96.   12 Brady, John, op. cit., 103.   13 Fenning, Hugh (ed.), 'Documents of Irish interest in the Fondo Missioni of the Vatican Archives' in *Archivium Hibernicum*, vol. 49 (1995), 17.

In the early 1760s the continuing war in Europe and elsewhere led to a manpower problem for the British Army, and catholics in Ireland, who hitherto had been ineligible for membership, began to be looked upon as a possible source of new recruits. Lord Trimleston opportunely put forward a proposal for raising Irish catholic regiments for the King's service, and to get around the prohibition on catholics joining, the British government proposed in 1762 that the regiments raised should be allocated to Britain's catholic ally, Portugal. The agrarian disturbances in Munster and the anti-catholic feeling thereby aroused in the Irish parliament, as well as the fact that the war was coming to an end, ensured that the proposal was not proceeded with.[14] But Ireland as a potential source of manpower for the British Army became an important factor in influencing the British government towards the need to cosset the catholic majority in Ireland whatever the feelings of the Irish parliament might be. It should be remembered that, with an Irish population at this time of about 3m,[15] about 2.3m of whom were catholics, and the population of Britain no more than 8m, the size of the Irish population *vis-à-vis* the British was proportionately of far more significance than it is today. On the catholic side the death of James Stuart in January 1766 and the non-recognition by the pope of his successor, Charles Edward, as king of Great Britain and Ireland was a further factor in easing the relationship of Irish catholics, particularly the clergy, with the British and Irish administrations. With the ending of the Stuart nomination of Irish catholic bishops, Irish catholics had at last been relieved of the deadly mill-stone of the Stuarts.

The earl of Halifax was succeeded as lord lieutenant by the marquess of Hertford but he resigned in 1766 after staying for only one session of parliament. His successor, Lord Bristol, was appointed lord lieutenant in August 1766 on the expectation that he would live in Ireland for the full period of his viceroyalty and not simply during parliamentary sessions as had been the practice hitherto. With a full-time lord lieutenant the old system of conducting business in the Irish parliament through what were known as undertakers, would be ended and the authority and interest of the British government would be re-established in Ireland. Bristol was to continue his predecessor's conciliatory policy towards catholics, but as their part of the bargain he would require from catholics a special oath of allegiance to the king.

Lord Bristol had a brother, Frederick Augustus Hervey, who was destined to play an important role in Irish affairs. The Herveys had their family seat at Ickworth in Suffolk. Frederick was born in 1730, was educated at Cambridge university and studied initially for the law before deciding on a clerical career.

14 Wall, M., op. cit., 119.   15 See note 9 for Chapter 3 where the population of Ireland in the 1730s is estimated at 2.4m. The estimate of 3m. for the 1760s has regard to K.H. Connell's estimate of 3.48m. for 1767 which is now generally considered an overestimate.

As will be seen he was chaplain to his brother, the lord lieutenant, before being appointed bishop of Cloyne in February 1767 and bishop of Derry in February 1768. The latter was a highly lucrative post which he was to retain until his death in 1803. He was responsible for some useful public works in Derry, including a bridge over the Foyle, and he took a keen interest in the welfare of his clergy. He was opposed to the tithe system, advocating that each vicar be provided with a farm of land instead. In December 1779 he succeeded to the earldom of Bristol on the death of his elder brother. Although he did not join the Volunteers until 1782, he nevertheless played a prominent role at the Volunteer Convention in Dublin in 1783. He advocated electoral reform and favoured the enfranchisement of catholics. With the collapse of the Volunteer movement he ceased to play any significant part in Irish politics, although he voted by proxy for the Union. He spent a large part of his life travelling on the continent, particularly in Italy, where at one level he was associating freely with cardinals, archbishops and even the pope and at another level with women of easy virtue. He died at Albano, near Rome in 1803. A highly colourful, larger-than-life figure, possessed of great resources of generosity and liberality, nevertheless Charlemont's estimate of the private man was no doubt accurate: 'He was a bad father, a worse husband, a determined deist, blasphemous in his conversation and greatly addicted to intrigue and gallantry'.[16]

It is said that the king himself asked Lord Bristol to appoint Frederick as his (Bristol's) chaplain for his period as lord lieutenant.[17] Frederick Hervey was holidaying in Italy at this time but apparently he was informed about his appointment as chaplain without delay, for he was able to inform his daughter of it in autumn 1766. It is probable that Bristol when informing his brother of his appointment assigned him also the task of formulating an oath of allegiance for catholics. It is difficult otherwise to explain why on his way home from Italy Hervey took time off to visit the principal Irish seminaries in France and Irish émigrés there in order to obtain their views on such an oath and what it should contain. Hervey also consulted at this time the French Cardinal de Bernis, Archbishop Arthur Dillon of Narbonne and Abbé Colbert.[18]

Despite the expectation that he would as lord lieutenant live permanently in Ireland, Lord Bristol in fact never came to Ireland. With the prospect of a new session of the Irish parliament opening in the autumn of 1767, a session which as lord lieutenant he would have to attend, he resigned his post in July 1767. But he had already secured the appointment as bishop of Cloyne for his brother in February 1767. The latter had apparently gone about the preparation of an oath for catholics with considerable alacrity. He must have had a draft available early in 1767, for Archbishop Fitzsimons of Dublin, writing to

16 *Dictionary of national biography.*   17 Frederick Hervey had been a royal chaplain – hence his influence with the king.   18 Walsh, John R., *Frederick Augustus Hervey 1730–1803*, Maynooth 1972, passim.

the Brussels nuncio in December 1768, states that he first saw a draft of the oath around the begining of the previous year.[19]

Hervey's proposals for an oath, as they were afterwards conveyed to the nuncio at Brussels, are set out as an Appendix to this chapter. He at a later date summarised these proposals as follows: – (a) an oath of allegiance, (b) an abjuration of the Stuart pretender and his family, (c) renunciation of the pope's temporal supremacy, of his power to depose monarchs and to absolve their subjects from their allegiance, (d) renunciation of the pope's personal infallibility and of his superiority over general councils of the church, (f) renunciation of the 'detestable doctrine' that no faith was to be kept with heretics and (g) disowning of mental reservations.[20] He communicated the proposed oath to Archbishop Fitzsimons and these two later had meetings at which they examined the proposals. Fitzsimons agreed to communicate the proposals to the other bishops and to certain of the catholic laity. After an interval of six weeks, according to Hervey, Fitzsimons reported back to him that, while there was a great variety of opinions, the majority of those consulted were prepared to take the oath. (We shall see later that the situation as outlined by Fitzsimons was somewhat different.) Hervey inferred that those clergy educated by the Jesuits in Spain and at Rome held firmly for the temporal rights of the pope, while the majority who were educated in France were generally in favour of the oath proposed.[21]

In his presentation of the draft oath to opposing catholic and protestant interests, Hervey was guilty of considerable double-dealing. In comments intended for protestant consumption he observed in regard to the dissension the draft oath had produced in catholic ranks:

> But dissension was the very object of this test because it is apprehended that such a schism produced among a party once so united will be a thunder-stroke to all that sect and be the strongest security to the Protestant interest, and the most effectual safeguard against a foreign invasion.[22]

On the other hand, in a letter dated 31 October 1767 probably to Fitzsimons, he held out to catholics 'the free exercise of their religion, the liberty of purchasing and inheriting lands and in general an exemption from all penal laws'. He continued:

> I am in hopes too that your clergy will be reasonable and ready to render unto Caesar the things that are Caesar's. But under pretence of rendering unto God the things that are God's, let them not intrude on us the Court

19 Moran, Patrick F. (ed.), *Spicilegium Ossoriense*, Dublin 1874–84, vol. 3, 315–7, where this letter, which is in Latin, is incorrectly attributed to Archbishop John Carpenter. 20 Walsh, J.R., op. cit., 15–16. 21 Ibid., 17. 22 Ibid., 18.

of Rome and call it the Church of Rome. In all spirituals let them listen to
the Church, but in all temporals, directly or indirectly, let them obey the
powers that be, for they are of God.[23]

Elsewhere Hervey stated that the privileges to be accorded to catholics who
took the oath were (a) a legal but decent exercise of their religion by registered
priests in registered chapels, together with a small government stipend for such
priests, and (b) a liberty for catholics to purchase such lands only as were forfeited in the great rebellion of 1641.[24] The state of play on the evolution of
the draft oath in 1767, as understood on the catholic side, was later summarised
by the leading secular clergy of Dublin as follows:

> What happened in 1767 under Archbishop Fitzsimons? Bishop Hervey was
> brother of the viceroy. The viceroy was well-disposed but required an oath
> of allegiance. We consulted with the regular clergy. The archbishop framed
> an oath in consequence, but we never saw it. Bishop Hervey and the
> Internuncio were in correspondence about the Four Gallican Articles, but
> what happened we do not know.[25]

Some time in the spring or summer of 1768 Hervey's proposals found their
way to the Brussels nuncio, Tomaso Ghilini. In a letter dated 14 October 1768,
addressed to the four metropolitans, but sent to Archbishop Fitzsimons in
Dublin, Ghilini set out in unequivocal terms the Vatican reaction to the proposals, or rather what Ghilini considered the Vatican reaction should be.[26] He
felt compelled, he said, to rouse the zeal of the four metropolitans in the face
of the gravest misfortune which had been contemplated, and in part executed,
for the spiritual damnation of their wretched Christian people. The most worthy witnesses had reported to him in all truth that a certain formula of an oath
had been conceived by an heretical man, drawn up by the same heretical hand
and offered by him to the catholics of Ireland on the flattering pretext that, if
they offered such an oath to the government, they could reasonably hope that
the penal laws, under which they had groaned for a such long time, would be
revoked. It was next put to him (nuncio) that some people, not only laity but
also ecclesiastics and even bishops, had already approved of this oath, so
thoughtlessly as not even to have blushed, and that others still were prepared

23 Ibid., 12–13. 24 Ibid., 15–16. 25 Archives of Propaganda Fide (APF), SC Irlanda
12, ff 513–14, NLI Pos. 5377. Letter from eight Dublin canons to Brussels nuncio
dated 3 March 1770. 26 Burke, Thomas, *Supplementum Hiberniae Dominicanae*, 1772,
925–7. This is a summary of Ghilini's letter which is in Latin. Ghilini's championing
of the papal deposing and dispensing powers has to be viewed in the context that the
reigning pope, Clement XIV, was later (1777) seen in his published letters to have dis-
claimed all jurisdiction over the temporal rights of princes.

to do so. He ought to be concerned that so great an irregularity was so commonplace that it would become quite widespread in a short time.

If the government brought in 'this pernicious novelty', Ghilini claimed, and enforced the taking of the new oath by threatening to banish those catholics who refused it, no catholic worthy of the name would surender to such irrational violence. Catholics, accustomed to suffer for a long time already with the greatest edification and exceptional constancy the penal laws in force, which though severe were not entirely hostile to the profession and exercise of the catholic religion, now with an incredible submission of mind submitted themselves voluntarily to a man from the flock of the so-called Reformation, urging them to carry out a public act condemned by many catholic leaders. This was the greatest deviation of all and indeed so intolerable and scandalous that the Holy See, the guardian of the integrity of the catholic religion, could on no account ignore it and felt compelled to restrain it with a public censure.

Ghilini was particularly incensed with the part of the proposed oath where the swearer was required to state that he abhorred, detested and denied from the bottom of his heart the pernicious and abominable doctrine that faith must not be kept with heretics or that princes excommunicated by the pope may be deposed or killed by their subjects. This doctrine, he said, had been defended and championed by very many catholic nations and the Apostolic See had often followed it in practice; it was foolhardy for a catholic man to declare it detestable and abominable and such a declaration was rash, false, scandalous and injurious to the Holy See.

He was very concerned by the requirement to take the oath acording to the sense intended by the legislature of Ireland because, since the laws of England and Ireland recognised the king as head of the church and fountain of all its spiritual authority, it followed that he who swears such an oath and promises fidelity to the king according to the prescripts of the legislature of Ireland, must thereby recognise the king as head of the church and fountain of all spiritual authority. If this was or could be the meaning of this requirement, then the metropolitans and catholics generally ought to realise that this was a manifest error and contrary to the principles of the catholic religion, which acknowledges one only head and fountain of all spititual authority, that is, the Roman Pontiff. Hence the proposed oath, by reason of this provision, was blameworthy and detestable since it called on God as a witness and a champion of the error.

Ghilini emphasises with what bitter sorrow the most pious mind of the Holy Father was upset when it came to his ears that the Irish catholic laity, ecclesiastics and bishops even, had offered to the government to take such an irregular and reprehensible oath. He recalled that in former times Irish catholics had not troubled the Holy See but had listened to her advice in accordance with the most laudable spirit of the filial observance and subordination owed to the vicar of Jesus Christ, their pastor and head, and of that conformity with which everyone ought to serve the centre of catholic union, and which was professed with exceptional veneration by the renowned Irish nation, with such glory to its immortal name.

Lest he should be seen in a matter so grave to fail in his duty, he considered it indispensable to write these things to the Metropolitans, so that he might excite their pastoral zeal. They should recall to their duty, with a view to repairing the scandal given, those who had already agreed to such an oath, which, just as it was illicit in its totality, so by its nature was invalid, null and void of value in so far as it could bind and oblige consciences. They were to see to it that it was made known by every opportune, efficacious and prudent means to their own suffragan bishops, and through them to all the faithful, how this new formula of an oath had originated and what a grave sin those, who were either preparing to take it or unfortunately had already taken it, had committed. Hence the metropolitans ought to incite everyone to continue to endure the penal laws, which up to then they had endured with such laudable constancy, rather than free themselves from the same by taking refuge in an illicit and sinful oath, with such damnation of their own souls and of that religion which was so insensibly and insidiously threatened that it would perish in the hearts of those catholics, unless they listened with benign ears to the true and safe doctrine of their true father and Supreme Pastor, rather than to the fallacious suggestions of the enemies of their Holy Catholic Religion.

Fitzsimons replied to the nuncio in a letter dated 20 December 1768.[27] Around the beginning of the previous year (1767) several formularies of an oath of loyalty to the king were shown to him and very great advantages were promised to catholics if only they would give some satisfactory oath to the government. In view of the importance of the matter he wrote to the other archbishops urging them and their suffragans to come to Dublin to discuss the best course of action. Meanwhile, since the author of the formularies (Bishop Hervey) constantly importuned him, and many of the catholic laity urged him to declare his thoughts on the question as early as possible, he called a meeting of some of the principal clergy of Dublin, both secular and regular. They weighed the formularies word by word and amended what they considered absolutely in need of correction. They thought that with such emendation, the resulting oath might be taken with a safe conscience and without injury to the faith, but awaited the opinion of the absent bishops rather than take any rash step in so serious a matter.

Fitzsimons went on to state that there were present at this discussion two bishops, then by chance in Dublin, who approved of the opinion of the others, although one of them afterwards absolutely denied among his friends that

---

27 Moran, P.F., op. cit. vol. 3, pp. 315–17. I am indebted to Fr H. Fenning for help in the translation of Fitzsimons's letter which is in Latin.

he ever consented. Certain of the laity, sick of their own disabilities and avid for any kind of relief, immediately reported this common opinion of all to the author of the formularies. Further progress, he said, was not made with that oath, nor up to that time was it proferred, nor could it be proferred to any catholic, because it had not yet been laid before parliament, then on the point of prorogation, nor had it obtained the force of law. He had yet to learn what further steps might be taken, but some thought that in the next session the oath would be aired again and perhaps passed into law. But whatever might happen that oath, there was no reason for the nuncio to be in the least solicitous about the recognition of the king as the spiritual head of the church. Rather, in the appendix to the oath, the primacy of the church was expressly accorded to the Roman pontiff and denied to the king by catholics.

The certain right of the Supreme Pontiff in the temporalities of kings had been bitterly defended by scholars and theologians of the first note, but Fitzsimons regretted to say that the opinions of these had been little regarded by the Irish faithful. These latter were more concerned with the penal laws, the hatred implacably conceived against themselves, persecutions, spoliation of property and the many other evils which from the beginning of the so-called Reformation to the present day stretched out interminably. They were pre-pared to compromise to an extent on their religious principles in return for toleration by parliament; they thought it preferable to surrender in some wise to the will of the authorities rather than that the catholic religion should be utterly extirpated in Ireland.

In Fitzsimons's opinion no one, whether bishops or ecclesiastics, approved of the Gallican Propositions attached by way of an appendix to the proposed oath. It was accepted that many of them, while they climbed the academic grades in French universities, subscribed to these propositions in line with the practice of other academics, but they believed sincerely, no less than the grad-uates of other countries, that no serious note was taken of their subscribing, having regard to the obedience due to the [French] monarch, and the fact that their action led to nothing more than contentions and discords with the 'incen-diaries' [regulars].

The foregoing and many other things, Fitzsimons wrote, were conveyed to the author of the formularies by certain intermediaries but he (Hervey) insist-ed that these propositions had been accepted for a long time by the French clergy, that they would soon be accepted by the clergy of Spain, Portugal and other kingdoms and that they must be subscribed to in their entirety, nor less accepted, by the Irish clergy. The nuncio would do them a very great favour if he would deign to suggest some plausible excuse, to be offered to the Irish government, to explain why the Irish clergy could not agree to propositions which were upheld by the ecclesiastics of other kingdoms who continued to enjoy the grace and communion of the Holy See.

Fitzsimons would have liked to have seen the Irish archbishops and their suffragans declaring their opinions openly on this subject. Only the archbishop of Armagh (Blake) had declared his views frankly and he had said that the oath, if slightly amended, would displease him very little. Fitzsimons judged that the amendment suggested by Armagh was not only just but very necessary. The other bishops, to judge from the reports of their opinions, were, according to Fitzsimons, solely solicitous of how much advantage would accrue to themselves from such an oath. He had commended the nuncio's principles seriously to his own suffragans, from whom he expected nothing other than that they should not fail in their duty when needed.

In the foregoing letter Fitzsimons was clearly at pains to play down the part he had played himself in favour of the oath. For example, there is no mention of a letter he wrote to Hervey through an intermediary in February 1768 in which he gave it as his expectation that the majority of catholics would accept the oath proposed by Hervey.[28]

In a further letter to Ghilini dated March 1769 Fr Richard Reynolds, vicar general of Dublin, stated on behalf of Fitzsimons that there had been no change since the latter's letter of 20 December 1768 in regard to the oath of allegiance, nor did Fitzsimons know what parliament, which was not due to meet until the following October (1769), would think of it.[29] Fitzsimons died in November 1769 and was succeeded as archbishop by John Carpenter, a Dublin tailor's son.

The views of James Butler I, archbishop of Cashel, and of the Munster bishops generally on the proposed oath, as conveyed to Ghilini in May 1769, were much more forthright than those of Fitzsimons. Butler said that he had read the formularies of the oath 'with indignant eyes', obnoxious as it was to the rights of the Holy See and so little in accord with dogma. He abhorred those who were prepared to accept such an oath. The copy of the oath sent to him from Dublin was, he said, much like that enclosed with the nuncio's letter of 14 October 1768. All his suffragans rejected the proposed oath, especially the bishop of Cork (John Butler) who called his clergy together to consider it.[30]

The extent to which Hervey had involved the catholic laity in these negotiations was at this point rather insignificant.[31] There is little evidence of consultation with the Catholic Committee nor with such catholic activists as Charles O'Conor and John Curry. Certainly, O'Conor, writing to Curry on 9 December 1767, implied that he had not been consulted when he stated:

---

28 Walsh, John R., op. cit., 18.   29 Fenning, H., op. cit., in *Archivium Hibernicum*, vol. 49 (1995), 29.   30 Ibid., 29–30.   31 I note, however, that Mrs M. Wall states (*Catholic Ireland in the eighteenth century*, p. 110) that 'early in 1768 Viscount Taaffe, together with prominent members of the Catholic Committee, were in consultation with ... the bishop of Derry on the wording of a test oath', but she does not give her source for this. Curry's letter of 9 July 1768 below does not imply any great involvement by Taaffe or the Catholic Committee with Hervey in this matter. Nor is there any reference to such an involvement in O'Conor's correspondence at the time in question.

In passing a test for our people (if any such should be in agitation) I apprehend that the practice in Holland and Germany will not influence much; pride mixes here as in other things, men choosing rather in such cases to make than follow precedents. Assuredly they will throw in an abjuration of the exiled family.[32]

In the same letter he again suggested, in a passage already quoted in Chapter 3, Fr Cornelius Nary's form of oath as the most suitable for catholics. O'Conor was later forwarded the form of oath being proposed by Hervey, when Curry wrote to O'Conor on 9 July 1768:

I gave Lord Taaffe the printed copy of the bishop of Dery's oath of allegiance which he will let our masters on the other side of the water know that we are ready to take on the approbation of our clergy, and he is prepared to make proper animadversions on the Gallican propositions which the bishop has luckily I think got printed on the opposite column – your and my friend, the worthy Mr Carpenter [later archbishop], will pay you a visit at your delightful hermitage in less than a fortnight and oh that I could be of the party.[33]

Curry wrote this note on the back of a printed copy of Hervey's proposed oath. It is strange that, although O'Conor in a letter to Curry on 12 August, reported that Carpenter had just arrived with him, he has nothing at all to say about Hervey's oath.[34] This oath, as it appears in this printed version, was an amalgam of the first and second formularies (see appendix), said to have emanated from Hervey, which Ghilini appended to his letter of 14 October 1768, summarised above. Hervey was particularly crass and insensitive when he headed this printed formulary 'An oath of allegiance, abjuration and *supremacy*' (italics mine); although the contents of the oath did not justify the inclusion of the word 'supremacy' in the title, he should have known that that word had a connotation sufficient of itself to damn the oath in catholic eyes.

As to why Hervey should have seen fit to more or less ignore the catholic laity and cultivate Archbishop Fitzsimons, he may have seen in Fitzsimons a man with whom he could do business and he probably also took the view that the catholic clergy, rather than the laity, were the ones to be convinced; if he could get the agreement of the clergy, the laity would present no problem. He did, however, have correspondence with the earl of Kenmare, who was emerging as a principal catholic leader. Kenmare in a letter from Lille in France in January 1768 welcomed Hervey's formularies but felt that the time was not ripe because of expected opposition in the Irish parliament.[35]

32 Ward, R.E. et al. (eds), op. cit., 211. 33 Royal Irish Academy MS B.i.2. 34 Ward, R.E. et al. (eds), op. cit., 213. 35 Walsh, J.R., op. cit., 18.

To revert to the lord lieutenant and the administration generally, Lord Townshend replaced Lord Bristol in August 1767. Townshend showed some initial, if simplistic, interest in the catholic question when he enquired from George Faulkner, the printer, as to where he could get a copy of the penal laws against catholics. The first lord lieutenant to occupy that post on a permanent basis, Townshend spent most of his five year stint in endeavouring to bring the power brokers in the Irish parliament to heel, in re-asserting the status and power of the lord lieutenant and in securing the English interest in Ireland. He was by all accounts well-disposed to catholics, but, constantly engrossed in a cat-and-mouse game with parliament, it was difficult for him to find the time or the opportunity to foster legislation for the relief of catholics, although a minor relief bill was put through in 1771, under which catholics were to be allowed to reclaim bogland. He was also instrumental in negativing two quarterage bills inimical to catholic interests, in 1768 when such a bill was thrown out by the English privy council through his 'benevolent intervention' and again in 1772 when another such bill was not trnasmitted to London.[36] But the principal legacy of Townshend's viceroyalty, as far as catholics were concerned, was that, by maximising the authority of the lord lieutenant, he paved the way for the administration, pending the advent of Grattan's Parliament, to push catholic relief measures through parliament despite the opposition of the members.

It does not appear that there was any opportunity of introducing a catholic oath bill in parliament during 1768 or 1769. The 1769 session turned out to be a brief one when, faced with the intransigence of its members, Townshend prorogued parliament in December 1769 and it did not meet again until early in 1771. Hervey had hopes that the heads of a catholic oath bill might be introduced in 1771 but was disabused of this by the duke of Leinster, who himself favoured an oath for catholics but believed that opposition to it in parliament continued to be too great.[37]

Later in 1771 Hervey went to Rome where he had several interviews with the pope when the question of an oath for Irish catholics was discussed. In April 1772 he set out for home but on the way he delayed for some time in France, notably with Cardinal Rochefoucauld of Rouen and did not arrive in Ireland until the autumn of 1773.[38]

Lord Townshend was succeeded by the earl of Harcourt as lord lieutenant in October 1772 and he was to remain in that post until 1776. An amiable, easy-going man, with no great ambition, Harcourt was content to carry out the orders of his masters in London and to continue the policy of his predecessor towards keeping the Irish parliament in check. The trouble in the American colonies, which was fast approaching a state of war between Britain and the

36 Wall, M., op. cit., 68–9.   37 Walsh, J.R., op. cit., 19.   38 Ibid., 19–20.

colonists, and the necessity to commit such a large number of troops so far from home, meant that a peaceful Ireland was essential if troops, badly needed in America, were not to be tied up in Ireland.

But although the middle and upper class catholics presented Harcourt with an address of welcome, emphasising their eagerness to express their loyalty by a test which would engage their civil duty without interfering with the religion of their consciences,[39] the situation of the lower class of catholic, particularly in Munster, was rather different. A contemporary account tells us that

a huge multitude of the destitute country people and of the lowest class of Catholic principally in this southern province and in neighbouring regions, disturbed for a long time the peace of the Kingdom with turbulent assemblies, nocturnal robberies and diverse crimes. Since they raged mostly against those who collected tithes for Protestant ministers, at the suggestion of our enemies the suspicion was forthwith mooted and propagated that the Roman Catholics contemplated something abominable.[40]

Harcourt was already twelve months in Ireland when he opened the 1773–74 session of parliament on 12 October 1773. He was under orders from London to bring in that session an act of a soothing and conciliatory tendency towards catholics.[41] Activists on the catholic side did not, however, have any such expectations. Charles O'Conor, writing to John Curry on 2 October 1773, stated that 'it was not indeed likely that our masters here will soon call upon us for a civil test of allegiance, as admitted by our religious principles'.[42] The hierarchy were still divided on the question of a renunciation of the papal deposing and dispensing powers. Burke of Ossory attempted to advance his opposition to such a renunciation and indeed to any oath of allegiance for catholics by publishing, in a supplement to his *Hibernia Dominicana* in 1772, nuncio Ghilini's uncompromising letter of 14 October 1768 to the four metropolitans, already outlined. Bishop O'Keeffe of Kildare, the same who was a signatory of the Trimblestown pastoral in 1757, was critical of Burke's upmanship in publishing Ghilini's letter, but O'Conor counselled that ' in the present temper and constitution of legislative minds, all that we offer on the subject of the Doctor's [Burke's] book should be only whispered among ourselves'.[43]

It must have come as something of a surprise, then, for O'Conor when, late in January 1774, Hervey sent him the following invitation, dated simply

39 Wall, M., op. cit., 122–3. 40 Moran, P.F., op. cit., vol. 3, 342. Letter in Latin dated 4 October 1776 from James Butler II, archbishop of Cashel, to Cardinal Protector Castelli. In this letter, which will be presented in summary later, Butler outlines the position in Munster for three to four years previously. The organisation behind the disturbances mentioned in this extract was of course the Whiteboys. 41 Mitchel, J., op. cit., 113. 42 Ward, R.E. et al. (eds.), 298. 43 Ibid., 297.

'Thursday noon'. O'Conor, on a visit to Dublin, was staying with his friend
Thomas Lee, merchant, in Pill Lane.

> The Bishop of Derry presents his compliments to Mr O'Connor and would
> be much obliged to him if he could take his breakfast with him at Barry
> house tomorrow morning, or if he could be kind enough to call on the bish-
> op at any hour in the course of the morning that he would be kind enough
> to name.[44]

At this initial meeting, at which there may have been other catholic representatives present besides O'Conor, Hervey recommended 'the propriety of our
[i.e. catholics] giving a Test of our allegiance to his Majesty, urging at the same
time that a declaration of our being united with our fellow subjects in the same
summary of civil faith might entitle us to some relaxation of those Penal Laws,
which tie up the hands of industry among a million of people in this ill-fated
country'.[45] It appears from subsequent correspondence that Hervey put forward, either at this meeting or at a later date, a draft oath.

Hervey's approach was brought to the attention of the Catholic Committee,
which at its meeting on 3 February 1774 in the Committee Room in Essex
Street 'resolved that it was expedient at that time for the catholics of Ireland
to prepare a profession of their civil principles' and that Charles O'Conor, Dr
Curry, Thomas Roche, James Reynolds, Thomas Braughall, Christopher Reilly
and Martin Gaven should prepare the same and lay it before the committee.[46]
Towards the end of February there was a confidential letter from Hervey to
O'Conor, the details of which have not been discovered.[47] There was a further
meeting of the Catholic Committee on Thursday 3 March when the subcom-
mitee appointed on 3 February reported back to the Committee, which after
consideration approved of the form of oath set out below.[48]

---

44 Royal Irish Academy MS B.i.2. The Catholic Committee responded to Hervey's
contact with O'Conor at their meeting on Thursday 3 February 1774. Hervey's invitation to O'Conor, dated simply 'Thursday noon', would therefore have been written
on Thursday 27 January or possibly on the Thursday before that, 20 January. O'Conor
was apparently incorrect in his recollection (in letter dated 20 March 1774 to Daniel
MacNamara, agent of the Catholic Committee in London) that Hervey had applied to
him and other catholics 'in February last'.   45 Ward, R.E. et al. (ed.), op. cit., 309.
46 Edwards, R.D. (ed.), 'Minute book of the Catholic Committee' in *Archivium
Hibernicum*, vol. 9 (1942), 16.   47 Ward, R.E. et al. (ed.), op. cit., 306.   48 The oath
proposed by the Catholic Committee was worded as follows: 'I, A.B., do take Almighty
God and his only son, Jesus Christ my Redeemer to witness, that I will be faithful and
bear true allegiance to our most gracious sovereign King George the third, and him
will defend to the utmost of my power, against all conspiracies and attempts whatever, that shall be made against his person, crown or dignity, and that I will do my utmost
to disclose and make known to his Majesty, all treasons which may be formed against

With regard to consultation with Archbishop Carpenter, the minutes of the Catholic Committee state that, some days before the meeting on 3 March, Carpenter was shown a somewhat different form of oath from that set out below and it was approved by him. When representatives of the association later consulted him about the form below, Carpenter is reported to have said: 'It is the same in substance with the former, you need not have brought it to me.' The representatives concluded from this that the archbishop had agreed that the form of oath below was 'orthodox'.[49]

Immediately after the meeting on 3 March O'Conor sent a copy of the Catholic Committee's form of oath to Hervey,[50] while, in a letter to Hervey, O'Conor mentioned, *inter alia*, that in renouncing the papal deposing power in this draft, they had overcome some qualms about mentioning the pope by name. They had no such difficulty in renouncing by name the Stuart claimant, Charles Edward, but they questioned whether he had in fact assumed the title of Charles III, as stated in Hervey's formulary.[51] They felt that this should be re-worded to read 'is said to have assumed the style and title of king of Great Britain and Ireland by the name of Charles III'. They agreed that the doctrine that 'no faith was to be kept with heretics' was unchristian and impious, but they disagreed that this doctrine could be grounded in the 19th session of the Council of Constance, as stated in Hervey's formulary.

him: and I do faithfully promise to maintain, support and defend to the utmost of my power, the succession to the crown in his Majesty's family, against any person whatever: hereby utterly renouncing and abjuring any obedience or allegiance unto the person, who is said to have assumed the stile and title of King of England, by the name of Charles the third; and to every other person claiming or pretending a right to the crown of these realms.

'And I do declare that I do not believe that the pope of Rome, or any other foreign prince, state or potentate, hath any temporal or civil jurisdiction, power, superiority or pre-eminence, directly or indirectly within this realm.

'I do also declare, that I do reject and detest, as unchristian and impious to believe that it is lawful to murder or destroy any person or persons whatever, for or under the pretence of being heretics; and also that unchristian and impious principle, that no faith is to be kept with heretics.

'I further declare, that it is no article of my faith, and that I renounce the opinion, that princes excommunicated by a pope, or by a pope and council, or by any authority of the see of Rome, or by any authority whatsoever, may be deposed or murdered by their subjects or any person whatever: and therefore I do promise, that I will not hold, maintain or abet such an opinion, or any other opinion, contrary to what is expressed in this declaration.

'Lastly, I do solemnly profess that I make this declaration, in the plain and ordinary sense of the words, without any evasion, equivocation or mental reservation: and I firmly believe that no pope or council, or any power on earth, can absolve or dispense with me, in the obligation I contract by this oath, or any part thereof. So help me God.'

49 Edwards, R.D. (ed.), op. cit., 19–20.   50 Ward, R.E. et al (eds.), op. cit., 309. 51 Ibid., 306–9.

Events moved very quickly after that for, according to O'Conor, the Association 'heard no more of it [their draft oath] or very little more of it' before Robert French,[52] member for Roscommon county, on 7 March 1774 presented to the house of commons heads of a bill to enable his Majesty's subjects of whatever persuasion to testify their allegiance to him. By 15 March a committee of the whole house had gone through the heads and French was ready to report back to the house. French duly reported from the committee on 16 March, when the proposed oath was read to a 'thin' house. After some slight amendments of the oath, the heads were passed and it was ordered that French should attend the lord lieutenant and desire him to transmit the heads of bill to Britain in due form.[53]

On return from London the bill, now duly approved by the English privy council, passed through all stages in the house of commons between 19 and 23 May when it was sent to the house of lords for their concurrence.[54] It was shepherded through the lords by Lord Longford and was passed on 23 May. With several other bills it was given the royal assent by the lord lieutenant on 2 June 1774.[55]

The act was short and to the point. The preamble, or section 1, adverted to the situation where many of his Majesty's subjects were desirous to testify their loyalty and allegiance to him and their abhorrence of certain doctrines imputed to them, but because of their religious tenets were by the laws then in being prevented from giving public assurances of such allegiance, and of their real principles, goodwill and affection towards their protestant fellow subjects. It was expedient, therefore, that legislation be enacted to give such persons an opportunity of testifying their allegiance to his Majesty and their goodwill towards the constitution, and, further, to promote peace and industry among the inhabitants of the kingdom.

The preamble went on to provide that from 1 June 1774 any person professing the popish religion could take the oath and declaration set out in the act (and printed below) before a judge in the court of king's bench in Dublin, or before a justice of the peace of the county in which he resided, or before a magistrate of the city or town corporate in which he resided. The second and only other section of the act provided for the furnishing annually of lists of papists, who had taken the oath, to the clerk of the privy council, or his deputy – these lists to show the quality, condition, title and place of abode of such papists.[56]

---

52 Ibid., 309. O'Conor here seems to be implying that there was a sizeable interval between the date on which he presented the Committee's form of oath to Hervey and the presentation of the heads of bill in the commons on 7 March. In fact only a weekend was involved and O'Conor appears to be here attempting to cloak the dilatoriness of the committe in drawing up their form of oath.   53 *Commons Journal Ireland*, vol. 9, part 1, 116–30.   54 Ibid., 147–53.   55 *Lords Journal Ireland*, vol. 4, 785.   56 Irish Statutes, 13 & 14 George III c. 35, an act to permit his Majesty' subjects of whatever

Many catholics were dissatisfied with the form of oath passed by parliament. They had hoped, according to Charles O'Conor, that the Catholic Committee formulary would be adopted without change, but they were to find that it was only used as a groundwork into which interpolations were made by the house. Indeed, the Catholic Committee took the precaution to put printed copies of their formulary into the hands of several leading members of parliament and some were 'just enough to confess nothing stronger or more express could be required from men of our principles'.[57] But the majority judged otherwise and the interpolations mentioned took place. However, the single objection mentioned by O'Conor at the stage when the bill was still being processed – he was to voice some others later – had to do with the expression 'no foreign

persuasion, to testify their allegiance to him. The new oath was worded as follows: 'I, A.B., do take almighty God and his only Son Jesus Christ my Redeemer to witness, that I will be faithful and bear true allegiance to our most gracious sovereign lord, King George the Third, and him will defend to the utmost of my power against all conspiracies and attempts whatever, that shall be made against his person, crown and dignity; and I will do my utmost endeavour to disclose and make known to his Majesty, and his heirs, all treasons and traitorous conspiracies which may be formed against him or them; and I do faithfully promise to maintain, support and defend, to the utmost of my power, the succession of the crown in his Majesty's family against any person or persons whatsoever, hereby utterly renouncing and abjuring any obedience or allegiance unto the person taking upon himself the stile and title of Prince of Wales, in the lifetime of his father, and who since his death is said to have assumed the stile and title of king of Great Britain and Ireland, by the name of Charles the Third, and to any other person claiming or pretending a right to the crown of these realms; and I do swear that I do reject and detest as unchristian and impious to believe, that it is lawful to murder or destroy any person or persons whatsoever, for or under pretence of their being heretics; and also, that unchristian and impious principle, that no faith is to be kept with heretics; I further declare, that it is no article of my faith, and that I do renounce, reject and abjure the opinion, that princes excommunicated by the pope and council, or by any authority of the see of Rome, or by any authority whatsoever, may be deposed or murdered by their subjects, or by any person whatsoever; and I do promise that I will not hold, maintain or abet, any such opinion, or any other opinion, contrary to what is expressed in this declaration; and I do declare, that I do not believe, that the pope of Rome, or any other foreign prince, prelate, state or potentate hath, or ought to have any temporal or civil jurisdiction, power, superiority or pre-eminence, directly or indirectly, within this realm; and I do solemnly, in the presence of God and of his only Son Jesus Christ, my Redeemer, profess, testify and declare, that I do make this declaration, and every part thereof, in the plain and ordinary sense of the words of this oath, without any evasion, equivocation or mental reservation whatever, and without any dispensation already granted by the pope or any authority of the see of Rome, or any person whatever; and without thinking that I am or can be acquitted before God or man, or absolved of this declaration, or any part thereof, although the pope, or any other person or persons, or authority whatsoever, shall dispense with or annul the same, or declare that it was null and void from the beginning. So help me God.' **57** Ward, R.E. et al. (eds), op. cit., 310.

prince or prelate hath, or ought to have, any jurisdiction ... ', where he contended that the words 'or ought to have' did not come properly or constitutionally out of the mouth of a Papist, 'a mere passive being in the community, who had certainly by the Constitution no right to declare who ought to have jurisdiction'.[58] It was an objection which can only be described as niggling and pettifogging.

On the question of whether the government took sufficient notice of the Catholic Committee's proposals, some blame must be ascribed to O'Conor and the committee for their dilatoriness in drafting their formulary. The handing over of this task to a sub-committee, which reported back to the main committee meeting normally only once a month, resulted in a whole month being lost and it meant that the government side had only a weekend in which to give consideration to the committee's proposals before the bill was introduced in the house on 7 March. Nor can it be said that the government completely ignored the Catholic Committee's proposals: these were taken on board to the extent that there was no reference to the Council of Constance in the oath included in the bill and the Committee's wording 'is said to have assumed the style and title' was accepted.

In a letter to Curry dated 8 July 1774 O'Conor further criticised the oath which by then had passed into law. He objected to catholics being required to swear 'that we have no previous absolutions for future occasional perjury when it is obvious that no law or oath on earth can bind any man who makes occasional perjury a principle of his religion'. He took exception to another proposition in the oath 'that no power whatsoever can dispense with this oath' since certainly the people of Great Britain could 'upon great emergency do it, as they have done recently in the code [sic] of the late King James'.[59]

In a letter dated 13 September 1774 'to a member of the Irish House of commons' and apparently intended for publication, though the member may have been imaginary, O'Conor praised the new oath as 'a noble effort of legislative wisdom'. The letter was said to be in response to a request from the member in question to sound out catholics on the subject of the oath. He stated that he could not find the slightest hesitation among the majority of catholics on the propriety of including in the oath an absolute renunciation of the pope's temporal power and of every other foreign pretender whatsoever. Catholics had expressed concern that tests of allegiance, found effectual for catholics in other protestant states, should not be deemed insufficient in their own. But O'Conor excused this by saying that Irish catholics, since they did not enjoy the privileges of citizens like their counterparts on the continent, required to be bound by stronger sanctions, 'it being natural to suppose that they are but little attached to a constitution from whose principal benefits they are legally excluded'. He

58 Ibid., 310. 59 Ibid., 312.

was prepared to grant that oversights in all new experiments were natural and might be easily supplied in a subsequent revision. While O'Conor presents himself in this letter as a liberal catholic engaged in arguing the case of the legislature against his less liberal co-religionists, he was not free from descending to what can only be described as a quibble when he objects to the absence of 'foreign' before 'authority' in the phrase 'that no authority whatsoever ...'.[60] One can call this sloppy drafting but that was about the size of it. With more plausible effect he argues against the provision in the oath to renounce any papal dispensations directed towards invalidating the effect of the oath, when he states:

They are sensibly grieved indeed when they are called upon to depose that they have no previous dispensation from the Pope for preconcerted treason or occasional perjury. Such an abjuration includes an odious charge, indecent in them to admit and the more, as it must help to confirm the idea many Protestants entertain that the charge has some foundation.[61]

In a subsequent letter to Curry in late September/early October 1774 he belittles his own efforts in this letter to a Member of the Irish House of Commons, arguing that a paper of such importance 'should come from the united strength of the most sensible men among us, not from the efforts of any single person'. He argues that this will have to be done without the assistance of the clergy, for 'they are coy, and some of the best have reason to be so till affairs come to a crisis'. He predicts (rightly, as it turned out) that Rome would not previously approve the oath but that she would 'ulteriorly acquiesce' and that this acquiescence would be sufficient for the Irish clergy. He is scathing about the Ghilinis of this world – 'the ignorant, dogmatic Ghillinis' – whose power he hopes is on the wane.[62]

But O'Conor continued to argue against catholics taking the new oath pending efforts to have amendments made in it in the next 1776–77 session of parliament. He feared 'lest some among us might be giddy enough to run Assizes and Quarter Sessions and subscribe before they took every caution to consult with their principals'.[63]

The new year of 1775 opened with not a single catholic having taken the oath. Hervey was plainly disappointed with catholic reaction and complained about their lack of courage and honesty in not taking the oath. He was later in July 1775 to make the valid point that there should be some advantage to be gained from taking the oath, and some disadvantage for not doing so, if the oath were to be successful.[64]

60 Ibid., 315–6. 61 Ibid., 317–8. 62 Ibid., 319–20. 63 Ibid., 321. 64 Walsh, J.R., op. cit., 23–5.

In June 1775, with a meeting of catholics scheduled for the Music Hall in Fishamble Street, Dublin to appoint a day for subscribing to the oath, O'Conor was still arguing against the oath in its then form.[65] He was to find himself over-ruled, however, when on 28 June 1775 'a very numerous and respectable body of Roman Catholic gentlemen', said to be led by Lord Trimleston and including John Curry, went to the court of king's bench in the Four Courts to take the oath.[66] On 5 August O'Conor wrote again to Curry hoping that their disagreement over the oath would not affect their friendship, but still insisting on his quibble that the word 'foreign' should be included in the oath.[67]

It is time to turn now to the attitude of the catholic hierarchy to the oath. Archbishop Carpenter of Dublin had opposed it from the beginning because it did not conform to the formulary prepared by the Catholic Committee which, as we have seen, had been agreed by him. He said in a letter to O'Conor in August 1775 that he had taken care to make his sentiments known to many of his brethren 'to prevent a division from taking place among us'. He added:

> But if some of them choose to differ in opinion from me, and to oppose [put forward] what I condemn, I have only to lament the misfortune of our disagreement in this point, my having done my duty, and that my behaviour on this occasion is certainly the most irreproachable and least exposed to error.[68]

Carpenter is here referring principally to the action of the Munster bishops who had taken a line on the oath diametrically opposite to his. James Butler I, archbishop of Cashel, had just been succeeded in that diocese by his namesake, James Butler II. The same name was about all these two archbishops shared, for while, as we have seen, James Butler I was vehemently opposed to the Hervey formularies of 1767–68, James Butler II was every bit as vehemently in favour of the oath passed by parliament in 1774. Descended from the house of Mountgarrett, James Butler II was a professor at the Jesuit College of St Omer in France when he was appointed coadjutor in Cashel in 1773. Whether designedly or not, he waited until the old archbishop had died before proceeding to the diocese where he took up residence in September 1774.[69] He came well versed in the pros and cons of the oath passed into law the previous June, and, with Butler flair and panache, well equipped to persuade his six suffragan bishops to agree with his views.

---

65 Ward, R.E. et al. (eds), op. cit., 324.   66 *Dublin Journal*, 4–6 July 1775. I can find no evidence, however, that Trimleston took the oath at this time. According to the index to the Catholic Qualification Rolls he took the oath in Dublin in November 1778 (see 2/446/3 National Archives).   67 Ward, R.E. et al. (eds), op. cit., 325–6.   68 Ibid., 326.   69 Power, T.R., 'James Butler archbishop of Cashel 1774–1791' in *Irish Ecclesiastical Record*, vol. 13 (1892), 302–18.

In letter dated 4 October 1776 to the Cardinal Protector, Butler outlined the experience of the Munster bishops for the previous three years and claimed:

It certainly was the plan of the King and his administrators to nullify the tricks and shut the mouths of certain people not less ill-disposed to his Majesty than most hostile to us, who in their public addresses and in pamphlets, offered on the occasion of the recall of parliament, gave vent to their hostility and contended bitterly that all the Catholics of this kingdom, most suspicious of a Protestant king, were completely unfaithful to him by virtue of their true devotion to the Roman pontiff. Consequently it would be most imprudent to mitigate on their account the very wholsome harshness of the laws, which were of course designated and established for the end that, in short, no opportunity would be left to the Papists of devising or occasioning anything nefarious against the King or his Kingdom.

He then goes on to refer to the unrest among the lower orders in Munster – an extract of this part of the letter has already been included above. He cites this unrest as the proximate reason for the Munster bishops agreeing to the oath, for, in order to protect themselves from the spite of the local magistracy, it was essential to distance themselves from the outrages being committed by the common people by a declaration in favour of the new oath.

Butler juxtapositioned the understanding atttitude of the king and the central administration in Ireland towards catholics with the sectarian bigotry of the local magistracy in Munster and of the protestant population in general there. He complained that the Munster bishops had not been consulted about the formulary of an oath prepared in Dublin by the Catholic Committee just prior to legislation for a catholic oath being introduced in parliament. He was under the (wrong) impression that very many catholics of the first note in the city of Dublin did not hesitate to subscribe to this new oath, being assured (incorrectly) that this new oath passed by parliament was in accord with the formulary prepared by the Catholic Committee and approved by Archbishop Carpenter.

Butler proceeded to complain about a pamphlet which appeared in Dublin around that time gravely critical of the new oath for catholics.[70] Dublin catholics

---

70 I have not discovered any pamphlet as such, published at the time in question, which fits the bill here. Butler may be referring to what appeared in *Hibernian Magazine* for October 1775 (p. 605) as an article entitled 'The oath of allegiance ... with the Roman Catholics' reasons against taking it', which may have been published separately as a pamphlet. The author of this article was chiefly concerned with what he called the fourth paragraph of the oath beginning 'and I do declare, that I do not believe, that the pope of Rome ... ', and the arguments advanced were broadly similar to those advanced at an earlier date by Charles O'Conor. However, O'Conor can scarcely have

who had already taken the oath, he claimed, were very annoyed at this. They greatly feared that this pamphlet, whose publication was not unknown to the archbishop of Dublin nor against his will, would be gravely detrimental to catholic affairs. It had the effect of restoking the fires of sectarian hatred in Munster. There was the further problem that, while many Dublin catholics proceeded to take the oath, none of the catholics in Munster did so, and this was interpreted by the 'principal Calvinists' there as deriving from the support of the bishops and priests of Munster for the pope's deposing and dispensing powers and for the restoration of the Stuarts.[71] Rumours such as these were being put about by the bigots, nor were there absent those among them who openly threatened the closure of catholic chapels, the incarceration of catholic priests and other vexations of that kind.

Meanwhile, prominent catholic laymen in Munster, Butler claimed, were urging on their bishops that the best way to offset the sectarian hatred threatening them, was for them (laymen) to take the oath, especially since, in the same way as Dublin catholics, they could do so with a safe conscience and a sound faith. Arguing that the silence of their bishops gave a very wrong impression in these dangerous times, these laymen maintained that it was of the greatest concern that the Munster bishops should declare openly to the people that there was nothing contrary to the catholic faith to be found in the new oath.

Butler was convinced that it was not the purpose of the Holy See that a more excessive yoke of conscience should be imposed on the oppressed catholics of Ireland than the subjects of catholic kings elswhere were accustomed to bear. Recent visits of the king's brothers to the pope had increased the goodwill of the king towards his catholic subjects, and allowed them to hope that after the next election legislation would be introduced for the removal of catholic disabilities, the injustice of which had compelled many catholics, anxious about their property, to flock from the bosom of Holy Church to the side of the protestants each year.[72]

been the author since by end-September 1775 he had whittled down his opposition to the oath to such an extent that he was admitting to Curry that he 'had no exception to the new Test, but that it was defective in two or three words'. (Ward R.E. et al., op. cit., 328).   71 Official figures (*Commons Journal Ireland*, vol. 15, part 1, Appendix CXXVIII) show that the number of persons who took the oath in Dublin city in 1775 was 100, while the number in Munster in 1775 was 553, made up of 391 for Tipperary and 162 for Waterford. Most of the 100 in Dublin city would have taken the oath on 28 June. The great surge to take the oath in Tipperary (about half of which county was in James Butler's diocese) and in Waterford began in December 1775. (see *59th report of the Deputy Keeper of the public records*, p. 52 seq.) In 1776 there were a further 120 subscribers in Cork and 106 in Kerry. A difference between the *Commons Journal* figures for these places and those in the *59th report of the Deputy Keeper of Public Records* will be discussed in the next chapter. When Butler speaks of 'Calvinists' he probably means 'Whigs' in the same way as 'Presbyterian' was used to mean 'Whig'. There were few real Calvinists in Munster.   72 There were two main categories of converts to the

Butler pointed out that they had gone to the trouble of consulting the first theologians of Paris and other universities, and the latter had pronounced unanimously that there was nothing in the new oath dangerous to the faith or contrary to the catholic religion. These were the circumstances in which the Munster bishops met near Cork city on 15 July 1775 and, having exchanged views, unanimously decided that the oath of allegiance passed by parliament contained nothing contrary to the principles of the Roman Catholic religion.[73]

The publication of the bishops' statement, Butler pointed out, had the desired result in Munster. The Calvinistic storm, which just before had threatened the catholics of that province, subsided and a better hope for their future safety dawned. But while this difficult business was being handled by the Munster bishops, they heard, to their great bewilderment and anguish of mind, that the archbishop of Dublin had taken care that the oath promulgated by parliament was taken serious note of by the Holy Father and the Sacred Congregation, and that the archbishop of Dublin had received a reply in the matter from Cardinal Castelli. Although Butler requested most earnestly to be informed of the tenor of Castelli's letter, the archbishop of Dublin did not deign to reply to him, while he [Dublin] wrote diffuse letters in the matter to others not only in Ireland but also in England.

Butler was concerned whether, by negligence or for secret purposes not helpful to investigate, the provisions of the oath passed by parliament had been accurately reported by the archbishop of Dublin to Castelli, and to put the matter beyond all doubt he was annexing to his letter the oath promulgated by parliament together with the preamble thereto (in fact Latin translations of these and of section 2 of the act).

Butler drew the attention of Castelli to the purpose of the oath as set out in the preamble, that is, to extinguish hatreds which had their origin in certain doctrines which the Roman Church did not really hold, but which were

established church at this time: (a) a son converting so as to get hold of a property by excluding his catholic brothers and making his father a tenant for life, and (b) owners of property converting so as to forestall the activities of discoverers.   73 The signatories of the declaration were: James Butler, Cashel; John Butler, Cork; Daniel Kearney, Limerick; Matthew MacKenna, Cloyne; William Egan, Waterford & Lismore; Michael Peter MacMahon, Killaloe and Francis Moylan, Kerry. It is a measure of James Butler II's persuasive powers and authority that three of these (John Butler, Michael P. MacMahon and Daniel Kearney) had supported James Butler I in his rejection of Hervey's formulary in 1768/69. At the meeting on 15 July 1775 James Butler II also read out a condemnation of *Supplementum Hiberniae Dominicanae*, 1772 in which Thomas Burke of Ossory had tried to embarrass and outmanoeuvre Butler and the other Gallican bishops by publishing Ghilini's letter of 14 October 1768 outlined above. All the Munster bishops, except MacMahon of Killaloe, signed this condemnation, MacMahon's refusal being no doubt intended to show solidarity with Burke, a brother Dominican.

ascribed to her by malevolent people with a view to promoting hatred of the Holy See. It was not, therefore, the intention of parliament that the oath promulgated by it should contain anything contrary to the dogmas of the catholic faith, or opposed to or insulting to the authority of the catholic church.

Butler went on to claim that, if, by the authority of the Holy Father and the Sacred Congregation, Irish catholics were prohibited, as was so vehemently desired by the archbishop of Dublin, from swearing allegiance to the king in accordance with the new oath, such prohibition would be taken by their enemies as a manifest sign that catholic doctrine was highly inimical to the peace and order of the realm, and that the penal laws, far from being abrogated on account of excessive severity, ought to have been more strictly executed and enforced. In a parenthesis Butler pointed out that initially Carpenter, without consulting Butler, had publicly approved a form of oath very similar to the one in the statute.[74] The form of oath referred to here was apparently that proposed by the Catholic Committee and approved by Carpenter, a copy of which Butler enclosed with his letter, no doubt to demonstrate to Castelli and the Sacred Congregation how little difference there was between it and that passed by parliament.

Thus Archbishop Butler writing to Cardinal Castelli on 4 October 1776.

It is necessary now to revert to Archbishop Carpenter's submissions to Brussels and Rome on the admissibility of the new oath. The taking of the oath by a number of Dublin catholics in June 1775 and the declaration of the Munster bishops in July 1775 were apparently the proximate causes of Carpenter's writing on 3 August 1775 to the Brussels nuncio, Ghilini, enclosing a copy of the new oath and requesting that it be transmitted to the Holy See for examination.[75] Ghilini was just about to finish a twelve year term as nuncio in Brussels.

In this letter Carpenter stated that from the time the oath was first promulgated he had laboured to persuade all catholics subject to him from taking

---

74 When Patrick Moran, later cardinal archbishop of Sydney, published this letter, which is in Latin, in *Spicilegium Ossoriense*, vol. 3, 341–9 he omitted the paragraph of which this is a summary as well as one anterior and two succeeding paragraphs. The four paragraphs in question can be read in Thomas England's *Life of Revd. Arthur O'Leary*, Appendix B. A microfilm of Butler's letter can also be read in National Library microfilm Pos. 5377, ff. 490–5, where the broadside entitled *Profession of allegiance and civil principles of Irish Roman Catholics*, enclosed with Butler's letter, can also be read. This broadside is in fact the form of oath, approved by Carpenter, and proposed by the Catholic Committee on 3 March 1774 to Hervey and is evidently the same as the printed copy of the Committee's formulary which Charles O'Conor tells us above had been circulated to MPs while the heads of the bill were still under discussion in the house. Fr H. Fenning, who has seen the original papers in the Vatican Archives, tells me that the following is written in Latin on the back of the broadside: 'the formula which his Grace the archbishop of Dublin approved'.   75 APF, SC Irlanda 12, f. 64, NLI Pos. 5376, Latin original.

it and he had tried to warn them of the danger to their souls of such an oath. He pointed out that there were not lacking false brothers, among them many prelates of the kingdom and their followers, who were not afraid to declare in public as well as in private that the new oath could be taken in its totality by all with a safe conscience. Hence a fatal schism arose which daily caused new scandals, and which crept in everywhere among the laity, many of whom, defying him, were not afraid to present themselves of their own accord for the purpose of taking the oath. Accordingly, he trusted in the Lord that, the wished-for decision having been taken once and for all by the Holy See on the oath, an end would be put to growing evils and happily peace restored to the catholics of Ireland.

As no reply was received to this letter, Carpenter made on 14 November 1775 a more elaborate submission to Cardinal Castelli, Prefect of Propaganda.[76] He referred first of all to Pope Paul V's condemnation in 1606 of an oath proposed for catholics by James I and to Nuncio Ghilini's letter of October 1768, already summarised, condemning Hervey's formularies, as precedents for the condemnation of the new oath. He was extremely concerned that the Holy See could remain silent for some months on the issue of this oath while evil daily gained strength and scandal grew through nearly all the kingdom. He was all the more astounded because the two oaths referred to in the precedents mentioned were much more tolerable than the present one, and these two having been condemned, he had no doubt but that the present oath should also be condemned. It occurred to him that the present silence of the Holy See might have proceeded from the ill-founded and untruthful machinations, complaints and representations of certain bishops, who, although pious and most zealous for the salvation of souls, nevertheless applied themselves with too much ardour for the temporal advantages of catholics in this kingdom, in the expectation that, if catholics could unanimously bind themselves to this oath, they could hope that in the fuuture the penal laws would be completely abolished and revoked – an expectation more wished for than hoped for in Carpenter's opinion. Supported in their judgement by certain doctors of the Sorbonne, these bishops preached everywhere, publicly and privately, that the new oath contained nothing contrary to faith and morals, and they had the perception that, positively and demonstrably, the Holy See would never come to any determination in this business, and consequently all catholics in these kingdoms, of whatever status or condition they might be, could bind themselves to this oath without loss of salvation.

Accordingly, Carpenter went on, so that there might not be a schism among them, that the peace of Christ, which surpasseth all understanding, might abound in their hearts, and that with one voice unanimously they might

76 Ibid., f. 262, Latin original.

honour God, they awaited a direct response from the Holy See, decisive and categorical. With all humility, submission and deference to the chair of Peter they earnestly and urgently demanded: Can catholics of this kingdom bind themselves to the aforesaid oath without violating faith or the honour due to God? The issues involved, he said, could be compressed as follows:

1 By no law, by no authority are catholics forced to take this oath.
2 By taking the oath nothing is acquired, by refusing it nothing is lost.
3 By taking the oath they will be more odious to the protestants themselves; by refusing it, they will show themselves more welcome.

The letter was signed by Carpenter himself, who also signed *ex commissione* on behalf of two of his suffragans, Sweetman of Ferns and Burke of Ossory. Bishop James Brady of Ardagh added the interesting superscription: All the bishops of this kingdom, except those of Munster and Kildare, would freely subscribe to this letter if they were present. For whom I with a full heart subscribe affectionately.

The catholic hierarchy thus found itself sharply divided into two camps, jurors and non-jurors. It is doubtful, however, if all those claimed by Bishop Brady to be on the non-juror side were in fact solidly committed to that view. There were probably a number who maintained a neutral stance, waiting to see how events would unfold. For instance, it is difficult to see Blake, archbishop *faineant* of Armagh, as a committed non-juror, considering he reputedly had given a guarded welcome to Hervey's formularies in 1768, and it is very strange that Fallon of Elphin and Irwin of Killala should have sided with the jurors on the question of the appointment of a bishop of Ossory (after Burke died in September 1776), if they were committed non-jurors. Furthermore, the juror faction were to gain important support with the appointment of Patrick Plunkett as bishop of Meath in 1778.

As to the degree of animosity between Butler and Carpenter, Hervey claimed that there was a strong contest between the two at 'a national synod' held in Dublin, and that there were 'great altercations' between them both in manuscript and in print, with the result that Butler was stigmatised as a schismatic whilst Carpenter, with more reason, had been twitted with disaffection to government.[77] On the other hand, Carpenter showed some appreciation of Butler when he introduced the latter's catechism to the Dublin diocese in 1777.[78]

Rome's reaction to the admissibility of the oath cannot have been very satisfactory to either side. In a letter dated 6 January 1776 Borgia, secretary of

77 Royal Historical Manuscripts Commission Report no. 8, Appendix 197–8.
78 McCarthy, D. (ed.), *Collections on Irish church history from the mss of ... Laurence F. Renehan*, Dublin 1861, 355.

Propaganda, set out in some detail the rather tortuous reasoning of the Holy See in regard to the admissibility of the oath.[79] After reviewing the case made for the condemnation of the oath, Borgia stated that, if the present oath were declared impious and inadmissible by the Holy See and if the pope issued a letter to that effect, as did Paul V in 1606, it was feared that such action would, in the present circumstances, be fraught with danger and do more harm than good to Irish catholics. Paul V had suited his mode of action to the conditions prevailing at the time, but in present conditions the approach used by the Holy See for the past century or so must be continued. In other places, and in particular in Holland, certain forms of oaths had been prescribed by the civil authorities which were very similar to the Irish form. The Holy See had not formally approved of such forms, nor had it condemned them publicly. The same approach was desirible in the case of Irish catholics, since there was a danger that a public declaration concerning the oath would arouse old hatreds and draw down the displeasure of the civil authorities on the Holy See, with the result that the catholic faith in Ireland would suffer greatly. Nevertheless, although the Holy See might refrain from issuing a formal declaration against the oath, it did not automatically follow that the oath was to be accepted; nor did it mean that it was not right for the bishops to dissuade the faithful from taking such a dangerous and obnoxious oath. Indeed, it was the duty of bishops to admonish the people, especially in private conversations with them, lest they be induced by a vain hope to substitute for their religion opinions which were harmful to the rights of the Holy See and damaging to the church and very truth itself.

There was no outright condemnation of the oath either in the reply sent by Propaganda to Butler, but he and his fellow jurors were severely reprimanded for having taken a decision of such magnitude without having first consulted the Holy See. It was pointed out to them that their action had been the occasion of no small pain to his Holiness and the Sacred Congregation.

As for translating their declaration of 15 July 1775 into the more positive action of taking the oath, the juror bishops found themselves in the difficulty that, according to the strict letter of the law, they were not supposed to be in the country at all – the Banishment Act had not been rescinded – and registering their names, addresses and occupations, as the test act required, might put them in some danger. However, having been reassured on this point, they proceeded to take the oath from December 1775. Butler, with fifteen of his priests and forty-seven laymen, took the oath at Thurles on 15 December 1775, while Egan of Waterford & Lismore took it at Clonmel on 18 December. O'Keeffe of Kildare took the oath at Borris, County Carlow with ten of his priests and seventeen laymen on 19 December 1775. Butler of Cork followed

---

79 Giblin, Cathaldus, op. cit., *Collectanea Hibernica* no. 11 (1968), 65–6.

with sixteen of his priests on 16 January 1776 and Moylan of Kerry on 7 March 1776.[80]

The stand-off between the two factions continued to manifest itself in some episcopal appointments in the following years. For example, in the case of Ossory, the non-jurors were to see their candidate, Troy, appointed instead of Molloy, the candidate of the jurors. Similarly, Richard O'Reilly, supported by the non-jurors, was appointed to Armagh in 1780 to the exclusion of the juror Patrick Plunkett of Meath, a far abler man.

Thus the oath, when at last it came, can be said to have been something of an anti-climax. As we have seen, there were deep divisions among catholics, particularly the clergy, on the question of its acceptability. But even those who found the oath acceptable were in no great hurry to subscribe to it since there was no tangible advantage to be gained by so doing, although as Plowden observed:

It gratified the Catholics, inasmuch as it was a formal recognition that they were subjects, and to this recognition they looked up as to the corner-stone of their future emancipation.[81]

Accordingly, once a definite benefit from subscribing was presented in the form of Catholic Relief Acts, there was a rush to take the oath, and some, like Carpenter, who had been loudest in its denunciation, found it expedient to pocket their principles, swallow their pride and take the oath.[82] The oath had been more than fifty years in the making and it is arguable whether the formulary settled for in 1774 was that much different from what might have been negotiated in the 1720s, if catholics had been prepared to ditch the Stuarts and to reject long outmoded papal claims.

APPENDIX

Hervey's Proposed Oath (1767)
(as set out by Thomas-Maria Ghilini, Brussels nuncio,
in a dispatch to Rome in 1768
and here now translated from the Latin into English)

Formula of a new oath which is proposed to be offered by the Government of Ireland to both the Ecclesiastics and Laity of that Kingdom in the hope that following such an oath, the penal laws, there in force against Catholics, will be repealed.

---

80 *59th Report of the Deputy Keeper of the public records*, passim.   81 Quoted in J. Mitchel, op. cit., vol. 1, 113.   82 Carpenter finally took the oath at the head of seventy of his clergy and several hundred catholic laity in November 1778.

I, N.N., most sincerely promise and swear on the Holy Evangelists in the presence of God and Men that I will be always faithful and loyal to his Majesty King George the Third, and that I will always defend the same with all my might against all conspiracies and endeavours attempted against his Person, Crown and Dignity, and that I will do all that is in my power to disclose and make known to his Majesty and his Successors all betrayals and conspiracies which anyone shall undertake or contemplate against him or his successors. And I promise and swear faithfully that I will defend with all my power the Succession to the Crown in the Family of his Majesty against any person whatsoever. I also swear that I abhor, detest and abjure from my innermost heart as pernicious and abominable the doctrine that faith ought not to be kept with, or a promise made to, Heretics or excommunicated Princes, or that those deprived by the Pope should be deposed or killed by their subjects or by any other person whatsoever. I solemnly swear and declare in the presence of God that I make this Declaration and this Oath according to the common and ordinary sense as it is understood by the Irish Legislature, without equivocation or internal reservation and that I have not obtained any anterior dispensation from the Pope or from any other authority whatsoever, and finally that I do not believe that I can be absolved at any time or dispensed from the onus of this Oath by the Pope or anyone whosoever who declares that no such like Oath ought of its nature to have been taken in the first place.

Another [following] formula of an Oath was shown to me [nuncio] which almost coincided with the preceding. We transmit it at the same time so that he [the Pope?] can investigate with all his sagacity and prudence how orthodox all this is and how far it can be sustained. Have a care to forward a prompt and efficacious remedy by returning instructions to me in regard to everything without delay.

Although I do not dare to take in the usual way for the sake of conscience an Oath of Fidelity, Abjuration and Sovereignty/Supremacy, as prescribed by the Irish Legislature, I wish nevertheless to assure his Majesty of my Faith and Fidelity. And therefore I, A.B., voluntarily testify to almighty God and to Jesus Christ His only Son that I will be faithful and will show true allegiance, that is, Fidelity, to George the Third and that I will defend him with all my might against all traitorous conspiracies and from all machinations whatsoever against his Person, Crown and Dignity, which treasons and machinations I will certainly endeavour diligently to detect and, having detected, disclose to his Majesty and his Successors. I declare also that no foreign Prince, no Prelate, no State nor any Power has any Jurisdiction, Power, Superiority or Pre-eminence, temporal or civil, direct or indirect, within the limits of this Kingdom, and in the presence of God I do solemnly profess, bear witness and declare that I make this Declaration in each and every part thereof in the plain and ordinary sense of the words just as they are understood by the Legislature of this Kingdom, without any evasion, equivocation or mental reservation whatsoever, and without any Dispensation already obtained at this time, whether from the Pope or from any other authority of the See of Rome or any person whatsoever. Neither do I believe that I can be absolved from the bond of this declaration, either in whole or in part, even if the Pope should declare it to be null and void from the beginning.

A third form of Oath [following] was also shown to me [nuncio] which tended equally to excite my vigilance, another Oath to be taken by the clergy and People:

Although I believe the Pope is bishop of Rome and is the Vicar of Christ, having spiritual jurisdiction in all the Catholic Church, nevertheless I am persuaded that he has no temporal power, direct or indirect, over the Temporal Affairs and Causes of this Kingdom, and that his jurisdiction ought not to be extended except to Spiritual Causes and Judgements [*Censuras*]. Hence I, A.B., heartily in the presence of God and Men subscribe to the Four Propositions to which the Clergy of France subscribed A.D. 1682.[83]

1 The Pope, or the Pope in Council, has no authority over the Temporalities of Kings or of their subjects.
2 Every General Council, according to the fourth and fifth Session of the Council of Constance, is superior to the Pope, and could, if expedient, depose him or reform him.
3 The Apostolic Power of the Pope must be regulated by the Apostolic Canons, without violating nevertheless the Liberties of the Church of Ireland, according as it was provided by Law before the year 1527.[84]
4 Even if the Pope can declare Articles of Faith, his decrees nevertheless are not irreformable until they have been confirmed in a General Council.

83 For a more accurate version of the Gallican Articles see Chapter 1.   84 This is of course an interpolation into the Gallican Articles and is intended to take account of the liberties wrested by the king from Rome for the English church prior to the Reformation. Whether these liberties applied also to the Irish church is highly questionable. The date 1527 should no doubt be 1537, the date of the original Act of Supremacy.

7

The Relief Acts and the Catholic Qualification Rolls

So among catholics, both clergy and laity, the debate continued on whether the new oath might be taken without offending faith and morals. Charles O'Conor continued to oppose it although he now admitted he found it defective in only two or three words. For the first time the people, he pointed out, were divided into subscribers (to the oath) and non-jurors, and yet the subscribers, he claimed, had as little attention paid to them as the non-jurors during a long session of parliament (1775–6) just then ended.

Propaganda's letter of 6 January 1776, mentioned in the last chapter, was sent to the Dominican, John T. Troy, later to be bishop and archbishop, but then attached to San Clemente, the Irish Dominican College in Rome, and it is not clear when it reached Ireland. It can hardly have come into the hands of Archbishop Carpenter prior to his writing once more to Cardinal Castelli on 12 March 1776 since, if Carpenter had seen Propaganda's letter, he could scarcely have remained so cocksure of the strength of his position that he continued to castigate Butler and the juring bishops in the terms in which it will be seen he did. Strangely, as will appear from this letter, the juring bishops had wind of Propaganda's letter before Carpenter.

At all events in this letter of 12 March Carpenter[1] accused Butler, with his suffragans and O'Keeffe of Kildare, of trying to remove all suspicion of error from the new oath, in order to induce the laity to take it. Butler, he said, had not been afraid to be seen publicly in the presence of magistrates, accompanied by his own parish priests, binding themselves voluntarily to the oath. It was not enough for Butler to show his zeal for the oath in his own diocese: he also felt compelled to intrude into Carpenter's diocese, and, forgetful of the reverence due to a bishop in his own diocese and with a total disregard for ecclesiastical discipline, he caused a pamphlet to be printed there in which he attacked Carpenter's arguments against the oath, tried to expose them to vulgar

1 APF SC Irlanda 12, ff 347–50, NLI Pos. 5376.

derision and finally endeavoured to rouse the indignation of parliament against the adversaries of the oath, declaring them unworthy to be allowed to live in the kingdom with the other subjects. Is it your Eminence's judgment, Carpenter asked, that this should be tolerated in the said prelate?

Henceforth, Carpenter went on, the flames of discord flourished everywhere and pervaded everything. He had received letters from these prelates in which they asserted that the Sacred Congregation, having given mature consideration to the oath, had solemnly declared that it contained nothing contrary to faith or morals, and that accordingly all catholics could bind themselves to it without any scruple. Moreover, by industriously propagating these reports in Dublin and by other machinations, they had studied to have him made, on account of his opposition to the oath, an object of contempt and hatred among the people. He argued that the majority of the people believed that the oath was completely contrary to the faith and they confidently and anxiously desired that it should be subjected to the censures of the Holy See. He firmly believed that not twenty catholics would be found in the whole kingdom disposed to take such an oath, had they not been deceived by the inducement and example of the aforesaid bishops into thinking that the dictates of their own conscience could be disregarded.

The pamphlet referred to in Carpenter's letter above may be *A vindication of the new oath of allegiance proposed to the Roman Catholics of Ireland by a steadfast member of the Church of Rome*, printed in Dublin in 1775. It has been attributed to Fr Patrick Molloy of Ossory who, supported by Butler and the juring bishops, was a year later unsuccessful in his bid to be bishop of Ossory. It is clear from a letter from the author to the *Hibernian Magazine* that this pamphlet was in the nature of a reply to the article which had appeared in that magazine's October 1775 issue citing 'the Roman Catholics' reasons against taking the oath', discussed in note 70 to Chapter 6. The author proceeded to make his case in favour of the oath by way of question and answer. He drew a parallel between an Irish catholic and a catholic in Canada or Silesia who had sworn allegiance to a protestant king, 'because it is not to the religion, but to the personage of the protestant king he swears allegiance to'. He contended that every catholic who declined the Test would wound severely rather than promote the real interests of his religion, because an obstinate refusal to take the Test must confirm protestants in their prejudices as to catholic belief. He claimed that 'no Pretender ought to wear the British crown, whilst George wears it by supreme authority of the British state and the sanction of Divine Providence, by which kings reign,' and that 'in short, the State from its supreme powers, can alter the succession of the crown, as Blackstone remarks'. He insisted that since 'it is not deemed to be unjust for any state to disqualify or disinherit the innocent son of a rebel convicted of high treason, so neither can it be said to be an act of injustice in the British state to disqualify suspected Papists, who abet and maintain certain darling doctrines, which are evidently obnoxious to the state'. Catholics, he pointed out, rejected the pope's power to depose princes while upholding his spiritual supremacy.

Harcourt resigned as lord lieutenant towards the end of 1776 and was replaced by the earl of Buckinghamshire in January 1777. Early in March the Catholic Committee presented Buckinghamshire with an address in which they expressed their loyalty most fulsomely to the king, their respect for the lord lieutenant and the hope of some evidence of royal favour to catholics. The reply gave catholics some grounds for hope when it informed them of the king's resolution to continue to extend his royal protection to all his loyal subjects, however they might differ in faith or modes of worship.[2]

But no matter how favourable the attitude of the king, the lord lieutenant and administration might be to catholics, there remained a sizeable body of members of both houses of the Irish parliament who were implacably opposed to any concessions to catholics. This opposition was further galvanised when France came to the aid of the American colonists and there was talk of a French invasion of Ireland which disaffected catholics might support. The militant protestant, George Ogle MP, proposed the establishment of a protestant militia to counter this situation, and while the prime serjeant, Hussey Burgh, hastened to the catholics' defence, he must have gone a bit too far when he claimed that 'protestants and papists were alike men and brothers'.[3] There was little sign of brotherly love when a motion on 12 March 1778 for leave to introduce a bill to enable catholics to take long leases of building sites in cities and towns met with such opposition from Ogle and others that it had to be withdrawn.[4] Clearly, the protestant land-owning class were still so fearful of the possibility, however remote, of losing their estates to catholics that even the smallest concession to them was not to be thought of.

However, it was evident that the contagion of American ideas had spread to Ireland in the rising impatience of the Patriot Party, and Lord North, the British prime minister, began to see in the conciliation of catholics a means of recruiting them to the English interest, as a kind of balance to the activities of the protestant Patriots. Furthermore, by 1778 outright war with France was increasingly likely and Hervey, writing from Rome in May 1778, warned that, if war with France took place, Ireland must almost inevitably be thrown into the greatest confusion, that the first blow would certainly be directed there and that Irish catholics, exasperated by repeated disappointments, were ripe for an almost general revolt.[5]

Since catholics were of little importance numerically in Britain – barely 1 per cent of the population at this time[6] – it appeared to the government that a

2 Wall, Maureen, *Catholic Ireland in the eighteenth century*, Dublin 1989, 125.   3 Ibid., 125.   4 Ibid., 125.   5 Royal Historical Manuscripts Commission (RHMC) Report no. 8, Appendix, p. 197.   6 See note 8, Chapter 3.

measure for the relief of English catholics could be introduced in the British parliament with relative ease and would provide a sort of dry run for similar reliefs for Irish catholics. The necessary bill was drafted by Edmund Burke and he was active behind the scenes in shepherding the bill through the house. However, since his catholic connections might antagonise certain MPs, he did not introduce nor second the bill;[7] those functions were performed respectively by Sir George Savile and John Dunning, Baron Ashburton. Cited as a bill 'for the repeal of certain of the penalties and disabilities provided in an act of William III', it provided for religious toleration for English catholics as well as for the removal of disabilities in regard to property.

The English bill passed without opposition and received the royal assent on 3 June 1778. Burke was apologetic as to its narrow focus but explained that 'it was necessary to come with simplicity and directnes to the point, and to repeal that act which, with the least apparent cruelty had the most certain operation; leaving those laws, which from their very savageness and ferocity, were more noisy than effective, to wait for a time of greater leisure'.[8]

The man chiefly responsible for bringing in a somewhat lesser measure of relief for Irish catholics was Luke Gardiner, member for County Dublin. On 25 May in the Irish house of commons leave was given to bring in the heads of such a bill and Gardiner together with Barry Barry, the member for County Cavan and Barry Yelverton the member for Carrickfergus were assigned the task of preparing it. Gardiner introduced the heads of the bill on 5 June when they were read a first time and committed to a committee of the whole house for consideration. The heads were further considered in committee on 15, 16, 18 and 19 June. A measure of the extent of opposition to the bill can be gleaned from the fact that the house sat until 3 am on 18 June and until 4 am on 19 June. On 20 June John Dillon, the member for Blessington, reported from the committee that they had gone through the heads paragraph by paragraph and had made several amendments thereto. These amendments were agreed to by the house with several other amendments and it was then ordered that Mr Gardiner should attend the lord lieutenant with the heads with a view to their transmission to London.[9]

The heads contained a clause, intended for the relief of dissenters, rescinding the requirement of receiving the sacrament of the Lord's Supper according to the usage of the established church as a necessary qualification for the holding of offices and places of trust and profit under the Crown.[10] This clause was dropped by the English privy council, but, although as a consequence it was open to the Irish parliament to reject the entire bill on its return to them,

7 O'Brien, Conor C., *The great melody: a thematic biography of Edmund Burke*, London 1992, 75–6.   8 O'Brien, C.C., op. cit., 76.   9 *Commons Journal Ireland*, vol. 9, Part 1 under dates mentioned.   10 Ibid. for 15 June 1778.

both houses accepted the revised bill and it received the royal assent with several other bills on 14 August.

The resulting act was couched in such arcane terms that it could be fully understood by few people apart from specialist lawyers. The only outright repeal in the act concerned the provision in 2 Anne c. 6[11] under which a son on converting to the established church could take over the family property and make his father a tenant for life. Otherwise it was a matter of immunity being granted from certain property provisions in 2 Anne c. 6 and 8 Anne c. 3[12] to those catholics who before 1 January 1779 took the oath provided in the 1774 act.

Thus under section 1 of the act catholics who took the oath might take leases not exceeding 999 years certain, but where leases were determinable on lives, a limit of five lives was provided for. Section 2 provided that catholics should be capable 'to take, hold and enjoy all or any such estate or estates, which shall descend, or be devised or transferred as aforesaid', notwithstanding anything to the contrary in 2 Anne c. 6 and 8 Anne c. 3. The effect of all this, for those taking the oath, was that, apart from the exceptions mentioned below, gavelling of catholic estates was at an end and discoverers were henceforth precluded from carrying on their nefarious traffic. Suits for discovery already instituted were, however, excluded and it was somewhat ironic that, because of this, the act failed to provide any relief for one of the main activists for catholic relief for many years, Charles O'Conor, whose younger brother, Hugh, had turned protestant and had sued in 1777 for the family estates as a protestant discoverer.[13]

Unlike the British relief act, there were no reliefs in the act aimed specifically at the catholic hierarchy and clergy. The Banishment Act remained on the statute book, although considered for many years a dead letter. Hervey, writing to Speaker Pery in May 1778, advocated that religious toleration should at least be granted to such as had taken the new oath of allegiance 'were it only to create a schism among them'. Such a measure, he claimed, 'would necessarily divide the Papists at present, and render them perfectly harmless hereafter'.[14]

But even without the carrot of religious toleration the catholic bishops one by one succumbed and took the oath, among the last being Carpenter in November 1778 and Troy in March 1779. The Sacred Congregation finally washed their hands of the whole business in a letter dated 22 November 1778 from Secretary Borgia. He noted that Carpenter and Troy had decided to take the oath as the other Irish bishops had done,[15] as also the vicars apostolic in

---

11 i.e. the act to prevent the further growth of popery 1704. 12 i.e. the acts to prevent the further growth of popery 1704 & 1709. 13 Ward, Robert E. et al. (eds.), *Letters of Charles O'Conor of Belanagare*, Washington DC 1988, passim. 14 RHMC Report no. 8, Appendix, p. 197. 15 There may, however, have been some bishops who never took the oath. For example, I have not been able to find any evidence that Mark Skerrett, archbishop of Tuam, did so.

England and Scotland. In view of this the Congregation had given no further directions to any of these prelates with regard to the oath, the position being that it had neither disapproved of what they had done nor much less approved of it, although in the difficult circumstances which prevailed acceptance of the oath was considered to be the better approach in the matter; indeed in the instruction issued by the congregation on 6 January 1776 it was recommended that the needs and circumstances of the time must be taken into consideration in deciding on a mode of action.

Section 10 of the new act provided that the concessions in the act did not apply to a convert relapsing to catholicism, or to a protestant becoming a papist or educating his children under the age of fourteen as papists, even if such people took the oath. Section 3 provided that the oath could be taken in any of the Four Courts in Dublin, at the quarter sessions of the peace for the County Dublin, or before the going judge of assize. While, therefore, the 1774 act provided for the taking of the oath in only one of the Four Courts, i.e. the court of king's bench, the 1778 act allowed it to be taken in any of the four courts of exchequer, common pleas, king's bench and chancery. There was provision for the keeping of a roll of those who took the oath and for depositing of these rolls in the rolls office.

Since the act had only received the royal assent on 14 August (although operative from 1 August), and since catholics availing of its provisions were required under section 3 to take the oath before 1 January 1779, there was a scramble to fulfill this requirement, which necessarily had to be telescoped into the months of October, November and December 1778, since the courts did not open until the start of the Michaelmas term in October. Thus of 1,250 catholic merchants, manufacturers, shopkeepers and tradesmen from the Dublin city area who took the oath under the 1778 act in the period 1778–1782, some 85 per cent of them took the oath in the months of October–December 1778.[16]

Although the 1778 act has been said by some to have been minimalist in its approach, nevertheless it had the merit of going to the root of the problem by eradicating those provisions of the penal laws, the effect of which had been most keenly felt particularly in more recent decades, that is, the laws concerned with catholic property. While the religious provisions of the penal laws had been for many years dead letters on the face of the statutes, the property provisions had continued alive and threatening and requiring only the greed of men to put them into operation. The 1778 act could be said to be one of those watersheds in history, following which it could be said that nothing was ever the same again. Edmund Burke, in a letter dated 12 August 1778 to Speaker Pery, was not perhaps after all too sanguine when he wrote:[17]

16 See Maureen Wall 'The Catholic merchants, manufacturers and traders of Dublin, 1778–1782' in *Reportorium Novum*, vol. 2, no. 2, 298–323.   17 RHMC Report no. 8, Appendix, p. 197.

The Irish house of commons has done itself infinite honour. Its longest session has been its best.... It gave me great pleasure to find, as I do from many accounts, that, without derogating from the talents of the gentlemen who dissented from the Toleration, the far greater weight of the abilities and eloquence of the house was on the side where eloquence and ability ought ever to be, on the side of liberty and justice. You are now beginning to have a country; and I trust you will complete the design. You have laid the firm, honest, homely rustic of property; and the rest of of the building will rise in due harmony and proportion.

Contemporary comments such as Buckinghamshire's that the act would 'benefit only the rich papist',[18] have led to the belief that the concessions granted were very limited in scope and applied to few people. The number of people who took the oath arising out of the act, belie this view. To take the case of Dublin, why would around one thousand merchants, manufacturers, shopkeepers and tradesmen rush off to take the oath in the months of October to December 1778 if they did not expect to benefit from the act? The majority of these could not be regarded as 'rich' in Buckinghamshire's sense of that term.

The removal of the thirty-one year limit on leases to catholics of land and property benefited potentially a vast number of people. It must have had a considerable effect on agricultural and industrial development in encouraging and rewarding hard work and initiative, which, as we have seen, Charles O'Conor claimed was stifled by the thirty-one year limit on leases

THE RELIEF ACT OF 1782

The following years were marked by the rise of the Volunteeers, the movement for free trade and, finally, in 1782 the declaration of the legislative independence of the Irish parliament.

The danger of foreign invasion by French or Spanish forces continued. The Catholic Committee in July 1779 formulated an address to the king in which they expressed their abhorrence and indignation at 'the insidious and base attempts of the French and Spanish courts to disturb the peace and distract the happiness' of his Majesty's dominions.[19] In an address at the same time to Lord Lieutenant Buckinghamshire they expressed 'their gratefull acknowledgments for the recent benefits conferred on us by the legislature'.[20] There were similar addresses from catholics in the town and county of Wexford and the city of Kilkenny.[21] Towards the end of the following year when Buckinghamshire

18 Quoted in R.B. McDowell, *Ireland in the age of imperialism and revolution*, Oxford 1979, 190. 19 Edwards, R. Dudley (ed.), 'Minute book of the Catholic Committee 1773–1792' in *Archivium Hibernicum*, vol. 9, 40–1. 20 Ibid., 41. 21 Brady, John,

was replaced by the earl of Carlisle, the committee were quick to present an address to the new lord lieutenant in which they again expressed their 'utter abhorrence of the insidious conduct of France and Spain and the unnatural and ungrateful hostility of Holland', and they recognised with thanks the liberality of what had already been done for their particular relief.[22]

Busca, the Brussels nuncio, informed the Sacred Congregation in February 1780 that Bishop Troy had learned for certain that there was to be a bill proposed in the Irish parliament to grant the same reliefs to the catholic clergy in Ireland as had been granted to catholic clergy in Britain in 1778, that is, the grant of religious toleration in addition to the property reliefs. Busca remarked that the greatest credit was due to Bishop Troy for the part he played in bringing about this advantageous state of affairs. He mentioned that Troy had become so friendly with many of the more respected members of the Irish parliament that he had been able to influence them to look favourably on the proposal to be put before them.[23] There is here evidence of the emergence of Troy as the leading member of the hierarchy, with the eclipse of Carpenter perhaps because of failing health or the failure of the line he had taken on the oath, and with Butler in Cashel to an extent *persona non grata* with the Roman authorities.

There had indeed been hopes that in the 1779–80 session of parliament measures for further relief for catholics, on the lines mentioned by Busca, might be brought forward by Luke Gardiner with help from Hussey Burgh, Barry Yelverton and Sir Hercules Langrishe, the attorney general. But following the anti-catholic Gordon riots in London and the possibility of similar anti-catholic unrest in Ireland, further action in the matter that session was suspended.[24]

The movement for independence for the Irish parliament at this time also had implications for the furtherance of the catholic claims, since Grattan, the main proponent of independence, had come around to Burke's concept of one nation. In a short speech in the house in December 1781, when Gardiner announced his intention of bringing forward a further relief bill, Grattan declared that 'it should be the business of parliament to unite every denomination of Irishman in brotherly affection and regard to the constitution'.[25] Later in the same speech he declared:

It had been well observed by a person of first rate understanding [Burke] … that Ireland could never prosper till its inhabitants were a people; and

Catholics and catholicism in the eighteenth century press, Maynooth 1965, 200.   **22** Edwards, R.D., op. cit., 54–5.   **23** Giblin, Cathaldus, 'Catalogue of material of Irish interest in the collection Nunziatura di Fiandra, Vatican Archives' in *Collectanea Hibernica*, no. 11 (1968), 63.   **24** Fenning, Hugh, *The Irish Dominican province 1698–1798*, Dublin 1990, 455–60.   **25** Mitchel, John, *The history of Ireland from the treaty of Limerick to the present time*, London, no date, 136.

though the assertion might seem strange, that three millions of inhabitants in that island should not be called a people, yet the truth was so, and so would continue till the wisdom of parliament should unite them by all the bonds of social affection. Then, and not till then, the country might hope to prosper.[26]

But even the liberal-minded Grattan did not have in mind full emancipation for catholics, for he later revealingly appealed to the house to tell catholics: 'We are willing to become one people – we are willing to grant you every privilege compatible within the Protestant ascendant'.[27]

The case for catholic relief gained further important support when the Volunteer convention in Dungannon in February 1782, in what amounted to a declaration of the independence of the Irish parliament, at the instigation of Grattan also resolved that 'as men and as Irishmen, as Christians and as Protestants, we rejoice in the relaxation of the penal laws against our Roman Catholic fellow-subjects, and that we conceive the measure to be fraught with the happiest consequences to the union and prosperity of the inhabitants of Ireland'.[28]

On the same day that this resolution was passed in Dungannon the heads of a catholic relief bill were read a first time in the commons and the house resolved itself into a committee to give them further consideration. They were further considered in committee on 20 February, when the house sat until past 2 a.m., on 26 February, 1 and 2 March. In the course of an intervention on the committee stage Grattan made the memorable declaration: 'The question is now, whether we shall grant Roman Catholics a power of enjoying estates, or whether we shall be a Protestant settlement or an Irish nation? Whether we shall throw open the gates of the temple of liberty to all our countrymen, or whether we shall confine them in bondage by penal laws?'[29]

The support of Grattan and the majority of the Patriots, as well as that of the Volunteers, was to be crucial in putting the measure through parliament, for there was considerable and sustained opposition to it centring around the question of whether catholics should be allowed to hold estates in fee, that is, outright ownership. Grattan pointed out that this question had been debated in the house four years before on the occasion of the 1778 relief bill, when there was a majority of three against granting catholics the fee and they were allowed to take leases of indefinite extent (999 years) instead. The argument at that time against granting them the fee was that they might influence elections, but it had been shown that a 999-year lease gave catholics as effectual an influence on elections as the right of holding estates in fee.[30] This argument as well

26 Ibid., 137.   27 Wall, M., op. cit. in note 2, 147.   28 Quoted in J. Mitchel, op. cit., 139.   29 Ibid., 141.   30 Wall, M., op. cit in note 2, 138–9.

as the continued, quiet behaviour of catholics was sufficient to secure a majority for this section of the bill.

Not surprisingly, the regular clergy continued to be the *bête noire* of many members in the house. There had been rumours that some bishops, notably Butler of Cashel, would not be averse to their suppression and banishment in any relief legislation but these rumours had been finally scotched by a certificate signed by all the hierarchy 'that the regular clergy of this kingdom are a respectable body of men, useful to the public, by instilling the principles of good morals, and therefore worthy of being protected under their own institutions'.[31]

The heads of the bill were finally passed on 6 March when Gardiner was asked to attend the lord lieutenant with the heads with a view to their transmission to London, where they were accepted by the privy council without amendment. The returned bill was formally passed by both houses during April and received the royal assent on 4 May.[32]

The section of the act allowing papists to purchase lands in fee has been mentioned above. Section 5 appeared to regularise at long last the position of the catholic clergy, in particular that of the bishops and the regular clergy, although there was still no outright repeal of the Banishment Act. Rather it provided that no popish ecclesiastic who took the oath provided in the 1774 act and who registered with the (protestant) registrar of the diocese in which he resided, giving certain particulars, should be subject to the Banishment Act and certain other acts. The particulars required to be given by each ecclesiastic were Christian name, surname, place of abode, age and parish (if he had one), time and place of his receiving first and every other popish order and from whom he received them.

The regular clergy were left in a rather unsatisfactory position in that those who were abroad could not claim the benefit of the act unless they returned within six months to take the oath prescribed. But considering the unfriendly attitude of the Irish administration and even of the secular clergy towards them, and the treatment of regular clergy about this time in catholic Austria, the provisions in the act were probably the best that could be hoped for in the circumstances. There was, however, a belated intervention in April 1782 by Busca, the Brussels nuncio, with Fitzherbert, the British minister in Brussels, to have the Irish regular clergy outside the ccountry treated in the same way as those within the country. The reply from Fitzherbert in May 1782 was that, apart from many other (unspecified) reasons, it would not be proper for the king at that particular time to make such fundamental changes in the bill because of the position in which Ireland then found herself in relation to Britain. At the

---

31 Fenning, H., op. cit., 464. 32 *Commons Journal Ireland*, vol. 10, part 2 under dates mentioned.

same time Fitzherbert was instructed to assure the nuncio in the most explicit terms of the sincere and friendly regard of the English court for the court of Rome.[33] The covert reference in Fitzherbert's reply to the declaration of legislative independence by the Irish parliament was a reminder that the day was gone when a successful Irish catholic lobby could be mounted in London to have anti-catholic measures passed in Dublin negatived by the British privy council. The Capuchin, Arthur O'Leary, was in the circumstances rather philosophical about the situation of the regulars when he noted that other countries, notably the United States, would be opening up to receive any unwanted Irish regulars stranded on the continent.[34] However, it was to be the cause of great surprise and alarm when it emerged at the time of the Emancipation Act of 1829 that legal advice to the government of that time was that the 1782 and 1793 relief acts did not legalise the existence of the regular clergy in Ireland.

Section 7 provided for the registrar of each protestant diocese to keep a roll of popish clergy in that diocese benefiting under the act, and to make yearly returns to the clerk of the privy council.

Section 18 provided for keeping rolls locally of those who took the oath with a view to benefiting under the property clause, citing their quality, condition, titles and place of abode, these rolls to be deposited yearly in the Rolls Office in Dublin. There was provision for certificates to be given to subscribers on payment of a fee of two shillings.

The reliefs granted under the act were hedged around by a number of petty and derogatory exceptions. Section 8 provided that the benefit of the act did not extend to priests officiating in chapels with a steeple or a bell, or exercising any rites save in their own chapels etc, or to those who used any symbol of ecclesiastical authority, or assumed any ecclesiastical rank or title whatsoever.

Excluded from benefiting, under section 9 of the act, were converts from the protestant to the catholic religion and catholic ecclesiastics who procured the conversion of a protestant to the catholic religion. There were a number of repeals of penal provisions which had become dead letters – the restriction on a catholic owning a horse worth more than £5, the restriction on catholics living in Limerick or Galway cities, the levying of catholic inhabitants of a county in respect of robberies by privateers in time of war, the requirement for catholics to say where they heard Mass and who celebrated it.

Contemporaneously with the foregoing John Dillon,[35] member for Blessington, presented to the house on 7 March 1782 heads of a bill for better regulating the education of papists. The heads were further debated on 13 and 14 March before being passed for submission to London. The bill received the royal assent on 27 July 1782. Section 1 repealed the parts of 7 William III c. 4 which

33 Giblin, C., op. cit., *Collectanea Hibernica* no. 11 (1968), 72.   34 Fenning, H., op. cit., 467.   35 *Commons Journal Ireland*, vol. 10, part 1 under dates mentioned.

prohibited foreign education for catholics and of 8 Anne c. 3 which prohibited catholic schoolmasters from teaching school. To qualify for benefit under
the act schoolmasters were required to take the oath provided in the 1774 act.
They were also required to obtain a licence from the relevant church of Ireland
bishop before commencing to teach school. Section 5 provided that papists,
excluding ecclesiastics, having taken the oath of allegiance in the 1774 act, might
have guardianship of their own or any papist's child.

The passing of the 1782 relief act coincided with the declaration of the independence of the Irish parliament. The Dungannon Convention had in a sense
opened the debate with the resolution that 'a claim of any body of men, other
than the King, Lords and Commons of Ireland, to make laws to bind this
Kingdom, is unconstitutional, illegal and a grievance'. On 16 April Grattan in
his address to the king asserting the independence of the parliament of Ireland,
which was passed unanimously, was characteristically upbeat when he stated:

> This house agreeing with the voice of the nation passed the popery bill, and
> by doing so got more than it gave, yet found advantages from generosity,
> and grew rich in the very act of charity. Ye gave not, but ye formed an
> alliance between the Protestant and the Catholic powers, for the security of
> Ireland. What signifies it, that three hundred men in the house of commons;
> what signifies it that one hundred men in the house of peers assert their
> country's liberty, if unsupported by the people.[36]

But Burke was less enthusiastic when, after recounting the many disabilities
which catholics still laboured under, he claimed that the new act had 'surely
more of the air of a table of proscriptions than an act of grace.'[37]

Clearly, there was a long way still to go in the matter of complete emancipation for catholics. Was an independent Irish parliament prepared to go the
extra mile? How far removed was the high-flown rhetoric of Grattan from the
realities at the protestant grass-roots?

THE RELIEF ACTS OF 1792 AND 1793

A Volunteer convention at the Rotunda in Dublin in November 1783[38] was
expected to react favourably to further reliefs for catholics. However, with the
connivance of government, a bogus message reached the convention that
catholics were willing to relinquish all ideas of pressing further claims, and this
provided an excuse for the convention to shelve further discussion of the matter.
Although there were some catholic members of the Volunteers at this time, the

36 Wall, M., op. cit. in note 2, 143.   37 Quoted in J. Mitchel, op. cit., 142.   38 Wall,
M., op. cit in note 2, 150.

majority of the leaders, with Hervey as an honourable exception, were opposed to granting catholics any political power.

Following William Pitt's appointment as prime minister in December 1783, the duke of Rutland came over as lord lieutenant in February 1784. He was faced with two major problems – the movement for reform of parliament and the threat posed by the existence of an armed volunteer force. Although the Catholic Committee presented an address to Rutland, it was insipid and vapid in tone, and an attempt by government to gain the support of the catholics through the intervention of the earl of Kenmare, failed.[39] When a parliamentary reform bill, supported by the Volunteers, was roundly defeated in parliament in March 1784, the more militant of the Volunteers turned to the catholics for support and some Northern corps openly invited catholics to join.

A large meeting in Dublin in June 1784, representative of all shades of opinion, supported the extension of the vote to catholics while still preserving in its fullest extent the protestant government of the country. A committee set up at this meeting to draw up a petition to the king seeking parliamentary reform, contained four prominent catholics.[40] But Rutland was so alarmed at the implications of such a meeting that he began to think of the union of the two parliaments as the only way to keep Ireland from going the way of the American colonies. He believed, quite wrongly, that if catholics were given the vote, the next parliament would be composed of papists, and if more protestants were given the vote to the exclusion of catholics, the latter, he was convinced, would 'run into rebellion'.[41] When parliament finally in February 1785 grasped the nettle of ridding the country of the Volunteers, Rutland was hopeful that catholics might be persuaded to resign en bloc from that organisation, but, despite pressure from government, the Catholic Committee refused to come out in favour of such a step.

A bitter pamphlet war between dignitaries of the protestant and catholic churches was not helpful in advancing the cause of further relief for catholics. In 1787 a clause in a Riot Bill that any catholic chapel, where Whiteboy oaths were administered, should be destroyed, smacked of the worst excesses of the penal code, but, following appeals by well-known catholics, the clause was withdrawn.[42] There was a recognition in government that acceding to Catholic Committee demands for admission of catholics to the bar, for commissions in the armed forces and for votes for better-off catholics, would mean nothing at all to poorer catholics, who were the vast majority, and that a reform of the tithe system might assuage lower-order unrest and act as a riposte to these middle/upper class catholic pretensions.[43] But nothing came of such ruminations.

Disagreements within the Catholic Committee led to gentry and clergy members leaving it and to the emergence in 1790 of a vibrant and active organisation

39 Edwards, R.D., op. cit., 90–1.　40 McDowell, R.B., op. cit., 315–17.　41 Wall, M. op. cit. in note 2, 154.　42 Ibid., 158–9.　43 Ibid., 158.

under the leadership of John Keogh, with the protestant Wolfe Tone as assistant secretary and organiser. The founding of the United Irishmen Society, with its aim of a brotherhood of Irishmen of all religious persuasions, also helped the furtherance of catholic claims. However, faced with opposition from all sides in the Irish parliament, the committee decided on direct recourse to the government in London towards the end of 1791, with a view to the latter intervening with the Dublin administration on their behalf.

This action was presumably in some measure responsible for Sir Hercules Langrishe, member for the barony of Knocktopher, County Kilkenny, presenting to the house a bill for certain reliefs on 3 February 1792. On 7 February the inhabitants of Belfast, 'convened in the town-house by public advertisement', petitioned the house 'to repeal all penal and restrictive statutes at present in existence against the Roman Catholics of Ireland' and for their restoration 'to the rank and consequence of citizens'. The petitioners were conscious that 'the prosperity, happiness and security of this country must eventually depend on an union of interests among all religious denominations'.[44]

On 18 February George Nugent, later earl of Westmeath, member for the borough of Fore in that county, reported progress by the committee examining Langrishe's bill. On the same date the gentlemen, clergy and freeholders of the four lower baronies of County Antrim petitioned the house, rejoicing in the indulgences hitherto shown to Roman Catholics, but relying on the wisdom of parliament 'that such indulgences as will be granted Roman Catholics will not affect the elective franchise, or endanger the Protestant religion of the kingdom'. There was also on the same day a petition from the Catholic Committee 'requesting relief from certain civil incapacities and the restoration of Roman Catholics to some share in the franchise, which they enjoyed long after the Revolution'. The petitions from the inhabitants of Belfast and the Catholic Committee were both rejected by the house, the latter by 208 votes to 25.[45]

On 23 February the bill was reported from the committee with amendments and was agreed to by the house. It was passed on 24 February and Langrishe was deputed to carry it to the lords for their concurrence. On 6 March it was agreed by the lords with an amendment and on 18 April it was accorded the royal assent by the lord lieutenant.[46]

The resulting act[47] referred in Section 1 to restrictions in 6 Anne c. 6 (in regard to solicitors) and 1 George II c. 20 (in regard to barristers) and provided that the oaths and declarations therein mentioned be no longer required after 24 June 1792 and substituted therefor the oath in the 1774 act. Section 2 removed restrictions on the employment by catholic barristers and solicitors of

---

44 *Commons Journal Ireland*, vol. 15, part 1 under dates mentioned.   45 Ibid. under date mentioned.   46 Ibid. under dates mentioned.   47 i.e. 32 George III c. 22, an act to remove certain restraints and disabilities therein mentioned, to which his Majesty's subjects professing the Popish religion are now subject.

apprentices and clerks, but these latter were required to take the oath in the 1774 act. Sections 3 and 4 removed the bar on barristers having catholic wives; the obligation on solicitors to educate their children as protestants was also removed. However, catholics continued to be excluded from the inner bar.

Section 9 repealed the act to prevent protestants intermarrying with Papists. Section 15 dispensed with the requirement in the 1782 relief act for school-teachers to obtain a licence from the church of Ireland bishop of the diocese where they resided. Section 16 removed the restriction on catholic solicitors keeping more than two apprentices.

The 1792 act was thus rather limited in scope and the Catholic Committee, not surprisingly, continued to keep up the pressure for further reliefs. In an effort to put an end to their being burdened with certain tenets no longer held by the catholic church, the committee prepared a declaration of catholic tenets. To support themselves in this they resurrected the answers of six catholic universities (Paris, Louvain, Alcalá, Douai, Salamanca and Valladolid) to three questions submitted to those universities in 1789 by English catholics. The questions were concerned with the papal claims to depose princes, and to absolve their subjects from their oaths of allegiance and the dictum that faith should not be kept with heretics. The answers from all six universities denied these tenets.[48]

The United Irishmen Society produced a *Digest of the popery laws* which emphasised what remained to be achieved in the matter of relief. To show they had country-wide support and were not simply Dublin-based, the Catholic Committee organised a national convention in Tailors' Hall, Dublin in December 1792 where the debate continued for a week. A delegation from the Committee, headed by John Keogh, was again sent to London where they petitioned the king and held discussions with government ministers, emphasising that their goal was full emancipation for catholics.[49]

At home on 18 February 1793 Troy, now archbishop of Dublin, on behalf of himself and the catholic clergy of Ireland, together with several laymen, petitioned the house that it might 'be pleased to take the whole of their case into consideration, and in conformity with the benign wishes of his Majesty for the union of all his people in sentiment, affection and interest, to restore the petitioners the rights and privileges of the constitution of their country'.[50] They pointed out that the system of injurious exclusion had operated not less to the depression of the catholics of Ireland than to the general obstruction of the true and manifest interests of the country. On the same date the chief secretary, Robert Hobart, introduced in the house a new relief bill, which was received and read a first time. On 25 February a motion was made that the committee examining the bill should receive a clause to enable catholics to sit

48 Mitchel, J., op. cit., 201.   49 McDowell, R.B., op. cit., 410–13.   50 *Commons Journal Ireland*, vol. 15, part 1 under dates mentioned.

and vote in either house, but it was defeated by 163 votes to 69. The only surprising aspect of this vote is that as many as 30 per cent of members were prepared to vote in favour of such a motion.

The opposition concentrated their efforts on the proposal to give catholics the vote in parliamentary elections. They believed that this was the thin end of the wedge of allowing catholics to stand for parliament. They were prepared to agree to wealthier catholics with £20 freeholds and upwards being granted the vote but baulked at the idea of forty shilling catholic freeholders, because of the multitude of such people, being granted the vote the same as protestant forty shilling freeholders.[51]

But, although seventy-two members spoke in the debates, the opponents of the bill did not call for a division in any of the readings. It was put through the house in a speedy and efficient manner and was read a third time and passed on 7 March. The lords returned the bill with several amendments to which the commons agreed and it received the royal assent from the lord lieutenant on 9 April.

Section 1 of the resulting act[52] provided that catholics should not be subject to any penalties and limitations in regard to estates and property save such as protestants were subject to. By the same section and section 2 catholics were placed on a par with protestants in the matter of voting in certain parliamentary elections. This meant that catholics, as was already the case with protestants, in possession of freeholds of forty shillings or more would in future have the vote in such elections. However, while certain features, anathema to catholics, of the oath administered to all voters would be omitted in future, and while catholic voters would not be required to take the simple oath of allegiance and the oath of abjuration, they would be required to take the oath set out in the 1774 act, together with an additional declaration and oath set out in the 1793 act, which will be examined more fully later. By section 4 of the act catholics were excluded from voting at parish vestries.

The extension of the vote to catholic forty shilling (and higher) free-holders was not in the short run of any great consequence since such people would

51 McDowell, W.B., op. cit., 415. Sir Lawrence Parsons, who would have been regarded as a liberal, put the situation rather bluntly when he stated in the house: 'Give then the 40s franchise to the Catholics, and they will become the majority of the electors in three provinces of the Kingdom; and consequently will elect catholic representatives for every county in these three provinces. Add a parliamentary reform to this by throwing borough representation into the counties collectively or divisionally, and then you will have all Catholic representatives for these provinces, and most probably also for some of the counties even in the fourth.' He went on to argue that catholics would use their votes to elect members favourable to the catholic cause, who in time would procure the admission of catholic members to the house. (*Parliamentary Register*, vol. 13, p. 209).   52 i.e. 33 George III c. 21, an act for the relief of his Majesty's popish or Roman Catholic subjects of Ireland.

have a vote only in county elections and in a few boroughs, accounting for around seventy seats in a house of three hundred. However, following the Act of Union, the extension of the vote attained major significance since it still affected around seventy seats but in a total of one hundred Irish seats in the British house of commons.

Section 6 provided that catholics might keep arms on the same terms as protestants if they were seized of freehold estates of £100 a year or more, or possessed of personal estates of £1,000 or more. Catholics seized of freehold estates of more than £10 but less than £100, or possessed of personal estates of more than £300, but less than £1,000, could keep arms on condition that they took the oath in the 1774 act.

Section 7 provided that catholics might hold, exercise and enjoy civil and military offices or places of trust and profit under his Majesty, and, on certain conditions, hold or take degrees, or any professorship in, or be masters or fellows of any college to be thereafter founded in Ireland (provided that such college should be a member of the university of Dublin). This section further provided that catholics might hold any office or place of trust in, or be a member of any lay body corporate, except Trinity College, Dublin. Instead of the oaths of allegiance, supremacy and abjuration and the receiving the Sacrament of the Lord's Supper according to the rites and ceremonies of the church of Ireland, normally a requirment in such cases, catholics were required to take the oath in the 1774 act as well as the new declaration and oath set out in the 1793 act. The most important organisations intended by the term 'lay body corporate' were the city guilds of merchants and other trades, but catholic expectations of becoming freemen of such guilds were to be sadly disappointed. Over the ensuing years only a very few catholics were successful in achieving that status.

Section 9 excluded catholics from the posts of lord lieutenant, lord chancellor, chancellor of the exchequer, the higher judgeships, privy counsellor, prime serjeant, attorney general, solicitor general, king's counsellor, the higher ranks in the armed forces and many other state posts.

Section 13 provided that from 1 June 1793 it should not be necessary for any person taking a degree in Trinity College, Dublin to take any oaths other than the oaths of allegiance and abjuration, and thus allowed for the entrance of catholics to that college for the first time.

Section 14 provided that no catholic should take any benefit by or under the act unless he first took the oath and declaration in the act and also the oath in the 1774 act in one of the Four Courts in Dublin, or at the general sessions of the peace for his county, city or borough, or before the going judge of assize for his county.

Section 15 provided for entering on rolls the names and certain other particulars of persons who took the oaths and for the transmission of these rolls annually to the Rolls Office.

Section 16 provided that a catholic should not be capable of voting in an election until he had produced from the Rolls Office or from the local officer of the court a certificate of his having taken and subscribed the oaths and declaration as set out in the act.

The oath and declaration included in section 7 of this act is set out below.[53] It was said to be the handiwork of Patrick Duigenan, king's counsellor and member for the borough of Old Leighlin, County Kildare. A former catholic who had converted to the established church, he had spoken most eloquently and most virulently against the bill when it was debated in the house. However, this oath and declaration appears to have been in circulation for some time, for what was apparently an earlier draft was examined by a committee of Dublin priests in May 1791.[54] This committee raised no objection to it, but there was no unambiguous denial of papal infallibility in this earlier draft but rather the quite acceptable statement, even to the ultramontane, that 'I acknowledge no infallibility, right, power or authority in the pope, or in any council of the church, save in matters of ecclesiastical doctrine and discipline only'. This committee were unanimous in accepting the references to the Sacrament of Penance, although they professed to be somewhat bemused by the suggestion that anyone but a priest could forgive sins.

53 The oath and declaration was as follows: 'I, A.B., do hereby declare that I do profess the Roman Catholic religion. I, A. B., do swear that I do abjure, condemn and detest, as unchristian and impious, the principle that it is lawful to murder, destroy or anyways injure any person whatsoever, for, or under the pretence of, being a heretic; and I do declare solemnly, before God, that I believe that no act in itself unjust, immoral or wicked, can ever be justified or excused by or under pretence or colour that it was done either for the good of the church, or in obedience to any ecclesiastical power whatsoever. I also declare that it is not an article of the Catholic faith, neither am I thereby required to believe or profess, that the pope is infallible, or that I am bound to obey an order in its own nature immoral, though the pope or any ecclesiastical power should issue or direct such order, but, on the contrary, I hold that it would be sinful in me to pay any respect or obedience thereto; I further declare, that I do not believe that any sin whatsoever committed by me can be forgiven at the mere will of any pope or any priest, or of any person whatsoever; but that sincere sorrow for past sins, a firm and sincere resolution to avoid future guilt, and to atone to God, are previous and indispensible requisites to establish a well-founded expectation of forgivenees, and that any person who receives absolution without these previous requisites, so far from obtaining thereby any remission of his sins, incurs the additional guilt of violating a sacrament; and I do swear that I will defend to the utmost of my power the settlement and arrangement of property in this country as established by the laws now in being; I do hereby disclaim, disavow and solemnly abjure any intention to subvert the present church establishment for the purpose of substituting a Catholic establishment in its stead; and I do solemnly swear that I will not exercise any privilege, to which I am or may become entitled, to disturb and weaken the Protestant religion and Protestant government in this kingdom. So help me God.'   54 Moran, Patrick (ed.), *Spicilegium Ossoriense*, vol. 3, 425–31 – 'statement of the clergy of Dublin regarding oath'.

Furthermore and more importantly perhaps, the Catholic Committee, following the review already mentioned of outmoded catholic tenets, at its meeting on 17 March 1792 approved a *Declaration of the catholics of Ireland*, which agrees in all substantial particulars with this oath and declaration, including the references to papal infallibility, the forgiveness of sins, the acceptance of the property situation and the promise not to subvert the established church.[55]

Duigenan may have hoped that the references to papal infallibility and the forgiveness of sins would have had the effect of dividing the catholic body, and twenty years earlier this oath probably would have done just that, for one cannot see Archbishop Carpenter, for example, accepting without demur an oath which contained a stark denial of papal infallibility as well as some gratuitous strictures on the sacrament of Penance. However, by the 1790s the Catholic Committee, as already pointed out, had become laity-driven and so would be more concerned with concrete reliefs being offered rather than with the admissibility of a new oath. Even among the clergy, with the old antagonists, Butler and Carpenter, both in their graves, a certain apathy may have set in.

Although papal infallibility was not defined as a dogma of the church until the Vatican Council of 1870, there were already many Irish Catholics, clergy and laity, who believed in that doctrine in the 1790s and it is strange that there was apparently no objection from them to this new oath, more particularly as it presumed to preempt any future decision by Rome on such a doctrine.

Not suprisingly, the reaction of the Vatican, when eventually it got wind of the new oath, was far from favourable. Fr Valentine Bodkin, agent in Rome for some of the Irish bishops, reported on 30 August 1794 to Archbishop Bray of Cashel that the oath was 'by no means nourished [*sic*] by Rome, but highly disproved [*sic*]' and that 'neither the answers nor all alleged here in defence thereof could satisfy Rome'. He went on to claim that Troy's failure to consult the Vatican beforehand in regard to the oath had lost him 'much of his former credit and vogue here with the Congregation'. Bodkin made the point that Troy's being a regular saved him from the castigations and complaints which he would otherwise have had to endure from the powerful Irish regular lobby in Rome. (Pos 5998 NLI)

The undertaking in the new oath to defend the settlement and arrangement of property in Ireland, the disavowal of any intention to subvert the protestant church establishment and to substitute in its stead a catholic establishment and the promise not to exercise any privilege, flowing from the act, to disturb and weaken the protestant religion and protestant government in Ireland, all smack of damage limitation in the expectation and fear of a catholic resurgence arising from the reliefs granted in the act.

55 Edwards, R.D., op. cit., *Archivium Hibernicum*, vol. 9, 157–9.

CATHOLIC QUALIFICATION ROLLS

As we have seen the 1774 act provided for catholics to take the oath of allegiance in that act before the court of king's bench or before the various justices of the peace and magistrates throughout the country, and for furnishing annually in December to the clerk of the privy council lists of those who had taken the oath, specifying the quality, condition, title and place of abode of such persons. The Relief Acts of 1778 and 1782 provided for the taking of the oath by persons wishing to benefit under those acts in any of the Four Courts, in the quarter sessions for County Dublin at Kilmainham or before the going judge of assize in the rest of the country. A person wishing to qualify for the reliefs and benefits in the 1793 Relief Act was required to take in open court the oath contained in the 1774 act together with the further oath and declaration in the 1793 act in any of the Four Courts in Dublin, or at the general sessions of the peace for the county, city or borough where such person dwelled, or before the appropriate going judge of assize. In the case of these relief acts the judge or magistrate was required to have a roll maintained of those who had taken the oath, specifying their quality, condition, titles and place of abode, these rolls to be deposited annually in the Rolls Office in Dublin.

The rolls came to be known as the Catholic Qualification Rolls since the taking of the oath qualified the swearer for the benefits and reliefs in the acts mentioned. These rolls were transferred by the Rolls Office to the Public Record Office (now the National Archives) shortly after the foundation of the Public Record Office in 1867.[56] The rolls were all destroyed in the fire in the Public Record Office in 1922 but alphabetical indexes (which will be later shown to be incomplete) of the names in the rolls did survive and are now held by the National Archives. These indexes give the names, the places where the oath was taken, the dates and, with some exceptions, the addresses and occupations of the persons taking the oath.

RETURNS MADE UNDER THE 1774 ACT

The returns made to the privy council of persons who took the oath under the 1774 act were a separate matter from the Catholic Qualification Rolls. These returns were entered up in a book in the privy council office described as *Test Book 1775–76*, which was also transmitted to the Public Record Office where it suffered the same fate as the Rolls in 1922. However, in the case of the Test Book an Inspector Jennings[57] of the Royal Irish Constabulary had prior to the 1922 fire transcribed the contents into a notebook which eventually found its

---

56 *42nd Report of the Deputy Keeper of the public records in Ireland*, Dublin 1911, 79.
57 This appears to be I.R.B. Jennings, a native of County Galway, who was born about 1850. He joined the R.I.C. in 1869 and rose to the rank of county inspector, retiring in

way to the library of the Christian Brothers School in North Richmond Street, Dublin. The note book was loaned to the Public Record Office in the 1950s and the contents were published in the *59th report of the Deputy Keeper of Public Records* (1962).[58]

However, prior to publication, it was discovered that the information which Inspector Jennings had so industriously committed to his note book, had already appeared in a publication, preserved in the British Library.[59] There were slight differences between the Jennings transcript and the publication in the British Library – five names in the British Library source were missing from the Jennings transcript and there were six names in the Jennings transcript which were not in the British Library source. The geographical distribution of the names in the Test Book, as transcribed by Jennings, was as follows:[60]

PROVINCE	COUNTY	NO. OF NAMES
Connacht	Galway	84
	Leitrim	1
	Mayo	1
Leinster	Carlow	93
	Dublin	95
	Kildare	45
	Kilkenny	189
	Laois	48
	Longford	1
	Louth	49
	Meath	70
	Offaly	9
	Westmeath	10
	Wexford	23
	Wicklow	1
Munster	Cork	139
	Kerry	103
	Tipperary	368
	Waterford	173
Ulster	Derry	12
	Fermanagh	1
County not known		11
TOTAL		1,526

1908. See National Archives, R.I.C. records, ref. MFA 24/16, 259.   58 There is an introductory note by Breandán Mac Giolla Choille, keeper of state papers.   **59** *59th Report of Deputy Keeper of the public records in Ireland*, 1962, 51.   60 The 59th Report

There is in fact a third source of information on the number, though not the names, of those who took the oath under the 1774 act in Appendix CXXVIII to *Commons Journal Ireland* vol. 15, part 1, where the geographical distribution is given as follows:[61]

> Galway 84, Carlow 96, Dublin City 100, Kildare 46, Kilkenny 193, Laois 61, Longford 1, Louth 51, Meath 68, Offaly 9, Wexford 23, Cork 128, Kerry 106, Tipperary 391, Waterford 162, Derry 12.

These statistics were laid before the Irish house of commons in response to an order of the house given on 2 February 1792.

It will be seen that in the case of only five counties the number of names was the same in the *Commons Journal* and in the Jennings transcript and that County Westmeath is absent from the *Commons Journal* list. However, the total number of names in the three sources was quite close, being as follows: Jennings 1526, British Library 1525 and Commons Journal 1531. The Jennings and British Library figures were not as close as the net difference of one suggests, since, as already stated, there were five names in the British Library source which were not in Jennings and six names in Jennings absent from the British Library source. Of the three total figures mentioned, that from the *Commons Journal* appears to be the correct one, since, if we add to the Jennings figure of 1526 the five which he missed out on, a total of 1531 is arrived at, and this is the total in the *Commons Journal*.

It will be seen that there were eleven counties where, according to the returns in the 59th report, no person had taken the oath. The fact that three-quarters of those who had taken the oath were from Munster and South Leinster must be due in large measure to the support of the Munster bishops and O'Keeffe of Kildare & Leighlin for the oath. The large number from Kilkenny shows that the opposition of Bishop Burke of Ossory to the oath counted for little and that the influence of Archbishop Butler of Cashel, who was a native of Kilkenny, was also felt in that county.

The very high number of names for Tipperary must be mostly due to the example of Archbishop Butler in taking the oath, but also in part to the need for better-off catholics in that county to demonstrate their loyalty in the teeth

states that the eleven unapportioned names were from the Carrick-on-Suir area and might belong either to Tipperary or Waterford. The names (one each) for Leitrim, Mayo and Fermanagh were originally included under Dublin; these were apparently people from those counties who took the oath in Dublin. The one name recorded for Wicklow was originally included under Waterford.   61 The heading to the information in the *Commons Journal* is: 'an account of the number of persons who have subscribed the oath and declaration of 13 & 14 George III c. 35 specifying the number in each county and the number in each year since the passing of the act to 1st February 1792.'

of the extraordinary hostility shown to them by the protestants there. This hostility stemmed from protestant chagrin at the very considerable number of catholics who had managed one way or another to continue in possession of large holdings in Tipperary.[62] It is difficult to understand why there should have been no returns at all for County Limerick, having regard to the fact that about one-third of Butler's diocese was in that county. The absence of any returns for County Clare is not too surprising, considering that the support of Bishop MacMahon of Killaloe for the oath was at best lukewarm, although he had signed the declaration of the Munster bishops on the oath in July 1775. He did not in fact take the oath until September 1778.[63]

The occupations of the persons concerned in these returns are valuable in furnishing a kind of profile of the extent and composition of the catholic middle/upper class, particularly in Munster and South Leinster, during the closing decades of the eighteenth century. An analysis of the returns shows five bishops, 115 priests, 82 esquires, 272 gents, 186 farmers, 18 physicians, 15 surgeons, 16 apothecaries, 47 inn–keepers/publicans, 88 clothiers/shopkeepers, 238 merchants, 18 chandlers, 15 coopers and 29 brewers/distillers. These account for 1,144 persons or 75 per cent of the total. The esquires would be mostly owners of large estates while a high proportion of the 'gents' would be what are called in modern times 'gentlemen farmers'.

A bewildering feature of the *Commons Journal* figures is that in addition to the totals for the different counties for 1775–76, there are also figures totalling 96 names for the years 1785–87 for Tipperary and figures totalling 82 names for the years 1783–86 for Limerick. Since there was no relief or benefit to be derived from taking the oath under the 1774 act *per se*, one would expect that the persons who took the oath in the years 1783–87, would have done so to qualify for the benefits and reliefs under the 1778 and 1782 acts, and that these latter returns should have been made to the Rolls Office and not to the privy council office. It may be a case of some local functionary not knowing what he was about.

SURVEY OF CATHOLIC QUALIFICATION ROLLS

Turning now to the Catholic Qualification Rolls, information on the extent of the rolls held by the Public Record Office prior to the 1922 fire is given at page 80 of the *42nd report of the Deputy Keeper*, issued in 1911, as follows:

62 Cullen, Louis, 'Catholics under the Penal Laws' in *Eighteenth Century Ireland*, vol. 1, 31.   63 Murphy, Ignatius, *The diocese of Killaloe in the eighteenth century*, Dublin 1991, 124.

Court of Chancery	1778–1815	Leinster Circuit	1778–95
Court of King's Bench	1778–1853	North East Circuit	1778–96
Court of Common Pleas	1778–1837	North West Circuit	1779–86

Leinster:		*Ulster:*	
Carlow	1793–1841	Antrim	1794–1801
Dublin	1778–1811	Armagh	1793–1808
Kildare	1793–1801	Cavan	1793–5 & 1830–31
Kilkenny	1793–1830	Donegal	1795–1812
Offaly	1794–96	Down	1793–1837
Laois	1793–1837	Fermanagh	1793–6 & 1830
Longford	1792–96	Derry	1795–1801
Louth	1794–1835	Monaghan	1793–1834
Meath	1793–1833	Tyrone	1801–11
Westmeath	1793–1814		
Wexford	1796–1818		
Wicklow	1795–1828		

Munster:		*Connacht:*	
Clare	1778–1797	Galway	1778–1814
Cork	1778–1837	Leitrim	1779–1795
Kerry	1778–1826	Mayo	1778–1826
Limerick	1778–1837	Roscommon	1779–1814
Tipperary	1778–1812	Sligo	1779–1837
Waterford	1778–1813		

It will be noted that there were then (1911) no rolls extant emanating from the court of exchequer and it may be that there were never any such rolls. Rolls emanating from the courts of chancery, king's bench and common pleas would be mainly in respect of Dublin city or county, with about one-third provincial. The item 'Dublin 1778–1811' presumably relates to rolls emanating from Kilmainham quarter sessions and would pertain mostly to County Dublin but there would be some from the city and a few provincial. The Leinster Circuit comprised the counties of Leinster excluding Dublin, Meath and Louth, the North West Circuit the counties of Donegal, Cavan, Fermanagh, Derry and Tyrone and the North East Circuit the counties of Antrim, Down, Armagh, Monaghan, Louth and Meath. The Munster Circuit did not include Clare, which was included in the Connacht Circuit.

It is apparent from the list above that even before the fire in the Public Record Office in 1922 there was a considerable gap in the information held by that office in relation to the counties comprising the North West Circuit.

Furthermore, there were seven counties – Kildare, Offaly, Longford, Clare, Antrim, Derry and Leitrim – where the rolls held ended in 1801 or earlier. Admittedly, in three of these counties – Kildare, Longford and Antrim – there was no county election poll in the period 1801–29 and thus the main reason by that time for taking the oath (i.e. eligibility to vote) may not have arisen during that period in those counties.

Following the 1922 fire, all that remains of the Catholic qualification rolls in the National Archives are alphabetical indexes contained in five large books as follows: (a) An index for the whole country for the years 1778–1790; (b) An index for Leinster for 1793–96; (c) an index for Munster for 1793–1801; (d) an index for Ulster for 1793–96 and (e) an index for Connacht for 1793–96.[64] It is clear from the 42nd Report that these indexes were originally produced in the Rolls Office and were handed over to the Public Record Office on its inception.[65]

The index at (a) above is contained in what can only be described as a gigantic book, with penmanship of an exceptional order. The names are entered under the following headings for the different letters of the alphabet: Dublin city, Dublin county, Leinster Circuit, North East Circuit, North West Circuit, Connacht Circuit and Munster Circuit. A big difficulty in analysing the entries and breaking them down between the different counties is that about one-third of the entries under Dublin city and county pertain to the provinces, predominantly the Leinster counties, and are entered in a higgledy-piggledly manner. There are a total of 10,600 names in this index, made up as follows: Leinster 5,045; Munster 3,015; Connacht 1,845 and Ulster 695.

The total number of names contained in the indexes at (b), (c), (d) and (e) above are: Leinster 4,000, Munster 3,865, Ulster 1,795, and Connacht 2,375 making a total of 12,035 for the whole country.

For the entire period of the five indexes there are thus a total of 22,635 names for the whole country, the break-down as between provinces being Leinster 9,045, Munster 6,880, Connacht 4,220 and Ulster 2,490. As to the break-down between counties, the following are estimated figures extrapolated from a count of one-third of all entries:[66]

---

64 The National Archives references for these indexes are: (a) Shelf 2/446/3 (23); (b) and (c) Shelf 2/446/52; (e) and (f) Shelf 2/446/53. 65 *42nd Report of Deputy Keeper of the public records in Ireland*, p. 81. 66 While the figures for the whole country and the provinces are the result of a full count of the entries, the figures for individual counties are based on a sample of one-third of all entries. While a sample of one-third might appear quite adequate, the preponderance of particular surnames in particular counties (e.g Byrne in Wicklow, Power in Waterford) could have such a distorting effect that I would not claim that the figures for individual counties are other than approximations.

Leinster:		*Munster:*	
Carlow	255	Clare	380
Dublin	3,390	Cork	2,910
Kildare	570	Kerry	–
Kilkenny	610	Limerick	615
Laois	1,290	Tipperary	1,185
Longford	370	Waterford	1,790
Louth	200		
Meath	465		
Offaly	425		
Westmeath	195	*Ulster:*	
Wexford	700	Antrim	265
Wicklow	575	Armagh	105
		Cavan	280
Connacht:		Derry	60
Galway	2,350	Down	1,400
Leitrim	225	Donegal	65
Mayo	545	Fermanagh	195
Roscommon	1,010	Monaghan	90
Sligo	90	Tyrone	30

The absence of any entries in respect of Kerry is very strange, considering that that county had been to the fore in the number who took the oath in 1776 under the 1774 act when there was no benefit to be gained from doing so. Furthermore, according to the list given in the *42nd report of the Deputy Keeper* (see above), the Public Record Office prior to the 1922 fire held rolls in respect of County Kerry for the period 1778–1826. We can only conclude that, for whatever reason, the Kerry names were not entered in the relevant indexes.

There are also deficiences for certain other counties for the period from 1793 onwards which are not apparent from the figures above. There are no entries at all for this period in the relevant index for the counties Sligo, Donegal and Tyrone, while Limerick and Armagh have only one entry each and Monaghan only six. But it will be seen from the information from the *Forty Second Report of the Deputy Keeper* that at the date of that report the Public Record Office held rolls for the counties mentioned extending well into the nineteenth century.

It will also be noted that the indexes at present held by the National Archives terminate on the following dates: Leinster, Ulster and Connacht 1796, Munster 1801, but again it is clear from the Forty Second Report that, apart from the seven counties named above, the Public Record Office prior to 1922 held rolls for the different counties covering periods terminating many years subsequent to the dates mentioned. As we have seen the 1793 Relief Act admitted catholic forty shilling, as well as larger, freeholders to the vote in certain parliamentary elections subject to their taking the necessary oaths; as before there was provision for the qualification rolls to be lodged in the Rolls Office. The relatively large number of entries recorded for certain counties in the figures above (Laois 1,290, Galway 2,350, Roscommon 1,010, Cork 2,910, Tipperary 1,185, Waterford 1,790 and Down 1,400) is no doubt attributable to the administration of the oath to such freeholders for the purpose of either a contested by-election or of a poll in the general election of 1797. The following extract from the Forty Second Report is of great interest in this connection:[67]

> For several years after the passing of this [1793] act the series is complete for practically all the counties; the rolls supplying the place to some extent of the registers of voters of modern days (vide 51 Geo. III c. 77). This was the period when the Catholic forty shilling freeholders became such a powerful factor in political life; these rolls show in what numbers they were admitted to the franchise.

The act, 51 George III c. 77, referred to in this extract provided in Section 4 for the administration of oaths 'in some convenient part of the court or place where the election shall be carrying on, so as not to interrupt the poll'. It provided in section 5 for the transmission before 1 January 1812 to the Rolls Office by the proper officer of all catholic qualification rolls 'as shall not have been duly transmitted' and for the transmission annually in future to the Rolls Office of all such rolls. Section 6 provided for keeping locally an alphabetical list, with addresses, of persons on the rolls, such list to be open to inspection by any person on payment of a fee of 2s 6d. This latter appears to be what the 42nd Report had in mind as supplying the place of a register of voters.

It is clear, then, that the indexes at present held by the National Archives must be regarded as seriously deficient mainly because the names of large numbers who took the oath in order to qualify for the vote are not recorded. As to the extent of this deficiency, it is a matter of attempting to compute the number of catholics who took the oath to qualify for the vote in county elections in the period 1793–1829; from the latter date the vote was restricted to those with freeholds of £10 and upwards. Some idea of how many catholics were involved can be obtained from the number of votes polled in contested county elections over that period.

67 *42nd Report of Deputy Keeper of the public records in Ireland*, 80.

In the period 1801–1829 there were polls in 25 of the 32 counties.[68] The seven counties which did not have contested elections were Kildare, Offaly, Wicklow, Roscommon, Tyrone, Antrim and Donegal. Polls in a number of borough constiuencies have been ignored since forty shilling freeholders were involved only in a minor degree. On the basis of one poll for each of these 25 counties – where there was more than one poll in a county over the period the largest poll has been selected – we arrive at a total of 150,000 votes polled. As to how many of these were protestants, the total county electorate in 1784, when it was exclusively protestant, was c.46,000.[69] But allowing for the increase in population and for the fact that the electorate was not the same thing as the number of voters (and noting that these are to an extent counterbalancing factors), the number of protestant voters included in the figure of 150,000 was probably around 50,000. This leaves us with about 100,000 catholic voters. But this is not the whole story. Account has also to be taken of the situation where there was more than one poll in a county over the period in question and where, in the case of some freeholds, there was a change of tenant as between the polls, resulting in two or possibly more voters to be counted for such a freehold instead of one. It is not possible to quantify what to allow for this, but at any rate it seems likely that the number of catholics who took the oath in order to qualify for the vote in the period 1801–1829 was over 100,000. There was a further unquantifiable number who took the oath during that period for purposes other than the vote.

When we put this figure of 100,000 alongside the total of 22,635 persons recorded in the indexes in the National Archives, the measure of the deficiency in those indexes is apparent, and it appears pedantic to mention the further unrelated deficiences noted in the case of Kerry and some other counties.

However, this is not to minimise the importance of the extant indexes as a barometer of the catholic dimension in the several walks of life in Ireland in the closing decades of the eighteenth century. These indexes are an indication of how far catholics weathered the storm in the matter of the property restric-

68 Walker, Brian M., *Parliamentary election results in Ireland 1801–1922*, Dublin 1978, passim. There is an element of double-counting (say, 7,000) involved in these calculations because some six (Laois, Galway, Cork, Tipperary, Waterford and Down) of the 25 counties above, to judge from the large numbers (already noted) who took the oath in those counties in the 1790s, either had during that period a contested election or had a situation where, due to the withdrawal of a candidate, a poll was avoided at a late stage, and the catholic voters had already taken the oath, as appears to have happened in a by-election in County Down in 1793. But this double-counting may be offset by some or all of the seven counties named (which did not have a contested election in the 1801–29 period) having had polls avoided at a late stage in that period, or having had contested elections in the period 1796–1800.   69 Jupp, Peter J., *British and Irish elections 1784–1831*. p. 153. Jupp estimated the total Irish county electorate at 160,000 in 1803 and at 203,000 in 1815.

tions in the Penal Laws, and the extent to which catholics made their mark in trade, commerce, manufacture and in the medical profession, when they were debarred from the legal profession and from state offices and employment.

As regards the occupations of those who took the oath, this information is given in nearly all cases for Leinster and Ulster, but in the case of Munster and Connacht there is a high proportion of cases where it is not given. From samples taken from pages selected at random in the five indexes, it appears that about half of those who took the oath were farmers. Interestingly, and especially in Munster, it was not that uncommon for labourers to take the oath. In view of the great numbers involved, however, it is not feasible to attempt a breakdown of the different occupations for the entire country as has been done above in the case of those who took the oath in 1775 and 1776. But, the profile of occupations which emerged in the latter case should hold good in large measure for the vastly greater numbers who took the oath from 1778 onwards.

The information in respect of occupations is particularly comprehensive and valuable in the case of Dublin city. Some years ago Mrs Maureen Wall extracted from the relevant index information on occupations for Dublin city in respect of 1,250 merchants, manufacturers and traders who took the oath in the years 1778–82, and published the information in the Dublin diocesan journal *Reportorium Novum* with an introductory note.[70] Although the information extracted is spread over a period of five years, in fact 85 per cent of those listed took the oath in the year 1778. As the information would be all the more valuable if the numbers of catholics in the various occupations could be compared with the total numbers in those occupations in Dublin around the time in question, it was felt that a comparison with relevant information in the list of merchants and traders in *Wilson's Dublin Almanac* should prove rewarding.

However, a number of limitations to the usefulness of such a comparison should be mentioned. While ideally the information in Wall's list should be compared with Wilson's list for 1778, it happens that the only year where Wilson's list is compartmentalised to show the numbers in each trade and occupation is 1768, and while the total numbers in Wilson's list remained constant at around 2,700 for the two years in question, there must have been some differences in the numbers in each trade or occupation. Secondly, there must have been some unquantifiable number of catholic merchants, manufacturers and traders who, for one reason or another, did not take the oath and so do not appear on Mrs Wall's list. On the other hand, a significant number on Mrs Wall's list do not appear on Wilson's, resulting in a deficiency in the latter's list. To some extent these are of course counter-balancing factors. Thirdly, neither list gives us any idea of the volume of trade carried on, a necessary factor should

70 Wall, M., op. cit. in note 16, pp. 298–323.

we wish to determine the proportion of trade accounted for by catholics. Fourthly, there are several trades and occupations on Wall's list which do not appear on Wilson's, apparently for the reason that they were for the most part people who rendered a service and so did not come within the scope of Wilson's list.

Subject to the foregoing caveats, we can now proceed to compare the two lists. As regards persons engaged in some form of trading, including merchants, a total of 589 on Wall's list compares with a total of 1,108 on Wilson's, indicating that catholics made up about half of such persons. For manufacturers and tradesmen there was a total of 560 on Wall's list compared with 1,392 on Wilson's, indicating that about 40 per cent of such people were catholics.

When we look at catholic representation in different trades and occupations, it ranges from a position of predominance in some to a situation where there were very few or none in others. Occupations where catholics predominated were baker (41 Wall: 53 Wilson), brewer (29 : 35), carpenter (40 : 46), grocer (160 : 180), skinner (30 : 50), tanner (34 : 36) and woollen draper/clothier (40 : 61). In the case of distillers a total of 15 on Wall's list compares with only 10 on Wilson's, which is of course a nonsense, but at any rate it emphasises the predominance of catholics in that industry.

Occupations where there was a moderate or low representation of catholics included apothecary (15 Wall : 44 Wilson), bookseller/printer (15 : 36), brazier (6 : 37), breeches maker (2 : 15), butcher (7 : 64), chandler (34 : 87), cooper (12 : 44), coachmaker (15 : 33), goldsmith (3 : 33), haberdasher (5 : 40), hatter (7 : 25), hosier (12 : 29), ironmonger (8 : 25), jeweller (4 : 35), linen draper (34 : 71), mercer (8 : 23), merchant (143 : 483), saddler (3 : 22), shoemaker (25 : 66), staymaker (2 : 29), tailor (19 : 100), tobacconist (12 : 31), watchmaker (7 : 34) and weaver (27 : 135). The low representation of catholics among the butchers may be due to the fact that the vast majority of butchers operated from stalls in the Ormond, Castle, New Hall and other such markets,[71] and catholics operating from such premises would not have the same need to take the oath as those in possession of valuable properties. Chief among the occupations on Wall's list which do not figure at all on Wilson's were publicans, inn keepers and vintners of whom there is a total of 62 on Wall's list, which must have been a significant part of the total in the city.

Since it did not come within her remit, the medical profession does not figure in Wall's list. However, figures extracted from the indexes by me show that 16 physicians and 11 surgeons from Dublin city took the oath in the period 1778–1794. These figures compare with a total of 70 physicians and 52 surgeons practising in Dublin according to Wilson's almanac for 1793.

71 This situation continued for many years thereafter. The *Dublin Pictorial Guide* for 1850 shows the butchers still heavily concentrated in the various markets.

RETURNS OF CATHOLIC CLERGY UNDER THE 1782 RELIEF ACT

It has already been noted that section 5 of the 1782 Relief Act provided that no Popish ecclesiastic who took the oath set out in the 1774 act and who registered with the registrar of the protestant diocese in which he resided, should be subject to the Banishment Act and certain other acts. Section 7 of the 1782 act provided that the registrar of each protestant diocese should keep a roll of Popish clergy in that diocese benefiting under the act, and make yearly returns to the clerk of the privy council.

On 17 February 1792 the Irish house of commons ordered the registrars of the several dioceses to lay before the house before 1 March following an account of the number of Popish ecclesiastics who had registered themselves pursuant to the 1782 act.[72] The response to this order was published in an appendix to the *Commons Journal* but it appears from the heading that the information published was what was already in the possession of the privy council office and not information sent in, following the order of the house, by the different registrars.[73] It was of course asking a bit much of the registrars to submit the information within less than a fortnight.

The list published in the *Commons Journal* gives the names and addresses of 225 catholic clergy, distributed among twelve protestant dioceses as follows: Dublin 84, Kildare 8, Ferns 8, Ossory 37, Tuam 25, Killala & Achonry 16, Cashel 11, Cork 10, Limerick 19, Cloyne 4, Ardagh 2 and Dromore 1. Included in these figures are a total of 52 regular clergy, 44 of whom were from Dublin, 6 from Tuam and 2 from Killala & Achonry. The 16 clergy included under the protestant united diocese of Killala & Achonry were in fact all from Achonry. The wardenship of Galway was included with Tuam. The list contains two archbishops (Carpenter of Dublin and Butler of Cashel), two bishops (Phillips of Achonry and Lennan of Dromore) and Warden Kirwan of Galway.

This list was followed by the following cryptic note signed by Henry Upton, deputy clerk of the privy council:

72 *Commons Journal Ireland*, vol. 15, part 1 under date mentioned   73 Ibid., Appendix CXXIX. The information appeared under the heading: 'A list of Popish ecclesiastics in this kingdom who have registered their names, abodes, parishes &c with the register of the diocese where their abode is, pursuant to an act passed in 21 & 22 George III, specifying the number in each diocese from the passing of the act in 1782 to 1st February 1792, as returned to the council office'. Virtually the same information was published by Fr Reginald Walsh in *Archivium Hibernicum*, vol. 1, 46–76 under the title 'A list of ecclesiastics who took the oath of allegiance'. Fr Walsh explained that the information was 'compiled from various diocesan lists which are also preserved in the Record Office, Dublin'. There is a slight difference between the two lists in that Fr Walsh's has one more for Ferns and one less for Limerick than the *Commons Journal* list.

It does not appear by these returns that the persons mentioned therein have taken the oath and declaration of the 13th and 14th George III, nor whether they have conformed to the said act.[74]

The 225 priests listed would represent only about one-eighth of the catholic clergy in Ireland at that time and so can hardly be regarded as the correct total of those who registered. One would have expected that the catholic clergy generally and the regulars in particular would have been anxious to avail of the provisions of the 1782 act in order to regularise their position *vis-à-vis* the Banishment and other acts, even though these latter had been dead letters for many years. It seems likely, then, that there was widespread neglect on the part of the diocesan registrars in furnishing returns to the privy council office. It may be that the order of the house of commons had some effect in impelling some registrars to send in returns subsequently to the council. Certainly, in the case of the diocese of Meath this appears to have happened for prior to the fire in the Public Record Office in 1922 Fr Thomas Mulvany, later bishop of Meath, copied out 'a roll for the registry of the Popish clergy' submitted in accordance with the 1782 act by the registrar for the diocese of Meath.[75] Together with Patrick Plunkett, the bishop of the diocese, the roll lists 69 priests, fifteen of whom were regulars. Included were two who were normally resident abroad – Jenico Preston, brother of Lord Gormanston, and Fr Stephen Taylor OP. In the case of each of the priests listed, details of parish, age, place and year of ordination and residence are given. There may be similar information for other dioceses which was retrieved from the Public Record Office prior to the 1922 fire and which may be available in such places as diocesan archives and the pages of local history journals.

74 Upton's remark appears to imply that the catholic ecclesiastics did not properly carry out the requirements of the 1782 act. This may have some bearing on the legal advice to the government at the time of the Relief Act in 1829 that the Irish regular clergy had never been legalised.   75 'Clergy of Meath diocese who registered in 1782–83' in *Archivium Hibernicum*, vol. 8, 216–22.

Epilogue

What has generally been called the Emancipation Act of 1829 was in fact something of a mixed blessing inasmuch as the relief act proper was accompanied by two other acts, one for the suppression of the Catholic Association as an illegal and dangerous society, and the other for the disfranchisement of the forty shilling freeholders and the restriction of the vote to persons with £10 freeholds and upwards. Furthermore, as will be seen later, the relief act itself fell short in some important respects of what one would expect in an emancipation act.

Section 1 of the relief act (10 George IV c. 7) repealed the declaration against Transubstantiation required before a person could sit in parliament or where required for the exercise and enjoyment of any office, franchise or civil right. Section 2 provided a new oath, set out below,[1] to be taken by catholic peers

---

1 The oath was worded as follows: 'I, A.B., do sincerely promise and swear, that I will be faithful and bear true allegiance to his Majesty King George IV, and will defend him to the utmost of my power against all conspiracies and attempts whatever, which shall be made against his Person, Crown and Dignity; and I will do my utmost endeavours to disclose and make known to his Majesty, his heirs and successors, all treasons and traitorous conspiracies which may be formed against him or them: And I do faithfully promise to maintain, support and defend, to the utmost of my power, the succession of the Crown, which succession, by an act entitled *An act for the further limitation of the Crown, and better securing the rights and liberties of the subject*, is and stands limited to the Princess Sophia, Electress of Hanover, and the heirs of her body, being protestants; hereby utterly renouncing and abjuring any obedience or allegiance unto any other person claiming or pretending a right to the Crown of this Realm: And I do further declare, That it is not an article of my faith, and that I do renounce, reject and abjure the Opinion that Princes excommunicated or deprived by the Pope, or any other authority of the see of Rome, may be deposed or murdered by their subjects, or by any person whatsoever: And I do declare, that I do not believe that the pope of Rome or any other foreign Prince, Prelate, Person, State or Potentate, hath or ought to have any Temporal or Civil jurisdiction, power, superiority or pre-eminence, directly or indirectly, within this Realm. I do swear, that I will defend to the utmost of my power the settlement of property within this Realm, as established by the laws: And I do hereby disclaim, disavow, and solemnly abjure any intention to subvert the present Church Establishment as settled by law within this Realm: And I do solemnly swear, that I

189

before sitting in the house of lords and by catholics returned as members of the house of commons. Section 5 provided that catholics, being in all other respects duly qualified, could vote in parliamentary elections on taking this oath.

It will be seen that the oath retained the more important features of the oath in the 1774 act and that to these were added the undertakings in the oath and declaration in the 1793 act to defend the settlement of property as established by the laws, and not to subvert the established church nor disturb or weaken the protestant religion or government.

Section 9 prohibited a catholic priest from sitting in the house of commons and by Section 12 catholics were barred from being appointed lord chancellor or lord lieutenant. Section 13 enabled catholics on taking the oath above, to be members of lay corporations, to hold any civil office or place of trust therein and to do any corporate act or vote at any corporate election. This cleared the way for catholics to take an effective part in, *inter alia*, local government.

Section 24 prohibited catholic ecclesiastics, on pain of a fine of £100, from using the titles of archbishop, bishop and dean. Such titles were reserved exclusively for the clergy of the established church. Section 26 prohibited catholic clergy from officiating, or, in the case of regulars, wearing the habits of their order, except in their usual places of worship.

Section 28 enacted that, 'whereas Jesuits and other members of religious orders are resident within the United Kingdom and it is expedient to make provision for the gradual suppression of the same therein', such a person resident within the United Kingdom should within six months from the commencement of the act (April 1829) deliver to the clerk of the peace a statement in the form set out in the schedule. The clerk of the peace was required to register the statement and transmit a copy to the lord lieutenant. A regular who happened to be out of the country at the time could rectify his position by furnishing the statement within six months; otherwise regulars were prohibited from entering the country except by special licence. As part of the gradual suppression of the regular clergy, sections 33–35 provided effectively for the banning of novitiates.

There were, then, some important provisions in the 1829 relief act which belied the sobriquet of Emancipation Act usually aplied to it. For the regular clergy it certainly was an odd kind of emancipation which provided for their gradual suppression by a system of monitoring the existing members and the banning of novitiates. The provisions of the original bill caused such alarm

never will exercise any Privilege to which I am or may become entitled, to disturb or weaken the Protestant Religion or Protestant Government in the United Kingdom: And I do solemnly, in the presence of God, profess, testify, and declare, That I do make this Declaration, and every part thereof, in the plain and ordinary sense of the words of this Oath, without any Evasion, Equivocation or mental Reservation whatsoever. So help me God.'.

among the regulars that a delegation was sent hot foot to London where they succeeded in arranging a meeting with the prime minister, Wellington. While professsing sympathy with their case, he said he had to take into account the legal advice available to him that the Irish regular clergy had never been legalised. This advice was contrary to the perception of the regulars that their position had been regularised by the 1782 and 1793 relief acts. In the end the only assurance Wellington was prepared to give was that the relevant clauses in the bill would not be made more severe in their further passage through parliament. However, there appears to have been a minor concession inasmuch as the statements required to be furnished by individual clergy were allowed to be collated into one comprehensive list of all the Irish regular clergy for submission to the lord lieutenant. Such a list was prepared and was published by order of the house of commons in June 1830. It consisted of 316 names but included among these were Christian Brothers. There were some notable absences from the list, for example, the Capuchins of Cork (including Fr Mathew, the temperance apostle) and the Franciscans of Multyfarnham, county Westmeath. As required by the schedule to the act, the list showed the name, age, place of birth, name of order and residence of the persons listed.[2]

Although little or no attempt was made over the ensuing years to enforce the provisions in the act in regard to the regulars, there could be serious repercussions deriving from the legal standing of the various orders. As late as 1865, in a case involving bequests to certain Dominican fathers, the judgment of the court, confirmed by the lord chancellor himself, was that the Dominicans, like the other orders, had been rendered illegal by the 1829 relief act and that the bequests were, therefore, invalid.[3]

It was also an odd kind of emancipation which prohibited catholic archbishops, bishops and deans from using their titles and prohibited any kind of religious display by the catholic clergy except within the confines of their churches. These provisions in the relief act were in fact reinforced by the Ecclesiastical Titles Assumption Act of 1851 which prevented catholic bishops in Britain or Ireland from using their titles. This measure had its origin in the perceived 'papal agression' in the establishment of a catholic hierarchy in England, with a newly appointed cardinal (Wiseman) at its head.[4] While the Irish hierarchy took the sensible course of ignoring both the 1829 and 1851 acts, it must have been the cause of some considerable annoyance that their status was demeaned and depreciated by such niggling, sectarian measures, which derived for the most part from the aim of the established church to maintain its privileged position. Full emancipation for catholics would not

2 The list was published by Fr Reginald Walsh in *Archivium Hibernicum*, vol. 3, 34–86, with the heading 'A list of regulars registered in Ireland pursuant to the Catholic Relief Act of 1829'. 3 Madden, R.R., *Historical notice of the penal laws against Roman catholics*, London 1865, passim. 4 Ibid., 167.

really materialise until that church was disestablished by Gladstone's Irish Church Act of 1869. Myles O'Reilly, member for County Longford, commenting on the effects of the latter measure, observed that catholics were now 'free to teach, to publish, to form what religious associations, to found and endow what institutions, we please', and that 'no royal exsequator is required before papal bulls or decrees can be published in this country, ... that no permission from the civil governor is needed to build or endow a church, a convent or an asylum'.5

The oath set out in the 1829 relief act was to continue in operation until the 1860s when a series of statutes, particularly the Parliamentary Oaths Act 1866, the Office and Oath Act 1867 and the Promissory Oaths Act 1868, simplified the law on the subject, and appointed short forms of oaths to be taken by all persons, irrespective of religion, on the various occasions indicated, such as taking a seat in parliament, or assuming a judicial or other office.

5 Vaughan, W.E., 'Ireland *c.* 1870' in Moody, T.W. et al. (eds), *A new history of Ireland*, vol. 5, 734.

Bibliography

Archdall, Mervyn, revision of John Lodge, *The peerage of Ireland*, London 1786

Anon., *Abstract of the number of protestant and popish families*, Dublin 1736

Anon., *The ax laid to the root*, Dublin 1749

Anon., 'The oath of allegiance ... with the Roman Catholics' reasons against taking it' in *Hibernian Magazine*, October 1775, pp. 605–8

Anon., *A vindication of the new oath of allegiance proposed to the Roman Catholics of Ireland*, Dublin 1775

Bartlett, Thomas, *The fall and rise of the Irish nation*, Dublin 1990

Bartlett, Thomas & Hayton, D.W. (eds), *Penal era and golden age*, Belfast 1979

Boulter Hugh, *Letters*, Dublin 1769

Bradshaw, John (ed.), *The letters of Philip Dormer Stanhope, earl of Chesterfield*, London 1892

Brady, John, *Catholics and catholicism in the eighteenth century press*, Maynooth 1965

———— , 'Proposals to register Irish priests 1756–57' in *Irish Ecclesiastical Record*, Jan–Jun 1962, pp. 209–22

Brett, John, *A friendly call to the people of the Catholic persuasion in Ireland*, Dublin 1757

Burke, Thomas, *Hibernia Dominicana*, 1762

Burke, William P., *The Irish priests in the penal times*, Waterford 1914, reprinted Shannon 1968

Cogan, Anthony, *Ecclesiastical history of the diocese of Meath*, Dublin 1867–74, reprinted Dublin 1993

Commons Journal Ireland

Connell, K.H., *The population of Ireland 1750–1845*, Oxford 1950

Corish, Patrick J., *The Catholic community in the seventeenth and eighteenth centuries*, Dublin 1981

Cullen, Louis M., 'Catholics under the penal laws' in *Eighteenth Century Ireland*, vol. 1, pp. 23–36

Curran, M.J., 'The Archbishop Linegar-Lincoln succession' in *Reportorium Novum*, vol. 2, no. 1, pp. 211–12

Curry, John, *An historical and critical review of the civil wars in Ireland*, Dublin 1793

Darcy, Garret, *Dr Father Darcy's reasons, showing that the clergy and laity of the church of Rome might safely take the oath*, Dublin 1710

Dickson, David, *New foundations: Ireland 1660–1800*, Dublin 1987

Dictionary of national biography, London 1895

Dobbs, Arthur, *Essay on trade and improvement in Ireland*, Dublin 1731

Donnelly, Nicholas, *Short histories of Dublin parishes*, Dublin, issued in parts, various dates

Edwards, R. Dudley (ed.), 'The minute book of the Catholic Committee' in *Archivium Hibernicum*, vol. 9, pp. 1–172

England, Thomas, *The life of Reverend Arthur O'Leary*, London 1822

Fagan, Patrick, *The second city: portrait of Dublin 1700–1760*, Dublin 1986

———, *Dublin's turbulent priest: Cornelius Nary 1658–1738*, Dublin 1991

———, *An Irish bishop in penal times: the chequered career of Sylvester Lloyd OFM 1680–1747*, Dublin 1993

——— (ed.), *Ireland in the Stuart papers*, Dublin 1995

Fenning, Hugh, *The undoing of the friars of Ireland*, Louvain 1972

———, 'The three kingdoms : England, Ireland, Scotland' in J. Metzler (ed.) *Sacrae Congregationis de Propaganda Fide Memoria Rerum*, Rome 1973, pp. 604–29

———, *The Irish Dominican province 1698–1798*, Dublin 1990

———, 'Documents of Irish interest in the Fondo Missione of the Vatican Archives' in *Archivium Hibernicum*, vol. 49 (1995), pp. 3–47

Finnegan, Francis, 'The Jesuits of Dublin 1660–1760' in *Reportorium Novum*, vol. 4, no. 1, pp. 43–100

Giblin, Cathaldus, (ed.) 'Catalogue of material of Irish interest in the collection Nunziatura di Fiandra, Vatican Archives' in *Collectanea Hibernica*, nos. 4–16

James, Francis G., *Ireland in the Empire 1688–1770*, Cambridge, Mass. 1973

Johnston, Joseph, *Bishop Berkeley's Querist in historical perspective*, Dundalk 1970

Jupp, Peter J., *British and Irish elections 1784–1831*, Newton Abbot 1973

Kenny, Colum, 'The exclusion of Catholics from the legal profession in Ireland 1537–1829' in *Irish Historical Studies*, vol. 25, pp. 337–57

Lecky, W.E.H., *A history of Ireland in the eighteenth century*, London 1892

Lords Journal Ireland

McCaffrey, James, *The history of the catholic church from the renaissance to the French revolution*, Dublin 1915

McCarthy, D. (ed.), *Collections on Irish church history from the manuscripts of Laurence F. Renehan*, Dublin 1861

McDowell, R.B., *Ireland in the age of imperialism and revolution*, Oxford 1979

Mac Giolla Choille, Breandán (ed.), 'Test Book 1775–6' in *59th Report of the Deputy Keeper of the public records in Ireland*, 1962, pp. 50–84

Mitchel, John, *The history of Ireland from the treaty of Limerick to the present time*, London *c.*1867

Moody T.W. et al. (eds), *A new history of Ireland*, 9 volumes, Oxford, various dates

Moran, Patrick F. (ed.), *Spicilegium Ossoriense*, Dublin 1874–84

Murphy, Ignatius, *The diocese of Killaloe in the eighteenth century*, Dublin 1991

Nary, Cornelius, *The case of the Roman catholics of Ireland* in Hugh Reily's *Genuine history of Ireland*, Dublin 1762

New Catholic Encyclopedia, Washington DC 1967

Nouvelle biographie générale, Paris 1863

O'Brien, Conor C., *The great melody: a thematic biography of Edmund Burke*, London 1992

O'Conor, Charles, *The case of the Roman catholics of Ireland*, Dublin 1755

——, *The principles of Roman Catholics, exhibited*, Dublin 1756

——, *Maxims relative to the present state of Ireland*, Dublin 1757

——, *A vindication of the political principles of Roman catholics*, Dublin 1760?

——, *The dangers of popery to the present government examined*, Dublin 1761

——, *Vindication of Lord Taaffe's civil principles* ... Dublin 1768

Ó Fágáin, Pádraig, *Éigse na hIarmhí*, Baile Átha Cliath 1985

Ó Tuama, Seán, *Filí faoi sceimhle*, Baile Átha Cliath 1978

Pastor, Ludwig von, *History of the popes*, trans. E.F. Peeler, London 1941

Power, Thomas P. & Whelan, Kevin, *Endurance and emergence: Catholics in Ireland in the eighteenth century*, Dublin 1990

Power, T.R., 'James Butler archbishop of Cashel 1774–91' in *Irish Ecclesiastical Record*, vol. 13 (1892), pp. 302–18, 522–38

[Prior, Thomas], *A list of the absentees of Ireland*, Dublin 1729

Radcliffe, Stephen, *A reply to Revd. Edward Synge ... wherein his sermon preached in Saint Andrew's church Dublin is further considered*, Dublin 1726

Simms, J.G., *War and politics in Ireland 1649–1730*, London 1986

Synge, Edward, *Sermon preached in Saint Andrew's church Dublin ... on 23rd October 1725*, Dublin 1725

Synge, Edward, *A vindication of the sermon preached ... on 23rd October 1725*, Dublin 1726

Synge, Edward, *Sermon preached in Christ Church cathedral Dublin on Saturday 23rd October 1731* ... Dublin 1732

Taaffe, Nicholas Viscount, *Observations on affairs in Ireland from the settlement in 1691 to the present time*, Dublin 1766

Walker, Brian M., *Parliamentary election results in Ireland 1801–1922*, Dublin 1978

Wall, Maureen, *Catholics in Ireland in the eighteenth century*, Dublin 1989

——, 'The Catholic merchants, manufacturers and traders of Dublin, 1778–1782' in *Reportorium Novum*, vol. 2, no. 2, pp. 298–323

Walsh, John R., *Frederick Augustus Hervey 1730–1803*, Maynooth 1972

Walsh, Reginald, 'Glimpses of the Penal Times' in *Irish Ecclesiastical Record*, 4th series, vols. 20, 22, 25, 27, 28 & 30.

———, 'A list of regulars registered in Ireland pursuant to the Catholic Relief Act of 1829' in *Archivium Hibernicum*, vol. 3, pp. 34–86

Ward, R.E. & Ward, C.C. (eds), *Letters of Charles O'Conor of Belanagare*, 2 vols., Ann Arbor, Michigan 1980

Ward, R.E., Wrynn, J.F. & Ward, C.C. (eds), *Letters of Charles O'Conor of Belanagare*, Washington DC 1988

Williams, Harold (ed.), *The correspondence of Jonathan Swift*, Oxford 1965

Wright, Thomas, *History of Ireland from the earliest period to the present time*, London 1854

Wyse, *Thomas, Historical sketch of the late Catholic Association*, London 1829

Index

Where a person was successively bishop or archbishop of two or more dioceses, only the last diocese to which he was appointed is mentioned. The following abbreviations are used: bp for bishop, abp for archbishop and Ld Lt for lord lieutenant.